The
Intelligence
Establishment

The
Intelligence
Establishment

Harry Howe Ransom

Harvard University Press

Cambridge, Massachusetts

1970

For Nancy

CONTENTS

Contents

Contents

Contents

Charts

Preface

In the years 1956-1958 I compiled information for a descriptive analysis of the United States intelligence community that had evolved in the decade since World War II. My attention focused primarily upon the Central Intelligence Agency. The result of my efforts, *Central Intelligence and National Security*, was published by Harvard University Press in October 1958. More than ten years have passed since I collected all available material on "the CIA problem" and timorously published my book.

My purpose was to explore a major *terra incognita* of American government, the national intelligence community, the original role of which was to bring the main facts of the outside world to the attention of policy makers. It was apparent that in this role the institution would be of crucial importance and great potential influence in decision making. Because of this, I felt that such an institutional phenomenon required as much description and analysis as its secret nature would permit.

A number of questions about such a study and its publication were raised then, as they will be now. Is it possible to write a scholarly book on a largely invisible intelligence establishment the archives of which are tightly closed, whose leaders and employees cannot be systematically interviewed, and the product of which is almost always secret? Is it in the "national interest" to collect and publish the material that is available, assuming that this might give some aid and comfort to present or future foreign adversaries of the United States? What good purpose can be served by publishing this information? It was at once apparent that America's new world role after World War II would demand a new system for decision making informed by a vast information-gathering organization. It was also apparent, particularly in the context of the ideological confrontation between United States and Soviet power, that the United States could be expected to enter into the back alleys of international politics to engage in the dangerous game of espionage and covert political action. The proper policy, organization, and system for control of this kind of activity subsumed under an intelligence organization were bound to confront the United States with new problems which would not be easily solved.

My assumption—bias if you will—about the "CIA problem" should be stated at the outset. I believe that in the contemporary world an intelligence system is required for effective decision making. But intelligence is also a source of ever-increasing influence in any governmental system. The secrecy of the apparatus abets its power. As a source of great influence, intelligence and covert operational systems demand the close attention of students of government and politics, just as they demand tight control by responsible policy makers. Too little serious attention has been given to, and inadequate controls have been exerted over, the intelligence establishment since 1947.

Perhaps no segment of the cold war apparatus that developed after 1947 has been more controversial or more misunderstood than the intelligence system—controversial because Americans with their sense of fair play have not been easily persuaded of the necessity of the compromises in moral-legal conduct represented in the duplicity required of secret services. And misunderstood because the secrecy surrounding the system has allowed the growth of legends, mythology, and a highly fictionalized image of the apparatus.

Many significant events have occurred since the research and writing of *Central Intelligence and National Security* were completed in 1958. There has been a continuing growth of the intelligence bureaucracy and a rise in its level of professionalism. The world-wide intelligence competition has been escalated in intensity and volume. Technology has continued to add to the techniques of collection, analysis, and communication of information. And under a balance-of-terror equilibrium, however stable or unstable, the use of secret services has continued apace.

In the process, the Central Intelligence Agency has become the whipping boy of American foreign policy and to some degree has come to be seen, if dimly so, in the role of the imperialist legions of old. In Communist nations and among developing countries with revolutionary leadership, the CIA represents the spearhead of American interventionism, as, indeed, it sometimes has been. And to American youth at home, goaded to activism either by idealism or by a negative revolutionary élan, the CIA has represented the ultimate in American governmental hypocrisy, this being particularly the mood in the latter half of the 1960's. This symbolic use of the CIA in the hyperbole of the new radicalism has been accompanied in large measure by ignorance of its true nature, its actual organization and functions. A decade ago it seemed useful to compile a survey describing this new phenomenon of American government; it seems even more useful and necessary today to bring this information up to date.

The decade after World War II saw the creation and development of governmental machinery for seeking integrated national decisions. At the apex of the new structure was placed the National Security Council in 1947, designed to give the President integrated intelligence to precede policy choices. The CIA therefore was made a subordinate part of the National Security Council system and a crucially important information-supplying arm of the decision makers.

Today the CIA rests at the top of a thriving intelligence "community," but it has come to have a dual responsibility. It collects, evaluates, and communicates information and at the same time performs the operational function of underground political action and psychological warfare overseas. Yet to most persons it remains a mysterious, supersecret, shadow agency of government. Its invisible role, its potential influence, and the secrecy enshrouding its structure and operations, have long raised important and as yet unresolved, questions regarding its place in the democratic process. For example: how can a democracy best insure that its secret intelligence establishment becomes neither a vehicle of conspiracy nor the perverter of responsible government in a democracy?

The intelligence establishment of the United States, with the CIA at the apex, has become a multibillion dollar annual enterprise. Yet even many serious students of public affairs, including most members of Congress, possess little or no accurate knowledge of this vast system. A best-selling textbook on American government, published in the 1960s, made no mention of a component of that system with a billion dollar annual budget, the National Security Agency. And textbooks in general still pay scant attention to the intelligence system.

No pretense is made that the following pages give a full and complete "inside story" of America's central intelligence system, particularly of the overseas espionage and covert political action operations. Of these we shall perhaps never see more than the top of the iceberg, at least in this generation. But diligent compilation of unclassified materials makes it possible to open the secrecy curtain sufficiently wide to reveal the structure and some of the methods of a pervasive intelligence system at work in Washington and around the globe.

Formidable difficulties confront any scholar who sets out to describe the history, structure, and principal methods of intelligence. Careful *library intelligence* permits many of these difficulties to be surmounted. I have never been an active member of the professional intelligence guild. Were I privy now, or had I been in the past, to secret information about the intelligence system, security inhibitions would impinge upon my scholarship.

Fundamental problems exist in even attempting an accurate historical survey of the intelligence experience because archives remain closed or certain kinds of documents have been destroyed systematically for security reasons. This problem is illustrated by Sir Kenneth Strong, writing about the intelligence experience in the Ardennes battle in 1944. He recounts in his book, *Intelligence at the Top*, how "Top Secret" intelligence digests containing the most up-to-date operational intelligence were destroyed as soon as they had been used during the Ardennes battle. And even though two digests were kept for the record, one in Supreme Headquarters,

Europe, and one in London, when the war ended both copies were destroyed for security reasons. While one is prompted to wonder whose security may have been at stake, this practice was so common as to make unlikely an objective review of the intelligence system and performance in many important past events. At any rate, this illustrates one aspect of the difficulty of scholarly research in this field. Nonetheless, the subject is far too important to be left unexplored. And on the question of whether this book will aid America's adversaries, I am convinced that they know far more about the United States intelligence system than American observers outside that system will ever know.

While there have been a number of publications on the subject during the 1960's, authentic works remain scarce. My bibliographic indebtedness will be detailed in footnotes and bibliography, but reference should be made here to some groundbreaking treatises on intelligence which have influenced the development of serious scholarship in the field and my own writing on the subject.

Included among these is George S. Pettee's *The Future of American Secret Intelligence* (Washington, 1946), an analysis of World War II deficiencies, with suggestions for the structure of a postwar intelligence system. Sherman Kent's *Strategic Intelligence* (Princeton, 1949), written shortly after the Central Intelligence Agency was established, is an incisive discussion of intelligence as a kind of knowledge, a type of organization, and a unique activity. Roger Hilsman's *Strategic Intelligence and National Decisions* (Glencoe, Ill., 1956) remains the only attempt to explore the nature of intelligence doctrine among policy makers in Washington.

I am indebted to each of these authors and to many more recent ones. Yet none of the works just cited, or those written more recently presents a detailed descriptive analysis of the contemporary intelligence establishment. The purpose of this book is to survey this ground.

My original book, *Central Intelligence and National Security*, was the outgrowth of materials prepared for use by the Defense Policy Seminar of the Defense Studies Program, Harvard University, and thus my debt remains to the students and guest lecturers who participated in those graduate seminars. This is true also for my Defense Studies Program colleagues, notably Professor W. Barton Leach of the Harvard Law School, and including Edward L. Katzenbach, Jr. and Maury D. Feld. Others who assisted me in various ways were the late Professor V. O. Key, Jr., and Walter Millis, Dr. George S. Pettee, and Professors Sanford M. Dornbusch, Samuel P. Huntington, and Walt W. Rostow.

This book bears the Harvard imprint primarily because the late Thomas J. Wilson, as Director of the Press, thought it should be published. I owe much, also, to Mark Carroll, present Director, who encouraged me to produce this new version. The reader will share my great indebtedness to M. Kathleen Ahern, of Harvard University Press, for editorial assistance.

In the preparation of this book I have been assisted by numerous other persons over the years, most of whom will be acknowledged in footnotes and bibliography. Special credit is due William R. Harris of Harvard University, who generously shared with me in recent years his extensive bibliographic knowledge. I am particularly indebted to the Research Council of Vanderbilt University for summer assistance over several years and to the Rockefeller Foundation for a research award in 1964-1965 permitting an exploration of the British intelligence system. My thanks are due also to the Council on Foreign Relations, New York, for an opportunity to participate in discussions of intelligence problems with experienced individuals in 1967-1968.

Typing assistance has been efficiently rendered by Betty McKee and Susan Gauthier. If this book has merit, all of these persons deserve credit; its faults are my burden. My wife Nancy knows how she has helped; perhaps she doesn't know that I know, too.

HHR

Vanderbilt University
Nashville, Tennessee
November 1969

The
Intelligence
Establishment

CHAPTER I

Intelligence in the
Space Age

In the summer of 1939 a group of senators met in President Roosevelt's White House office. The President had hoped to persuade them to repeal the arms embargo provision of the Neutrality Act. He spoke of the strong possibility of war and of the need for American assistance to her natural allies. Senator William E. Borah, an isolationist and an articulate opponent of Roosevelt's interventionist attitudes, finally spoke: "There's not going to be any war this year. All this hysteria is manufactured and artificial."

Exasperated, Secretary of State Cordell Hull declared, "I wish the Senator would come down to my office and read the cables." Borah silenced the Secretary of State, almost to tears, with the comment: "I have sources of information in Europe that I regard as more reliable than those of the State Department."[1]

Neither Roosevelt nor Hull had as a counterweapon to Borah's claim of superior information the vast intelligence apparatus now available to an American president and his principal national security advisers. Today the product of an intelligence system with a multibillion dollar annual budget is available to government

1

officials as they take policy decisions, while trying to persuade legislators, the press, and the public that such decisions are based upon superior information.

No longer can a single powerful senator effectively challenge the president's information, although some may still try. Indeed, it can be argued that not only have senators lost much of their influence in shaping foreign and defense policy, but even secretaries of state and presidents must yield heavily to the "estimates of the situation" produced by the intelligence apparatus.

Consider, for example, how a president—any president—in the quarter-century since World War II has been potentially entrapped by the intelligence system: The president normally begins his day by viewing a picture of world affairs as depicted by the enormous intelligence system. Into his hands each morning comes a booklet labeled FOR THE PRESIDENT. INTELLIGENCE CHECKLIST. TOP SECRET. The information in it represents the amalgamated selection of supposedly the best and most important and pertinent information available from the government-wide "intelligence community."

An American president also receives each day several cables from ambassadors in crisis areas, marked "PRESIDENT'S EYES ONLY," as well as the highly secret "Black Book" produced by the National Security Agency and containing important information distilled from world-wide electronic eavesdropping and code-breaking activities. Also available are special intelligence summaries from the Defense and State departments. Thus the President's view of the outside world is partially circumscribed by these products of a highly organized informational system.

All presidents, will also be aware in varying degrees of the major competitors of the formal intelligence system—press, radio, television, and other commercial news services, as well as their own personally chosen advisers and any other private sources from which they solicit information. So the intelligence system does not have an absolute monopoly as the supplier of information. But its influence is likely to be formidable, and its information difficult for others to challenge in many cases. And this will be the case increasingly in the years ahead.

At the initial meeting of the newly created National Security Council on September 26, 1947, Admiral Roscoe Hillenkoetter, the first Director of Central Intelligence, "presented a thumbnail review of the world situation in the order of priority and importance."[2] Since that time, almost invariably, whenever a group of presidential advisers assembles to discuss foreign or defense policy, the first step is a summary of foreign intelligence on the agenda presented by the Director of Central Intelligence to establish the informational framework in which decisions are taken. This is not to say that the intelligence necessarily determines the decision, but often it is the dominating ingredient.

The routine presence of the Director of Central Intelligence at National Security Council deliberations and the primary place of the intelligence estimate in deliberative proceedings are demonstrable evidence of a pivotal and unique role for intelligence in national decision making.

The intelligence estimate, injected in a crucial phase of national security policy making, is the end product of the now vast and complex machinery for gathering and evaluating information, presided over by CIA and encompassing the many separate intelligence agencies of government. A daily intelligence digest is prepared every twenty-four hours for distribution to about forty of the top officials of the national government. These digests together with intelligence in various other forms, are derived from the labor of tens of thousands of individuals and the expenditure of several billions of dollars annually for activity ranging from library research to dangerous espionage maneuvers in foreign lands.

Intelligence: Key to Decision

Nothing is more crucial in the making of national decisions than the relationship between intelligence and policy, or, in a broader sense, between knowledge and action. Few Americans, even those reasonably well informed about public affairs, know of the existence and vital role in the contemporary Washington decision-making machinery of such groups as the United States Intelligence Board, the Board of National Estimates, the Watch Committee, the National Security Agency,* or the "Special Group." Indeed, there is more misinformation and myth than need be about the key or-

---

* Routinely, I ask groups of college students to identify the National Security Agency. Most have never heard of it.

ganization, the Central Intelligence Agency, which was described in a *New York Times* survey in 1966 as "one of Washington's most discussed but least understood institutions."[3] Yet these are the agencies of the executive branch of the American government that have evolved to meet the comtemporary requirements for information which, it is hoped, will precede and guide government policy and action. Even so, a survey by a group of Washington's ablest journalists concluded that "despite the [Central Intelligence] agency's international reputation, few persons in or out of the American government know much about its work, its organization, its supervision or its relationship to the other arms of the executive branch."[4]

Other agencies or adjuncts of government exist to produce information on operational requirements, such as the Institute for Defense Analysis, the various research and analysis groups affiliated with the army, the navy's Operations Evaluation Group, the air force's Office for Operations Analysis, and the USAF affiliate, the RAND Corporation. Intelligence is an important ingredient in, and by-product of, the work of these groups. Strictly speaking, however, they do not engage in national intelligence production.

What are some of the contemporary requirements for information? Highest in priority among the nation's defense needs is the prevention of a surprise nuclear attack—in a more general sense, strategic deterrence. Maintenance of this categorical imperative depends heavily upon intelligence. Today, American bombing planes patrol the skies day and night, and intercontinental missiles are stationed in their underground silos, armed with hydrogen bombs capable of incinerating societies. Who is to give the word to these agents of deterrence or destruction to attack or not to attack in a given situation? Intelligence plays a key role here.

If, for example, it is learned that nation X, allied to the United States by solemn treaty, has decided to invade by a certain date nation Y, politically hostile to the United States, American officials must decide upon a course of action. What is to be the basis of such a decision? And what will be the effect of alternate decisions upon nation Z? Decision makers look to the intelligence estimate, though it cannot always supply the answer.

Or suppose it is learned that a fleet of hostile submarines, armed with missiles of megaton power and a range of hundreds of miles, has suddenly left its home pen. How do United States officials ascertain the meaning of this move, or the countermeasures required? Faulty intelligence could threaten national survival as much as enemy weapons. Or, in a different area, what will be the political, economic, or demographic shape of the world five, ten or more years hence? What are plausible, as opposed to desirable, future foreign policy objectives? Increasingly, an intelligence system has an awesome potential for determining mankind's future.

All such questions directly or indirectly affect the survival of the United States. Survival in the nuclear age with basic values intact will test all American instruments of foreign policy, as well as political institutions and processes. None faces a more severe and constant testing than the intelligence services. Important as its function of around-the-clock daily watch upon world events may be, of equal importance is the central intelligence function of providing long-range estimates to policy makers. No development in American government institutions in recent years is more important than the evolution of the mechanism for producing the informational foundation for national security policy.

Intelligence and Policy Planning

Such long-range estimates are of incalculable value to officials responsible for making plans and building and implementing programs for the security of the United States. Policy planners must continually look into the future. Answers must be provided to a variety of questions: Will the Soviet Union continue to be a hostile opponent of the United States? In which of various ways and where will hostility manifest itself in future periods? Will cracks in the Kremlin Wall widen or be patched up successfully? To what extent are the unrest and disputes among the various Communist nations now important strategic factors? What is the future of Sino-Soviet relations? Will the declaratory hostility between China and the United States continue indefinitely? What are the timetables and the major trends in the development of Soviet or Chinese military weapons? What are the fundamental facts which should govern United States policy on armament limitation? What will be the significant trends in the drive for economic and political progress in the less developed areas of the world? What relative political,

5

economic, and military strength will be maintained by former great power centers such as Western Europe (particularly Germany) and Japan? What future developments in the Middle East, Latin America, Africa, and Southeast Asia will impinge upon the interests of the United States?

Central intelligence has the unenviable responsibility for pointing the way to the correct answers to these questions. The broad strategic doctrine of the United States must be geared to the best attainable intelligence forecasts. United States success in fulfilling commitments and attaining foreign policy objectives will depend heavily upon the quality of such intelligence, for the accuracy of the pictures drawn for decision makers of the future face of world politics has a profound impact upon the adequacy of planning.

The successful use of any of the major instruments of national policy also depends heavily upon the quality of the intelligence estimate. In the use of diplomacy, military power, economic pressure, propaganda, psychological warfare, or covert political action—or any combination of these—accurate intelligence is a key to success, particularly in a period of complex international tensions. Thus a heavy burden of responsibility rests upon those who create the national intelligence estimates, those who sit as the Board of National Estimates or as members of the U. S. Intelligence Board.

A sure way to court national disaster is to remain in the dark today about the present status, the capability, or the probable intentions of foreign nations, particularly potential enemies, and of allies and neutrals as well. To avert disaster, a massive American intelligence bureaucracy works around the globe to supply the federal government with the abundance of information required. At least twelve major departments and agencies of the government today are engaged directly in the intelligence process, with some ten additional units also engaged in some form of intelligence work. At the apex of this structure is the controversial Central Intelligence Agency, overseeing and coordinating what is known inside government as the intelligence community; from outside it is best termed the intelligence establishment.

A president, a secretary of state or of defense, or a congressional committee, may make decisions apparently contrary to the "facts" supplied by the intelligence system, but never before have national policy makers had the benefit of such a wide range of processed information or highly refined intelligence estimates. Certainly the vast institutional apparatus for the gathering, evaluation, and communication of intelligence has in the past twenty years radically altered the policy-making environment, and perhaps even the basic nature of our constitutional system.

Defining Intelligence

What is intelligence? Seeking a definition, a Hoover Commission task force surveying the national intelligence community in 1955 arrived at the following: "Intelligence deals with all the things which should be known in advance of initiating a course of action."[5] This is indeed a broad concept of intelligence, describing an ideal situation which very few decision makers can expect to find. Such a definition also suggests a comprehensiveness which few intelligence estimators would claim to be attainable.

Admiral William F. Raborn, Director of Central Intelligence from 1964 to 1966, has defined the term as follows: " 'Intelligence,' as we use the term, refers to information which has been carefully evaluated as to its accuracy and significance. The difference between 'information' and 'intelligence' is the important process of evaluating the accuracy and assessing the significance in terms of national security."[6] As a highly placed Pentagon official once stated, "A decision is the action an executive must take when he has information so incomplete that the answer does not suggest itself."[7] If this is a proper concept, it underscores the enormous potential power to determine decisions that an intelligence system may come to possess. It also seems to refute the argument that intelligence professionals are not concerned with or involved in policy making. Perfect intelligence would ease the pain of decision making. The ideal of the intelligence expert—of the intelligenc community—is to supply the policy maker with complete and accurate information. If having this will not automatically produce a decision for the executive, it at least may increase the probability of the "correct" decision.

A somewhat less idealized and more useful definition of intelligence than the ones cited may be found in the *Dictionary of United States Military Terms for Joint Usage*:

Intelligence—The product resulting from the collection, evaluation,

7

analysis, integration, and interpretation of all available information which concerns one or more aspects of foreign nations or of areas of operations and which is immediately or potentially significant to planning.[8]

It is clear from this definition that each of the many agencies of government concerned with national security will have its own particular intelligence requirements in order that its responsible leaders may make and implement decisions on plans and programs.

The pursuit of intelligence is the pursuit of information required for decision or action. The information gained—the product— is substantive intelligence. The same word, "intelligence," is used interchangeably, however, sometimes referring to the process, sometimes to the product. And as we shall see in the next chapter, the term has so loosely expanded in common misuse as to mean, in some contexts, espionage, secret or covert operations, or other forms of clandestine activity overseas. In a general sense, the term has lost a precise meaning.

The intelligence process, crude or refined, instinctive or conscious, is common to almost every level of policy planning. All types of decisions involve an "intelligence" ingredient and must be based in part upon factors in which precise predictions are not usually possible, such as chance events or human behavior. The intelligence process and product required for national security policy making is infinitely more complex, yet it has characteristics common to lower level decisions.

The Knowable and the Unknowable

The primary goal of intelligence, as the definitions above suggest, is to provide foreknowledge, to supply national policy makers and operators with sound evaluations of the present and future status, capabilities, and intentions of foreign powers. In pursuing such information, a distinction must be made between the knowable and the unknowable, and between what can be predicted with reasonable certainty and only in degrees of probability. It is one thing for central intelligence to be able to supply the President and National Security Council with the hard facts that the Soviet Union almost certainly possesses x number of ballistic missiles, with a maximum range and destructive power of y, and capable of being launched from z locations; it is even possible to make reasonably reliable estimates of such capabilities some years hence. It is quite another thing to be able to give officials more than an estimate of probable Soviet intentions of using such weapons, or more than a qualified prediction of the probable effects their possession will have upon our own strategic capability or upon the actions of other nations. Even if this could be done, it is important to note here, the intelligence estimate does not automatically suggest what action should be taken by the President in the light of such information.

The production of hard facts or qualified predictions is the end result of the intelligence process. This process involves the countless systematic steps by which intelligence requirements are set, and raw data are collected, assembled, and refined into a useful information product which is to be communicated to intelligence consumers.

The body of information offered under the label of strategic, or national, intelligence to governmental leaders as they ponder national security policy issues is merely one element in the intellectual process by which responsible officials reach a decision or make policy. Certainly, the intelligence ingredient in this process must compete with other factors to be considered and other "pictures in the mind" of the decision maker. These include not only his receptivity to, and faith in the accuracy of, the proffered intelligence estimate, but also his own assumptions, biases, perceptions, and knowledge from other sources and from experience. In a sense, the official intelligence estimate must compete also with the sometimes unconscious evaluations made by the decision maker from his reading of the *Washington Post* or the *New York Times*. Undeniably, such influential newspapers are a major intelligence source for decision makers.

Reliability of intelligence data and the reception accorded them by policy makers and operators are only two of the many problems concerning the intelligence function. The purpose in the chapters that follow is to survey some of the more important problems created by the growth of an enormous intelligence establishment in the two decades after World War II.

How may one define "the CIA problem"? Some of its major elements involve questions of policy, organization, and control.

Also involved are questions about the proper limits of secrecy, of international ethics and morality, and of the net effectiveness of the intelligence system. What *are* the potentialities and limitations of any intelligence system? How should the various intelligence functions be organized in the governmental structure? Particularly, should covert *political* operations be organized under the same roof as *intelligence* operations? Who should supervise or control the process of collecting and utilizing secret information? What degree of secrecy is required for efficient performance of the intelligence function? What are the consequences of authorized disclosure and of secrecy in a democratic society? What moral and ethical questions confront a democratic nation utilizing in "peace time" the ruthless techniques of covert operations? What generalizations can be made about the effectiveness of the present system? If, as the Hoover Commission of 1955 has stated, "The fate of the nation may well rest on accurate and complete Intelligence data,"[9] then these are problems of the most urgent concern.

The philosopher, the student of the administrative process, or the observer of the political process will find challenging and fundamental questions in the relationship between national intelligence and public policy, as well as in the practical and moral problems involved in the use and control of secret instruments of policy. There is no attempt in the present volume to perform the task of the philosopher or theorist of politics and government. A much more limited goal has been set—to describe objectively contemporary central intelligence insofar as this can be done from non-secret sources.

The pages following contain a descriptive analysis of the nature of intelligence, the development of the central intelligence structure, an overview of the national intelligence community, intelligence in the military services and other major government agencies, top-level coordination of intelligence, the issue of secrecy and congressional surveillance, a description of how the British have managed similar problems and functions, and a discussion of some major problems of organization, procedure, and performance.

This study is not *pro-* or *anti-*CIA. If there is a bias, it is in favor of the notion that national decision makers should have the best attainable information prior to decisions. There are certain assumptions which underlie this study:

First, the intelligence and covert political action functions will continue to expand both in scope of activity and in importance to decision making.

Second, technology not only will expand enormously the potential capabilities of intelligence systems, as it has already done, but will make decision makers increasingly the potential prisoners of these systems.

Third, knowledge can be power; secret knowledge is potentially secret political power; and secret political power is a threat to democratic government. If a secret instrument of governmental policy exists, it is likely to be used, its size continually expanded and its techniques refined.

Fourth, to neglect to examine and discuss these developments, even in the face of great obstacles in the way of obtaining all the facts, would add to the dangers that threaten the viability of democratic values.

CHAPTER II

The Nature of Intelligence

Information labeled "intelligence" occupies a pivotal point on a simple triangular concept of foreign or defense policy decision making. The other two crucial points are "objectives" (goals or ends) and "means" (power or instruments).

To explain this concept with utmost brevity: a nation-state, as represented by its leaders, has a set of foreign policy objectives which range from a minimum of territorial survival to a maximum of having its values accorded universal application or respect. "Objectives" somewhere along this spectrum will be pursued in accordance both with the "means" of power available for their attainment and the information possessed by the decision maker about the external environment and the probable consequences of alternate courses of action. The information element is the product of an intelligence system, combined with the decision maker's perception of both the information and the wider reality of events.

As indicated earlier, intelligence as a term is variously used to apply to disparate functions or activities. Even in the context of its *information* meaning, the term connotes a process as well as a product. The nature of intelligence has been confused somewhat by a *mystique* surrounding the word and the activity. Misunderstanding abounds also from the many varieties and categories of sources for, and methods of, its collection. Some misapprehension also results from the fact that, as Sherman Kent has so well illustrated in his treatise, *Strategic Intelligence*, intelligence is knowledge, is organization, and is activity.

The intelligence process has been described in nonacademic terms by Lieutenant General James H. Doolittle: "The acquisition of intelligence is one thing; the interpretation of intelligence is another; and the use of that intelligence is a third." Yet the important point the general does not make is that these three basic elements in the process are, or should be, highly interrelated. And he fails to include a crucially important element in the process: the setting of informational requirements.

"There's nothing esoteric about the word 'intelligence,'" declared Allen Dulles, speaking as the Director of Central Intelligence.[1] This may be true to an experienced intelligence expert—Mr. Dulles had been active in intelligence work since World War I —but the layman is often confused not only by the wide misuse of the term but by a myriad of descriptive adjectives classifying various types of intelligence according to its use or with reference to methods of collection. We find such categories as strategic, tactical, flak, target, air, photo, economic, radar, and electronic.

Categories of Intelligence

Three useful major categories are strategic (or national), tactical (or combat), and counterintelligence.

Strategic intelligence is the broadest in scope. It refers to information regarding the capabilities, vulnerabilities, and intentions of foreign nations required by planners in establishing the basis for an adequate national security policy in time of peace. It includes both long-range forecasts of political, economic, and military trends and early warning of impending political or military actions. It also provides the basis for projected over-all military operations in time of war. As Sherman Kent has put it:

If foreign policy is the shield of the republic, as Walter Lippmann has called it, then strategic intelligence is the thing that gets the shield to the right place at the right time. It is also the thing that stands ready to guide the sword.[2]

It is impossible to set precise limits upon the scope and kinds of information needed in the strategic intelligence process. It may be fair to say there are no limits. This view, if not challenged, leads to an ever-expanding intelligence system. Basic categories of information include geographic, political, economic, scientific, military, sociological, psychological, and biographical factors, and many others.

Tactical, or operational, intelligence is sometimes termed combat intelligence because it usually concerns information required by a commander in the field engaged in tactical operations. The distinction between tactical and strategic intelligence, however, is decreasingly clear-cut. For example, the movement of a Chinese Communist field army across the Yalu River during the Korean War was tactical intelligence vital to the field commander, but it was also of prime "strategic" importance to the National Security Council. Indeed, a major field commander today requires much of the same intelligence available to Washington's top policy makers.

Counterintelligence denotes that phase of intelligence activity devoted to countering the effectiveness of hostile foreign intelligence operations. Essentially it is a police function. More specifically its purpose is to protect information against espionage, to guard one's intelligence operations from infiltration by the adversary, and to secure installations or material against sabotage. Counterintelligence is, in a sense, a negative, defensive function. Sometimes, however, it turns up information of significance to those concerned with "positive" intelligence. Many intelligence professionals do not want to draw too distinct a line between intelligence and counterintelligence. Their argument is that the adversary's attempts to penetrate your system are highly revealing with regard to his information gaps as well as his capabilities and intentions.

These various categories and distinctions in types of intelligence have precise meaning to the intelligence community. But the purpose of this book is to examine as a whole the national intelligence organization and process to which all types of intelligence contribute.

The Nature of Intelligence

Steps in the Process

The intelligence process can best be described in terms of the various procedural "steps." These are commonly grouped into four general phases:

Setting of Requirements—The crucially important task of intelligence management which determines what types of information are needed and assigns procurement to the various intelligence arms.

Collection—The procurement of information believed to be pertinent, sometimes called "raw" intelligence data.

Evaluation and Production—Sifting, sorting, and judging the credibility of collected information, drawing pertinent inferences from its analysis, and interpreting such inferences in keeping with the requirements of the planners, policy makers, and operators.

Dissemination—Communicating the intelligence findings in forms most suitable—oral, graphic, or written—to appropriate planners, decision makers, or those responsible for implementing decisions.

All links in the chain must be securely fixed or the intelligence system will be ineffective. A nation may have an efficient system for collecting intelligence data but its evaluation or the inferences drawn may be faulty, as may be its system for dissemination to the proper consumers. And all of this activity can turn out to be of little use if the intelligence system cannot answer those questions of greatest importance to decision makers. The importance of setting the proper "requirements" cannot be exaggerated. American experience in World War II, from its beginning at Pearl Harbor to the end of the conflict, was characterized by a loose and sometimes ineffective organization either for setting requirements or for utilization of available information. Certainly the use of intelligence immediately prior to the attack on Pearl Harbor can be described as "casual."[3]

It would be misleading, however, to picture the intelligence process merely as routine steps in a well-defined set of procedures as outlined above. A more accurate picture may be had by considering intelligence production in comparison with the inductive method, or with any intellectual process in which there is a high degree of "input," "output," and "feedback," and interrelationship between the elements of knowledge and the "steps" in the process. Certainly the collector of raw data needs guidance from the policy maker as

15

well as from the evaluator. Channels of communication must always be kept open between collector, coordinator, and consumer. Certainly the collector and coordinator must have some idea what the intelligence consumer needs to know. The consumer, in turn, must be supplied with sufficient basic facts to be able to know when certain elements in the picture are missing. This is only to suggest the limitations of viewing the intelligence process as a clear-cut performance of routine, isolated tasks.

Procuring Raw Intelligence

Because the intelligence process is both dynamic and interacting, there is no clear-cut starting or stopping point. It may be compared to a huge jigsaw puzzle the solution of which is complicated by the fact that many of the pieces submitted to the puzzle solver do not fit into the picture at all. Data collected by the nation's far-flung intelligence operations cover a multitude of items of enormously varying utility to decision makers and with varying degrees of relevance to the problem faced by the analyst.

The secret movement of Soviet submarines through the Skagerrak or out of the Kuriles may be of immediate strategic import. The removal of permanent naval delegates from the Russian Communist Party's Central Committee, on the other hand, may lack immediate critical importance but may fit significantly into a long-range study of the relative position of army, navy, and air force officers in the Soviet strategic planning apparatus.

The size of this year's graduating class at a Peking engineering institute must be included in any long-range estimate of Chinese capability for industrial expansion. A public announcement in *Pravda* of a railroad being laid in a heretofore barren area may stimulate a drive for collection of information on this area to ascertain whether or not a landing field, a steel mill, or a uranium mine may lie at the end of this iron rainbow. It should be clear that intelligence—strategic or tactical—involves more than military secrets, clandestinely gathered. The movement of freight cars, discovery of a new oil field, or development and application of a new industrial process are of interest to intelligence agents all over the world. The influence of such facts, usually gathered from "open" rather than secret sources, may be just as significant to our military—foreign policy planning as a spectacular May Day demonstration in Moscow of a new missile.

"A cable from the State Department regarding political developments in a country is intelligence," as Allen Dulles once observed.[4] So, too, are scientific, technical, military, and other data, whether collected from an American reconnaissance aircraft flying along the East German border with a long-range camera and electronic sensing devices, from a translation of a Russian scholarly journal, from interviews with refugees or political defectors from Communist countries, from such highly technical methods as particle-analysis, micro-analysis, from electronic information-gathering devices, from globe-circling reconnaissance satellites, or from intelligence agents, operating either in the open or secretly. Intelligence, like knowledge, knows no boundaries either as to substance or source. Yet the procurement of data to be fed into the intelligence mill is a difficult management function. The intelligence apparatus would soon become useless if the raw data were gathered at random and stored without plan. To be efficient, data-gathering must be planned and purposeful. Those who collect, evaluate, and assemble intelligence reports must be keenly aware of the important unanswered questions in the mind of the decision maker.

Sources

Wartime intelligence leader William J. Donovan reminds us that World War II taught Americans that good intelligence is neither mysterious nor sinister.[5] During the war, agents of the Office of Strategic Services learned that a few minutes spent with the brakeman of a freight train destined for Occupied France produced more useful data than Mata-Hari could learn in an entire evening. And in one instance an item in the society column of a German garrison-town newspaper revealed the location of a German division which the Allies had been seeking.

Reflecting on his days as an attaché of the British Foreign Office, Harold Nicholson recalls how very little information of value he could have conveyed to the fictional Slav countess who might have approached him on the Baghdad Express, offering, in return for valuable information, a half-million dollars, safe passage to Chile, and the favors of the lady herself. "There was little I could reveal to her which her employers could not have gathered from the London press."[6] The professional spy's more fruitful target is not the young attaché, Nicholson suggests; rather it is "the worker in some munitions factory, the dock hand at Scapa or at Kiel, even the Flemish peasant tilling the land and counting the military trains as they rambled along the railway embankment above him." Even sources of this kind generally produce less useful information than that pieced together by research and analysis far behind the front lines of secret intelligence operations. And the classical spy on the ground is being made rapidly obsolescent by technological innovation, or what might be called "automated espionage."

The decline of the classical espionage agent in gathering raw intelligence data was unmistakable even before the era of the "spy-in-the-sky." Today there are far more scholars and scientists, lawyers and former college professors, who work a nine-to-five day at intelligence jobs in their Washington offices than there are secret agents. The undercover foreign agent still exists however, and sometimes can supply the vital link in the information chain. The major part of the intelligence function over the past two decades has been performed by the college graduate sitting at his desk creating a mosaic from multicolored data gathered from around the globe, most likely from nonsecret sources.

Recent Developments

Since about 1957, emphasis has been shifting from the social sciences to the physical or "hard" sciences, from "ivory tower" research toward operations, from theoretical analysis toward technical means of collecting, collating, and interpreting data. Once the social scientists occupied the center of the stage in intelligence work. Now he is being displaced, for better or worse, by the technician, the electronics expert, the physical scientist, and the specialist in technical means of collecting, collating, and interpreting data. As our capacity to collect, communicate, and automate hard data increases, the nature of the intelligence process changes, as do the kind of specialized skills required. This means that an increasing amount of "hard" intelligence should become available. It means further that the intelligence system ought to be increasingly precise about another nation's power capabilities. But it still leaves open

18

the question of intentions, and on such questions the social scientist ought to have something to offer; for the same reason the classical spy can continue to claim an important role.

The shift of emphasis from spying to scholarly research and analysis, whether in the physical or social sciences, has been due to the growing complexity of war and society and to the increasing effectiveness of state security systems. A kind of technological race now is being run between offense and defense, with increasingly sophisticated instruments and techniques both for gathering information and protecting it.

One intelligence expert, Ellis M. Zacharias, a World War II Deputy Director, Office of Naval Intelligence, once wrote that in the navy 95 per cent of peacetime intelligence came from open sources, another 4 per cent from semi-open sources, and only 1 per cent, sometimes less, from secret agents: "There is very little these confidential agents can tell," he wrote, "that is not accessible to an alert analyst who knows what he is looking for and knows how to find it in open sources."[7] Twenty years of cold war have elapsed since those words were written. During that time, intelligence operations by secret agents have greatly increased, though it is debatable whether the information they supply has increased accordingly. The fact remains, however, that the great proportion of intelligence is gained from nonsecret sources, or, increasingly, from mechanical instruments.

A rough breakdown of the sources of United States national intelligence for most of the 1947-1967 period would indicate the following magnitudes with respect to sources and collectors:

	Per cent
Clandestine operations, covert sources, and secret agents	20
Press, radio, tourists, published documents, and other standard sources	25
Routine reports, Department of State and other government agencies abroad	25
Military attachés accredited by foreign governments and from routine military operations	30

Much material which may have been given a security classification by government agencies, such as the cables of foreign service officers or reports from other government agencies operating in foreign nations, is nonetheless collected by overt, above-board methods, and would normally be available to anyone with a well-organized information-gathering system.

While it is clear that 80 per cent or more of intelligence raw material in peacetime is overtly collected from nonsecret sources such as newspapers, libraries, radio broadcasts, business and industrial reports, or from accredited foreign service officers, the importance of secret sources should not be underestimated.

Because secret sources and methods are the intelligence system's most sensitive subject matter, the various forms of electronic spying and espionage by United States intelligence operations cannot be described here in more than very general detail. If the total operations of the national intelligence community are carried on, as they are, with a high degree of secrecy, its espionage activities are inevitably classified as TOP SECRET. One United States senator declared that it "almost chills the marrow of a man to hear about" clandestine activities of American CIA agents.[8] In addition to the hazardous activities of American foreign agents in hiding or masquerading under various guises or covers in foreign nations, scientific advances in electronics, photography, and various forms of communication are being brought into play in the intelligence process. Recall, for example, the Russian allegation in the early 1950s that the United States was drifting balloons across Soviet territory, carrying special cameras to photograph Russian installations and industry. Again, reliable information is scarce on such methods and devices, although it can be assumed that use has been made of them. Electronic intelligence, long-range and microphotography, and other possible devices suggest to the imagination many possible uses.

Prior to the disclosure of the CIA's U-2 program in May 1960, Allen Dulles had publicly hinted, for example, that there are "certain types of special projects of a unique and important nature which this agency [CIA] undertakes from time to time in the research and development field."[9] Mr. Dulles disclosed this much to Congress in requesting authority to make five-year contracts with manufacturers for special devices, some of which undoubtedly would seem to be science fiction come true.

Out of such research and development have come massive programs for espionage over the past twenty years in the effort by the

United States, and the Soviet Union as well, to use technology to bring the whole world under surveillance. Orbiting satellites, rapid advances in photographic equipment and sensing devices, and computer technology are radically changing the capabilities of intelligence systems. Code-breaking, for example, is one of the most important and least publicized techniques of modern espionage. Specific details of these developments are not easily obtainable; usually the information about them has resulted from the failure and exposure of a mission. But it is known that cameras aboard missiles which now are launched at regular intervals have the capacity of depicting, from heights of more than a hundred miles, cars parked on a Moscow street or even human beings on the ground. Numerous other devices are in use, such as "ferrets" for electronic eavesdropping and instruments capable of monitoring conversations on the other side of the globe. Similar devices are even more extensively ground, or ship-based, so that governments may try to keep under surveillance the widest range of electromagnetic emissions.

The public was made very much aware of this kind of activity in January 1968 when the *U.S.S. Pueblo*, which the government of the United States acknowledged was an intelligence ship, was captured by the North Korean government near Wonsan and its crew imprisoned. The ship was what may be called an electronic scavenger, seeking information by offshore monitoring of (a) North Korean tactical radio communications, (b) North Korean (Russian) radar equipment and procedures, and (c) miscellaneous naval intelligence, especially Russian submarine "signatures"—the telltale noise of a submarine, permitting its quick identification. The U. S. Navy operates a dozen or so such ships; the Russians operate many more, often disguised as fishing trawlers. Both nations pursue such ship-bound intelligence functions in the presumed sanctuary—in international law—of "free" international waters. Few subjects are more secret than some of the details of these international ELINT (electronic intelligence) programs, although techniques for local eavesdropping or surveillance are well known.

In the Vietnam War, tens of thousands of photographs have been taken daily, weather permitting, by military reconnaissance aircraft, both manned and unmanned. In the latter category are the camera-equipped "drones" that fly over territory, such as mainland China, where the risk of a mishap would be costly. Reportedly the Military Museum in Peking exhibits several crashed drone planes. It will be recalled that the Department of State announced the testing of the first Chinese atomic bomb before it occurred at Lop Nor in the Takla Makan region in 1964. This intelligence "scoop" was the result of combined intelligence efforts in which aerial reconnaissance played a major role. Modern techniques also enabled American officials to learn promptly the Chinese bomb's ingredients, how it was detonated, its force, and its exact location.

For certain kinds of covert missions, the U-2, a high-altitude, jet aircraft has been used extensively, even after its exposure in May 1960, when one was brought down deep within the Soviet Union. Since then the U-2 has been known to be used by Chinese Nationalists for mainland China overflights, and by the United States for flights over Cuba during the tense crisis in September–October 1962. A successor to the U-2, the twin-jet SR-71, also built by Lockheed but capable of much greater speed and altitude, and of carrying more sophisticated spying instruments, has been developed.

Meanwhile, the SAMOS missile, an orbiting "spy in the sky," since the early 1960s has been placed routinely in orbit, once a month, bringing virtually the whole world into the range of its cameras and other detection devices. For example, a multispectral camera employs several lenses at the same time and may use film sensitive to infrared light, making difficult the concealment of almost any form of human activity on the ground. After a week of orbiting, the SAMOS photographic "take" is ejected over a designated spot in the Pacific Ocean, where it is either caught in midair by special aircraft or retrieved from the ocean. In addition to optical cameras, various electronic scanning devices are in wide use, ranging from radar to thermal sensors. The latter could detect from great heights such things as Viet Cong campfires in a Vietnam jungle or the heat from a jet plane hours after it has flown away. Computers have been of additional assistance. Deductions from evidence revealed in photographs or other sources can, with the use of high-speed computers, allow for accurate estimates of factory production, missile launchings, economic growth rates, and a wide range of strategically important information. For example, photographs of crops, floods, drought areas, or plant diseases give excellent capability for making accurate predictions of future national productivity.

For a time Manned Orbiting Laboratory (MOL) was under development by the U. S. Air Force. The plan was to place in orbit a two-man crew who would be prepared to manipulate cameras and other sensing devices, giving greater intelligence versatility. Budget cuts eliminated this plan in 1968. The Soveit Union has had major programs, too, for aerial reconnaissance both by orbiting satellites and conventional aircraft. Russian requirements for information about this country may demand far less espionage than vice versa, but Soviet COSMOS satellites have been overflying the United States since 1962.

Espionage activities of American intelligence agents are unavoidably obscured in secrecy. They remain the most romantic aspect of intelligence and provide stimulus to the imagination of film and television script writers. But the serious work of cloak-and-dagger operations must be planned and carried out with the greatest possible efficiency. A United States secret agent caught in certain kinds of espionage obviously could cause serious diplomatic and political difficulties for this country if a plausible disavowal could not be made. It would obviously be a waste of effort and money—and possibly of human life—to attempt to procure information within the Soviet Union or China which might be available otherwise from a translation of *Pravda*, or from monitoring Chinese or Russian radio broadcasts.

Duplication of intelligence effort and overlapping jurisdiction in foreign areas cause problems for a multi-agency intelligence system and have pointed to the need for central intelligence. Similarly, there also may be a danger of overemphasizing the value of information obtained from secret sources.

When he visited the United States in 1959, Soviet Premier Nikita Khrushchev jokingly suggested that CIA and the Soviet intelligence system join forces in order to eliminate the "middle man." Khrushchev bragged to Allen Dulles, then CIA Chief, that he had obtained secret United States codes and had intercepted messages at the government's highest level. "You're wasting your money," declared Khrushchev; "you might as well send it direct to us instead of the middleman, because we get most of it anyway." "Your agents," he told Dulles, "give us the code books and then we send false information back to you through your code. . . . We send cables asking for money and you send it to us."[10]

The degree of truth in Khrushchev's remarks will perhaps never be known. Doubtless much that happens in secret services at times resembles a farce, at others a tragedy. Unless properly directed, undercover agents can furnish masses of trivia, or may even fabricate data in order to meet their "quotas" or remain in the employment of a government agency. Such a dangerous and "dirty" business must be handled with great delicacy by a nation still striving for professionalism in such matters.

Effective and trustworthy undercover agents may, of course, be valuable as intelligence sources. The tale of the combination valet and German spy who served Britain's Ambassador to Turkey during World War II has often been told and the results perhaps exaggerated, but few will deny that it was the kind of investment which might have repaid handsomely the German intelligence system.

But the investment did not in fact pay off because of a fundamental difficulty which plagues all intelligence systems—the problem of credibility of source and data. The British Ambassador in Ankara was a career diplomat with the storybook name of Sir H. M. Knatchbull-Hugesson. His valet at the time was a man known only by the name of Cicero, who obtained and offered to the Germans at a very high price photographs of highly secret documents, some of which included details of Allied war negotiations and strategy. The Germans purchased these documents (with counterfeit British sterling notes, as it turned out), but skepticism and disagreement, and competition between rival Nazi intelligence agencies, dominated their evaluation in Berlin, and the Nazis downgraded their validity. The purloined papers were viewed by the Nazis as documents deliberately "planted" by British agents.[11] At any rate, placing an undercover agent of this sort is a very long-range project, the result of cleverness, or good luck.

During the American War for Independence, Benjamin Franklin headed a mission to France to secure French assistance for the colonial cause. One of his principal assistants was Edward Bancroft, who was in the pay of the British to spy on Franklin and to keep London informed of the progress of the American mission in Paris. The record remains unclear as to the degree of Bancroft's success or the effectiveness of Franklin's security finesse in this episode.

Another classical and probably apocryphal example is that of the "Watchmaker Spy of Kirkwall," who, so the legend goes, was dispatched to Scapa Flow in 1927 and whose detailed wartime reports on the British harbor defenses enabled the German Navy to slip its submarine *U-47*, commanded by Lieutenant Prien, into the highly protected British Harbor at Scapa. On October 14, 1939, the *U-47* sank the battleship *Royal Oak* as she lay at anchor. For years this story was used in intelligence training schools to illustrate a method of "advance planning" for espionage, the point being that it was a dozen years before the Watchmaker sent in his first report. Once presented as true, recent research suggests that the story is a myth.[12] Because the United States was a latecomer to clandestine operations on a world-wide scale, it has been confronted by a disadvantageous lead-time factor. Thus it may be some years before its network of secret agents is firmly entrenched in rewarding locations. In the intelligence trade these agents are called "sleepers," or "stay behinds." Reports of intelligence agents may not always result in spectacular success or even contribute much original information. But they often return excellent dividends by confirming intelligence gathered by other means or by pointing up leads which can be followed by other collection methods.

Aside from the difficulties and long-range planning involved in procuring reliable personnel and locating them in a fertile area, manifold problems are encountered in collecting secret information. In the mid-twentieth century it is difficult to place agents in the heart of a foreign government or in vital areas of a military training or research and development establishment, although this has been successfully done and evidence is continually revealed that it is being attempted. The polygraph, or "lie dectector" test, for example, makes it difficult for an agent to directly locate himself by employment with his "target" institution. Such tests have long been routine in the Central Intelligence Agency. Internal security procedures of this type have continued to gain in efficiency in recent decades, particularly in totalitarian systems of government. And many of the devices, such as electronic equipment, which may seem to facilitate clandestine procurement of data, also aid those charged with the security of such information.

In the contemporary atmosphere of tight state security systems, heavy reliance in international espionage is placed upon that immeasureable secret asset, the defector in place—that is, the disloyal American, Canadian, Englishman, or Frenchman who is willing to supply secret information to a foreign nation. Or the defector may be a Communist who has broken with the Party without its knowledge but who remains in a position to supply an American intelligence officer with secret documents or oral reports. In the former category, examples include Julius and Ethel Rosenberg, Morton Sobell, and others, all of whose activities were eventually detected. The cases provide chapters in an espionage story undoubtedly not yet finished. In the latter category, American intelligence utilizes today any person who can be enlisted as a trustworthy defector in place (as well as the publicized defectors who flee from Communist states), but on these there are few details for obvious reasons.

Totalitarian governments maintain very efficient counterintelligence systems, and their disregard for the conventional civil liberties, honored in most Western nations, enable these security officers to operate with deadly effectiveness in peace as well as in war. The United States Director of Central Intelligence paid tribute to the effectiveness of Communist counterintelligence when he declared, in 1954, "It's the toughest job intelligence has ever faced—getting good information from behind the Iron Curtain."[13] American intelligence pipelines to the Kremlin are scarce, if they exist at all.

The never-ending problem of getting good information from foreign sources is often heightened by diplomatic factors. The affair of Commander Lionel Crabb, famous British frog-man who mysteriously vanished near the Soviet cruiser *Ordzhonikidze* at Portsmouth, England, in 1956, provided considerable embarrassment to Her Majesty's Government.* The Russians did not hestitate to charge that Crabb was in the employ of United States Naval Intelligence. The Soviets also generated much anti-Western propaganda over an attempt by United States intelligence agents in 1956 to tap the main underground cables between Moscow and Soviet military headquaters in East Berlin. A 1000-foot-long tunnel was dug into the Soviet zone, and an elaborate telephone exchange was set up and reportedly attached to Soviet wires. The Russians accused United States agents of doing this. The Soviets, for their part, have been far more embarrassed by exposure of their more extensive

* This episode is discussed below in Chapter VIII.

operations in Canada and Australia, to say nothing of their apparent espionage forays from the Soviet Embassy in Washington, from United Nations headquarters in New York, and from other espionage *avanpost*.[14] The problem in covert operations is not only to avoid detection but to be able plausibly to disavow connection with adventures in espionage which are exposed or which fail.

An example is the widely publicized case of Colonel Rudolph Ivanovich Abel, an officer of the Soviet Russian State Security System, the "KGB" (Komitat Gosudarstvennoi Bezopasnosti), the foreign intelligence arm of which is roughly analagous to the American CIA. He was arrested in the late summer of 1957, arraigned in a Federal Court in New York, and indicted, convicted, and sentenced on charges of operating a military and atomic espionage ring for the Kremlin in the United States for many years. He had been living in Brooklyn under cover as an artist and photographer, using assumed names. His indictment charged that he, with several co-conspirators, had plotted to send secret defense information to the Soviet Union. Such data were transmitted (presumably as micro-photographs) to Russia in containers cleverly fashioned from bolts, nails, coins, pencils, cuff links, and other devices of modern espionage.[15] At the time of his indictment, Colonel Abel was ignored by accredited Russian diplomats in this country, who were "plausibly disavowing" connection with his activities.[16] Later he was exchanged for Francis Gary Powers and subsequently decorated as a hero of the Soviet Union. Another revealing case was that of Yuri A. Rastvorov, who operated an extensive Soviet spy ring centered in Japan under the cover of a special Soviet "Mission." He defected to the West on January 24, 1954.[17]

The use of "legal" cover by intelligence agents is a well-established practice and has been practiced by both sides in the cold war. J. Edgar Hoover once testified that foreign intelligence agents

. . . seek admittance to the United States on diplomatic passports. They seek assignments to some official foreign agency and thus conceal themselves under the diplomatic cloak of immunity. To further avert suspicion, a high-ranking espionage agent may very well be employed as a clerk or in minor capacity in a foreign establishment.[18]

Replying to congressional inquiry, an unidentified executive agency also has reported on individuals in the United States from Com-

munist countries, either as officials or employees in foreign embassies or the United Nations. This report indicated that between 1946
and 1953, some forty-five of these individuals had "records of active work for the intelligence services of their respective countries."[19]
The following exemplifies what has become an almost routine announcement: On July 22, 1960, the Department of State requested
the immediate departure from the United States of Petr Y. Ezhov,
a Third Secretary of the Soviet Embassy at Washington. His title
would suggest a diplomatic assignment, but he was asked to leave
because he "had flagrantly abused his diplomatic status by engaging
in espionage activity."[20] Ezhov had paid a commercial photographer
more than a thousand dollars for intelligence information, including
aerial photographs of American cities; had paid for flying lessons
for the photographer; and had indicated that Soviet authorities
might purchase an airplane for carrying out systematic aerial
photography.

Other modern techniques of espionage in the cold war were disclosed in the spring of 1958 when two Oxford University under-
graduates were prosecuted by the British Government for violating
the Official Secrets Act. The two students, in fulfilling National
Service obligations, took part in secret intelligence operations of
the Royal Navy. Their duty, according to details published by them
in the Oxford undergraduate magazine, *Isis*—for which they were
being prosecuted—involved participation in Iron Curtain "frontier
incidents" deliberately provoked by the British.

A scenario for such a probe might read as follows: A plane or
sea craft crosses the Soviet Russian defense line. The purpose of
provocations is to obtain intelligence about the nature of Russian
military defenses, tactical behavior, and communication procedures
and secret codes. Such provocations allegedly occur on land and sea
and in the air. Thus it becomes clear that many such incidents which
arouse Soviet response—often reported in the press as "unprovoked"
Russian attacks upon Western forces "accidentally" encroaching on
Soviet territory, are deliberately provoked for intelligence purposes.[21] Defense systems when provoked normally do respond,
yielding intelligence. This dangerous game continues.

Espionage attempts are made at the highest levels of government;
adversaries in the espionage game overlook no opportunity to gain

information. When West German Chancellor Adenauer visited Moscow in September 1955 to negotiate resumption of Soviet-German diplomatic relations, he chose to travel in an official German train. Upon arrival he insisted upon remaining in his train rather than to accept the hotel accommodations his hosts had arranged. His train had been equipped by German technicians with devices to prevent audio-surveillance. Doubtless he was aware that his hotel rooms in Moscow were wired for sound.

The search for secret information by all conceivable means has continued. In April 1964 a network of microphones was discovered embedded in the walls of the United States Embassy in Moscow. The State Department assumed that some were in operating condition when discovered. In announcing that the American ambassador in Moscow was protesting formally to the Soviet Government, the State Department described this as merely "the most recent instance of a continuing effort to penetrate American posts in Eastern Europe with listening devices and microphones." Prior to the spring of 1964, according to the department, "over 130 listening devices of various types [had] been located and removed from American Embassy buildings in [Eastern European] countries by Security Officers of the Department of State since 1949."[22] Such espionage efforts produce counterespionage activity, even to the extent of specially constructed rooms inside certain embassy buildings where sensitive discussions can be held without audio-penetration. It seems clear that a highly secret battle is continuously waged between electronic specialists feverishly designing intelligence and counterintelligence techniques. One might imagine a future scenario in which diplomats converse in sign language behind shuttered windows in order to maintain privacy.

In 1965, when Vice-President Humphrey was visiting friendly capitals in Asia, Secret Service agents, according to the *New York Times* found at least three listening devices installed in his private quarters by one of his "allied" hosts.[23]

In July 1966 it was revealed that accredited Czechoslovakian attachés in Washington had sought to use a State Department employee in a plan to place a listening device in the office of a high official in the State Department building in Washington. The ultimate objective was to "bug" the office of George W. Ball, Undersecretary of State. The attempt was thwarted by a State Department employee who had pretended to cooperate with the Czechs while working in cooperation with counterintelligence officers.

Traditional American Misgivings

There is relatively less reliable information, understandably, about United States secret operations in gathering intelligence data from foreign nations. One United States senator, for example, designated by the Senate to keep informed of the program and activities of the national intelligence community, has indicated a strong hesitancy about asking such questions of CIA for fear that he might, in his own words, "obtain information which I personally would rather not have."[24] The existing supersecrecy about these and other aspects of CIA operations overseas has the necessary advantage of protecting such activities from exposure that would rapidly dry up sources of vital information. Yet it has the simultaneous effect of arousing public and congressional suspicion.

Traditional American misgivings about government support of espionage activities are illustrated in an experience cited in the memoirs of former President Harry Truman. Shortly after becoming Chief Executive in 1945 he had a discussion with the Director of the Budget, who brought up the matter of an item of twelve million dollars in the President's special fund. It was for unvouchered use in intelligence operations outside of this country. "I told Smith [Harold D. Smith, Budget Director] I did not want the fund enlarged and that I wanted a study made of all the agencies and services engaged in intelligence work. I told him what my thinking was on the subject of our intelligence activities and my misgivings about some of the fields of these activities. I again wanted to make one thing clear: 'I am very much against building up a Gestapo.' "[25] Even though this comment reveals some confusion of intelligence and counterintelligence, here, nonetheless, was an expression of traditional American misgivings about government-sponsored espionage.

On the same subject, Hanson W. Baldwin once commented:

To most Americans the idea of an espionage system—a spy system— is abhorrent, at least in time of peace. The Office of Strategic Services [World War II] and the adventures and accomplishments of its agents did much to "sell" the public on the wartime necessity of espionage, yet there is still a native repugnance to the permanent establishment of a peacetime system. It smacks too much of duplicity and hypocrisy and poses hidden danger to the social system. It implies an "unfairness" foreign to the American mind, and some details of any intelligence system unquestionably are a "dirty" business.[26]

This was written in 1947. The intervening two decades doubtless brought an increasing awareness of the pervasiveness of international espionage and perhaps a wider public acceptance of the argument that the United States needs its own international espionage network. But the suspicion still lingers. Indeed, Mr. Baldwin himself and his newspaper, the *New York Times*, have been leaders among those advocating a closer congressional surveillance of the government's foreign intelligence operations.[27]

In contrast to the period prior to World War II, today the United States is expending hundreds of millions of dollars annually for espionage equipment, research, travel funds for agents in foreign lands, radio monitoring of foreign broadcasts, purchase of bits of information from foreign informants, and many other activities in the intelligence process known only to a few American officials. As has been said, "the spy business is booming." This may be an inevitable outgrowth of twenty years of cold war; yet its compatibility with the American democratic system remains open to question.

Overt Collection Methods

The value of overt collection methods was suggested by President Truman in commenting on the ease with which Soviet Russia is able to gather intelligence about the United States. Writing of the 1951 Senate investigation of the dismissal of General Douglas MacArthur, he stated: "For the price of a good clipping service an enemy of the United States can acquire untold items of information about our plans and intentions and even about our installations and our equipment."[28] Mr. Truman added that if a potential enemy wanted to know even more, he could hope for nothing better than a congressional probe of foreign–military policy. Said the man who had access to most of the nation's top secrets, "Then he will probably receive at no extra charge all the information he wants."

A 1960 FBI report quotes an unnamed Communist defector as stating that the ease with which information is obtained in the United States has resulted in the reduction of hazardous clandestine operations that would otherwise be thought necessary. Another defector, says the FBI report, "has estimated that the Soviet Military Attaché's office in the United States is able to legally obtain 95% of the material useful for its intelligence objectives. He stated that, in fact, 90% of an intelligence agent's time in any other country in the world would normally be consumed clandestinely obtaining information which is readily available in the United States through Government agencies or commercial publishing houses."[29]

The open societies of Western nations stand in sharp contrast to the closed systems of Communist governments. United States intelligence agencies seeking foreign data obviously do not enjoy the intelligence opportunities to be found in an open society. Many officials today feel that the American system makes the Soviet intelligence process far too easy. Allen Dulles, Director of Central Intelligence in 1954, stated, "I would give a great deal if I could know as much about the Soviet Union as the Soviet Union can learn about us by merely reading the press. . . Sometimes I think we go too far in what our Government gives out officially and in what is published in the scientific and technical field. We tell Russia too much. Under our system it is hard to control it."[30]

Dulles's predecessor, General Walter Bedell Smith, was so disturbed by the difficulty of maintaining secrecy that he planned a test of the degree of security of United States defense secrets. He commissioned the services of a group of college professors for several weeks in the summer, and provided them with a stack of published information from newspapers, congressional hearings and reports, and government press releases. Their assignment was to determine how accurate an appraisal of U. S. military power could be assembled by a foreign intelligence system utilizing the same sources. After a few weeks of analyzing the open literature, they produced a highly accurate estimate of American military strength. When the findings were shown to the President and other top officials, they were deemed so accurate that, according to Allen Dulles, "the extra copies were ordered destroyed and the few copies that were retained were given a high classification."[31]

As previously suggested, the United States in pursuing vital data from foreign areas does not resort entirely, or even largely, to clandestine operations. Communist officials have not been hesitant, for example, in boasting about their progress in the field of long-range bombers, missiles, space exploration, or other achievements in science and technology. One major task of the intelligence system is to attempt to verify or disprove the facts behind such chest-thumping. Like their Western adversaries, the Communists have a proclivity for talking, and their public, and perhaps some private, communications are well monitored by the American intelligence community.

Even so, 80 to 90 per cent of the information collected in the American intelligence process is obtained by methods and techniques which involve no greater risk or difficulty than those arising from the handling of massive amounts of data. The wide scope of the problem is illustrated by the fact that as many as five million words monitored from foreign radio broadcasts are processed into a one-page daily summary of Soviet propaganda highlights for the busy policy maker. Such a process may be compared with that of mining nickel ore; the concentrate may be no more that 0.03 per cent of what must be dug out, but the end product is essential and worth the effort. Such analogy may be applied not only to the monitoring of foreign radio broadcasts but also to the over-all process of central intelligence.

To recall again William J. Donovan's remarks, at the end of World War II, intelligence work is mostly a matter of "pulling together myriad facts, making a pattern of them, and drawing inferences from that pattern."[32]

The premium is actually not so much on whether the facts are overtly or covertly gathered or even how many facts are collected. The emphasis in the collection phase of the process must be on developing a purposeful collection plan. Here guidance from the policy makers is essential. Keen analysis by intelligence community administrators of long-range information requirements is vital. To say that the information needed in the process knows no boundaries as to source and substance is not to say that masses of information should be collected indiscriminately.

Functional Categories

The existence of certain functional categories of intelligence is helpful in maintaining a purposeful collection plan. Three such categories have been suggested: (1) basic descriptive or general information type of intelligence; (2) current reportorial, or current estimate category; and (3) speculative-evaluative, or the forecasting or warning kind of intelligence.[33] Such categories are, of course, closely interrelated, and the same mass of intelligence data will normally contribute to all of them.

Basic descriptive intelligence is that contained in the numerous and constantly revised intelligence encyclopedias available both to policy makers and to intelligence analysts.

These several categories have been refined in Sherman Kent's trail-blazing book, *Strategic Intelligence*. The descriptive element is referred to as "the groundwork which gives meaning to day-to-day change and the groundwork without which speculation into the future is likely to be meaningless."[34] The basic descriptive function is, therefore, performed by the intelligence community in the production of the government's own special set of secret encyclopedias. Rather than being organized alphabetically in the fashion of an ordinary encyclopedia, they are divided by nations or by special categories, and further subdivided into introductory national surveys, advanced surveys in depth, and *spot intelligence* such as "How good is the water supply at an air base in Libya?"

This basic descriptive element is embodied in the National Intelligence Survey (NIS), a publication series which succeeded the Joint Army-Navy Intelligence Studies produced during World War II (JANIS). Volumes of NIS have been published and continually revised since 1948. By 1966, the NIS had grown, in the words of a CIA Director, so that they add up to "more than 10 times the size of the *Encyclopedia Britannica*." Much of their contents is not based upon secret information, but is designed to supply basic information on "virtually every country in the world." The set of NIS "comes in handy when our customers start playing '20 questions.' "[35] The prospect of nuclear-armed adversaries in an endless era of competitive coexistence makes it necessary that foreign-military policy planners have information available that goes beyond military forces, terrain and general political factors. All-inclusive basic descriptive studies also are needed for such purposes as foreign aid planning, economic, political, and psychological warfare, effective diplomacy, propaganda, strategic bombing (deterrence) plans, and military government planning.*

* For more details on the National Intelligence Survey, see pp. 114-115.

The Nature of Intelligence

The National Intelligence Survey inevitably must go to press from time to time, thus in a sense stopping the clock while national and international events continue their dynamic process. This makes necessary the *current reportorial* category of intelligence which can give policy planners and decision makers up-to-date information. While the "basic descriptive" category may contain a very full biographical account of the current Soviet premier, it would be a current reportorial function to be able to answer a hypothetical query from the secretary of state: "What is the Soviet premier's position today in the political power structure of the Soviet Union?"

An actual example of *current reporting* was the detection on September 3, 1949, of unexpected radioactive dust by the Air Force Long Range Detection System. This system was created with the specific purpose of obtaining intelligence on Soviet developments in atomic energy, and its discovery in September 1949 was given the highest priority for scientific analysis. The results led to the dramatic presidential announcement on September 23 that the Soviets had succeeded in detonating an atomic bomb. This kind of reporting fulfills both the requirements of keeping the basic descriptive element up to date and of informing policy makers of developments which might affect the national interest. It also provides what has been called "a bridge between the past and future."[36] The past is embodied, essentially, in basic descriptions of the National Intelligence Surveys. The future is represented in that function of intelligence which puts the greatest demand upon the capacities of intelligence analysts. And it is in this function that the work of the intelligence expert is most fallible—the speculative-evaluative, or forecasting, function. It is one thing to be able to forecast the future rate of production of Red Chinese nuclear bombs;[37] it is quite another to be able to predict with certainty the future intentions and actions of leaders of foreign nations or even of American leaders.

The *speculative-evaluative* category is that very important and difficult element in the intelligence process devoted to forecasting the future and giving adequate warning to responsible officials of government. In a perfect grand strategy, it is often argued, the unexpected never happens. It seems clear from the record of the past dozen years that neither American intelligence nor strategy has even approached such perfection. But it is the function of this third category of intelligence to develop a very elaborate set of *indicators* which permit the operation of an effective forecasting or warning system. Efficient gathering and processing of raw data obviously are vital steps in the performance of this function, just as the existence of reliable national surveys provides the middle ground for competent forecasting.

An example of an indicator in a warning system would be the movement of Russian submarines through the Dardanelles. This would normally be considered an indicator of a possible Russian adventure. It would have been established in advance as an indicator based on previous surveys of the Soviet strategic potential, particularly the Russian capability to wage submarine warfare. Undergirding this would be prior analyses of the previous history of Soviet courses of action, an estimate of probabilities and of the likelihood that the Russians would behave according to historical patterns, and, among other things, an appraisal of the existing state of international affairs. Other indicators of possible aggressive action would be the mobilization of troops in Russia, tightening of food rationing, increases in the frequency and violence of propaganda broadcasts, or the revision of Russian secret codes.

Such indicators, added to others, would have real significance, however, only in the light of previous knowledge of Soviet capabilities, specific vulnerabilities, and its leaders' interpretations of these factors. This latter must be based upon a continuing study of Communist ideology. Knowledge of the potential of other nations involved in the strategic situation would also be essential. Possessing such knowledge, intelligence specialists ought to be able to read the latest indicators and make at least educated guesses as to the probable course of action of a foreign nation, or at least of prospective trends and tendencies. But the impossibility of making a forecast on a basis of certainty is readily discernible.

It is important to stress here the critical importance of an integrated collection plan as a first step in the eventual production of sound estimates or speculative forecasts of another nation's capabilities and intentions. An effective set of indicators—a set of "essential elements of information"—which can be applied promptly to a foreign power's actions might be termed the apex of the intelligence process triangle. But it must be re-emphasized that such indicators, to have validity, can be established only on a base of detailed and accurate descriptive studies, coupled with the latest significant intelligence reports. An intelligence prediction based upon a foundation of sand—of bias or hunch—can destroy the utility of a national policy generated by such an estimate.

Over the first twenty years of CIA's existence, the intelligence system continued to suffer from the kind of information pathology that causes intelligence professionals—but particularly policy makers —to interpret events in terms of how they prefer things to be rather than as they actually are. There is always a tendency to predict the actions of others—particularly adversaries—on the basis of "what we would do if we were in their shoes" rather than upon clear understanding that "they" and not "we" are in their shoes.

Processing the Data

In discussing the collection and sources of intelligence data the question of its processing inevitably has been anticipated and touched upon indirectly. Clearly, the functional categories of intelligence influence the collection of the raw data, just as they have an effect upon its evaluation—the third step in the intelligence process.

The collection of the massive amount of data described above, for the functions also described, is only the beginning of the process. An equally challenging problem is properly storing and meaningfully digesting this wide assortment of data.

Although much information is accumulated and filed by an intelligence agency with an immediate purpose in mind, many additional data must be kept as insurance against future requirements. It is comparable to the problems of the institutional library, which must continue to acquire books and documents for possible future use while satisfying predetermined needs. The best libraries are those which can afford to, and do, anticipate the present and future requirements of the scholarly community. So an efficient intelligence system must anticipate the present and future needs of foreign-military policy planners, while placing some reasonable limits on acquisition.

The processing stage in intelligence procedures, although vital to the usefulness of the final product, is to a certain extent a mechanical process. It is, in effect, primarily a problem of librarianship, albeit a highly specialized one. It is librarianship involving a careful interplay of modern machine handling of data and human judgment. This judgment must be injected into the processing of the data to determine whether, for example, digests of material will suffice or the entire mass of the original data be stored. Similarly, the cross-referencing system must be skillfully organized so as to insure a balance betwen security and the maximum utilization of existing information. So, too, must there be an efficient system of cataloguing all the material which exists in the various departmental intelligence libraries. With the contemporary emphasis accorded to America's security commitments by treaty to more than two score other nations, an interallied system of cataloguing and exchange of material also must be a working reality.

The use of electronic devices for handling, cataloguing, and cross-referencing data has not been overlooked by the CIA as an efficient, though fallible, method for rapidly supplying essential data to intelligence analysts.

A congressional study in 1960 reported that the Central Intelligence Agency, along with the Atomic Energy Commission, has "made the most progress and achieved the greatest advancement of all Federal agencies in the field of information processing . . . it is obvious that some of the country's leading systems engineers, scientists, and information technicians have been consulted or have worked with the officials of CIA in developing . . . the most comprehensive information system now in operation, many aspects of which have been mechanized."[38]

Over the years the CIA has developed a processing center which indexes and stores incoming information from all over the world. This center supports the work of analysts in all parts of the government-wide intelligence community. It functions as a central reference service and is subdivided into four main branches: a central library of books and documents; specialized "registers" of biographical, graphic, or industrial information; a document section; and a machine unit supporting the center by controlled processing of data by machine methods.

One may get a glimpse of the scope of the storing, indexing, and retrieval operation by noting that, as of 1960, the CIA reported the receipt in the document center of thousands of different intelligence documents *each week* in numbers of copies running into the tens of thousands. This was exclusive of newspapers, books, maps, and other such open material which was being acquired on the average of 200,000 pieces per month.

The open literature is catalogued and filed centrally in the CIA library according to the Library of Congress classification system. The secret documents go through a different process and constitute a major management problem: their volume fluctuates, their formats vary enormously, their length and quality also vary as does the degree of secrecy to be accorded them. Those documents judged to have future value—about 50 per cent—are subject to control by an elaborate punched-card system. The CIA continues to experiment with systems for effective indexing, storing, and retrieving of this mountain of classified information, using punched cards, microphotography, and automated data-processing.[39] Although automation has undoubtedly been incorporated to a degree into the process, an electronic library will be unlikely to serve as a substitute for competent human judgment at many of the crucial steps in the intelligence process. And a pressing problem of more recent years has been that of trying to make the information storage and retrieval systems compatible among the various separate agencies of government.

Establishment of a central library outside the CIA for the national intelligence community was ruled impracticable in 1955 by the various intelligence units of government and by the Hoover Commission. The 1955 Hoover Commission, however, urged that all intelligence units within the Defense and State departments adopt a single-index system based upon the intelligence subject-code used by the CIA and the Air Force.[40] And, in fact, it is CIA policy that its information center—at least the unclassified section—serves not only CIA but twenty other government agencies. The cost of a more unified system may be high but the best intelligence data are useless if they lie buried in forgotten vaults or if one agency is unaware that essential data are held by another department. Incompetent or careless management in processing raw data could result in a serious breakdown of the entire intelligence cycle, just as the whole system might be made inefficient by improper cross-referencing or interdepartmental ignorance of information existing within the intelligence community.

Evaluation and Analysis

Although in a strict sense evaluation of intelligence takes place at the point of collection and continues all during the process, a second major evaluation occurs inevitably when the information is subjected to analysis, which may be separated out as another step. This occurs after information has been gathered, indexed, and boiled down into manageable form. Evaluation at this stage is one of the most critical phases in the intelligence cycle. Both source and content of each item of information require careful evaluation as to reliability and accuracy. While it is true that the originator of an item may evaluate the source, content evaluation is usually reserved for an intelligence middleman whose sole job may be such evaluations, or for the central intelligence topical specialist. Also, at another crucial stage, the presentation of the intelligence product to the consumer, a re-evaluation in effect may take place. In the intermediate stages, to be described below, evaluation and re-evaluation also occur.

In order to standardize evaluations and to protect clandestine sources, a letter-numeral scheme is commonly used. A letter designates reliability and a numeral indicates assumed accuracy. The standard rating system is illustrated as follows:

SOURCE RELIABILITY	INFORMATION ACCURACY
A—Completely reliable	1—Confirmed
B—Usually reliable	2—Probably true
C—Fairly reliable	3—Possibly true
D—Not usually reliable	4—Doubtfully true
E—Unreliable	5—Improbable
F—Reliability cannot be judged	6—Accuracy cannot be judged

Thus an item of information classified as A-5 means that the source is completely reliable (based on past performance) but the information is improbable (based on available evidence). The most frequent complaint from intelligence consumers is that this system is too mechanical; they would like to know more about the source of material as an aid in their own evaluation of the contents. Another complaint is that too frequently a middle-ground evaluation, such as "undetermined" is given. The counterargument is that consumers should trust the intelligence experts who do the evaluating. And, of course, secret intelligence sources, particularly persons, must be protected from disclosure. Both positions suggest a fundamental and perhaps never-to-be-resolved controversy between intelligence specialists and the makers and implementers of policy.[41]

A continuing question is: "How far do intelligence analysts go beyond presenting the 'facts' "? Professional intelligence men can be heard to say in private: "Having a high-grade intelligence product is fine, but if the consumer doesn't believe it, if you aren't able to 'sell' your product, you might just as well not have collected, evaluated, and presented it." A growing professional group of highly competent intelligence specialists in Washington undoubtedly meet with frequent frustration when national policy is made seemingly without regard to the intelligence available. It is perhaps impossible to prevent policy preferences of the intelligence corps from coloring the entire intelligence process, from its collection to the final step of communication to responsible policy makers. Yet an efficient intelligence system must try to maintain a spirit of objectivity.

Decisions all along the line must be made on how the data are to be analyzed, about their significance to United States national interests, about the best form in which to present them to policy makers; or, in fact, whether to disseminate the information at all, or when to do so. For example, information was available to the CIA on Monday night, October 15, 1962, that Soviet missiles had been emplaced in Cuba. This information was transmitted to McGeorge Bundy, the President's Special Assistant for National Security Affairs. He decided not to notify the President until the following morning.[42] Decisions must frequently be made whether to present the raw data or an analytical digest of them that would point up the events they portend; whether and how data should be collated with other relevant information, coupled, at some stage, with an overlay of data on United States policy, whether implications of United States policy (and strategic capability) must always be left to the politically responsible decision maker. Such complex questions pervade the intelligence process and will be discussed below.

The difficulties and scope of the evaluating process may be illustrated, for example, by the report of a large-scale movement of Soviet armor into East Germany. Such a report would be forwarded immediately with the necessary evaluation to the appropriate military commanders, to an Indications Center in Washington (a perpetual guard-duty apparatus established under the Watch Committee within the intelligence community), and to other interested consumers. The report would then be followed by an analytical report indicating whether this movement was occurring in conjunction with military maneuvers or was a secret Soviet military operation; whether East Germans were staging uprisings; whether similar military movements were being encountered elsewhere within the Soviet orbit; whether Soviet tanks were being accompanied by air forces and infantry; and whether the pattern of such movements had ever occurred in the past, and so on. The full-blown evaluated report, which would be sent to the President's desk or to the National Security Council, would have to be further matched against other diplomatic and military events around the globe. Had such an Indications Center existed at the time of the Pearl Harbor attack, there would have been sufficient "indicators" to sound a government-wide alarm.

Recall also the example previously mentioned of the 1949 Air Force report on the discovery of radioactive dust in the atmosphere. President Truman writes that "the scientists went to work and analyzed the data. The Air Force specialists, the AEC's [Atomic Energy Commission] experts, and consultants called in from the universities went over the available information." Mr. Truman adds that their collective findings were then reviewed by a board of scientific authorities, who concluded that between August 26 and August 29 "an atomic explosion had been set off somewhere on the Asiatic mainland."[43] It was the analysis in this case rather than the raw data that produced the ultimate finding; and note also the large number of participants in the process.

Not all or even most of the data collected is of the type eagerly sought by decision makers. A truly efficient intelligence system will anticipate the needs of the policy makers without wasting effort in attempts to gather every fact under the sun. Doubtless intelligence men on more than one occasion have been confronted with the policy planner's exasperated question: "Why haven't you got information on this?" Likely as not, the same policy planner had failed to give previous guidance to the collector on his possible future needs. So the intelligence process must produce considerable information that is fed into bound volumes or other information storage systems as insurance against future requirements. During World War II, American strategic planners found that the cupboard was almost disastrously bare of *basic descriptive* information on many crucial parts of the globe where American forces had to fight. One intelligence expert has complained of a World War II tendency to weaken intelligence program planning by "a heavy schedule of miscellaneous customer demands."[44] Too much emphasis can be placed upon spot studies and answers to requests on a "crash" basis, thus interfering with carefully researched long-range projections.

The importance of projecting long-range intelligence requirements cannot be overestimated. The long lead-time in producing either economic development or new weapons systems, for example (five to ten years is not unusual), puts a heavy burden on intelligence. As the Chairman of the Joint Chiefs of Staff testified in 1956, military-foreign policy planning involves "estimating capabilities of weapons and intentions of the enemy 4 or 5 years in advance."[45] Indeed, technology continues to require projections of ever-increasing range.

A somewhat separate problem in the intelligence process is that of dealing with hypothetical questions involving the intentions of foreign leaders. This is in the previously mentioned category of "unknowable" intelligence, as contrasted with a question, for example, about prevalent diseases in Thailand. A question of the unanswerable variety would be: What will be Red China's policy objectives in Southeast Asia by 1975? Obviously, Chinese leaders themselves may not know what their policy will be under conditions which they would have difficulty in predicting. Yet an estimate of probabilities has great relevance, for example, to American officials planning a long-range program of military and economic aid to Asian nations.

Intelligence analysts faced with such a question must move out of the factual into the speculative-evaluative arena. Few intelligence men will claim that an infallible forecast can be given to speculative questions, but policy planners can gain some benefit from knowledge of the courses of action which seem most likely to be available to leaders of other nations. The intelligence community claims that efficient collection, evaluation, and analysis can provide at least educated guesses in answer to "unknowable" questions. This, they argue, is preferable to policy making based upon untutored hunches.

Expectations of the intelligence community remain high, but it is a mistake to expect the impossible. As General Walter Bedell Smith is reported to have said prior to becoming Director of Central Intelligence in 1950, "America's people expect you to be on a communing level with God and Joe Stalin . . . They expect you to be able to say that a war will start next Tuesday at 5:32 p. m."[46] Certainly the American people can expect a performance better than that rendered by the intelligence system in the first week of December 1941, in which there was a major failure in the final and crucial step of the intelligence process—dissemination of known information to the commanders who badly required it in a hurry. Yet, after three decades and the expenditure of many tens of billions of dollars, intelligence failures, as judged by one level of expectations, continue to abound.

Dissemination of Intelligence

Of the lessons to be learned from Pearl Harbor, none was more critical than the necessity for proper and timely dissemination of intelligence. For the most important kind of military intelligence, in time of crisis, is, by definition, foreknowledge. It is information which should be known in advance of action—action by our own policy makers or action by a potential enemy. Clearly a most essential and crucial step in the process is dissemination of the intelligence product.

A principal, though not entirely convincing, defense of the army and navy commanders at Pearl Harbor, made during the congressional investigation of the December 7 attack was that they were not kept informed of the information available in Washington. A major difficulty appeared to lie in Washington's preoccupation with security. Brigadier General Sherman Miles, then army chief of intelligence, testified that no distribution outside of Washington was made of decrypted Japanese diplomatic messages in order to protect the famed "Magic" system of cryptanalysis.[47] That is to say, natural desire existed to safeguard the fact that Japanese diplomatic codes had been broken. The desire to protect Magic also contributed to General George C. Marshall's decision to alert Pearl Harbor through commercial telegraph rather than by telephone.[48] The result of this decision was that the RCA messenger (Japanese by birth) bearing General Marshall's message to the Pearl Harbor commander was on his two-cylinder motorbike covering his rounds when the bombing attack sent him scurrying for cover. His message, alerting Pearl Harbor commanders to "possible" danger, was delivered around noon on December 7.[49]

Intelligence today is disseminated to decision makers and operators through briefings, daily digests, and systematic routing of summaries and estimates.

There are now seven major categories of information disseminated by the intelligence system: (1) "Raw"—unevaluated and "unfinished"—information of such immediate importance that the responsible leaders should have it at once. Intelligence professionals admit that often the commercial news services report such information first. (2) The written memorandum, a kind of informal, quick analysis which may be sent to decision makers at once, prior to a more thorough analysis or search for confirming data. (3) The oral briefing in which an intelligence leader or specialist appears before a decision maker so that questions may be asked and opinions exchanged. (4) A digest with an "Eyes Only" (that is, for the President's or Secretary of State's eyes only) classification, published six days a week and circulated to about three dozen of the highest officials concerned with national security. (5) Weekly, biweekly, or monthly publications, highly classified, but circulated to a somewhat wider group of officials. These are intelligence digests dealing with major trends, background information, and special functional questions. (6) National Intelligence Estimates, which range from annual reviews to quickly prepared summaries representing the best information on a given topic from the government-wide intelligence system. (7) National Intelligence Surveys referred to earlier in this chapter. Additionally, there is a wide range of special studies and reports, as well as publications and house journals available only to intelligence insiders.

Every effort is made to maintain rapport between those responsible for intelligence collection and analysis and those concerned with policy making and operations. To this end, as we have seen, almost every meeting of the National Security Council opens with a briefing by the Director of Central Intelligence. President Truman used to start each work day with a similar briefing, also by the Director,[50] who gave the Chief Executive a digest of the most important and up-to-date intelligence. Subsequent presidents have received daily intelligence digests, and all theater and area commanders and important United States officials overseas are kept up to date on national intelligence. Since 1952, intelligence estimates have been given to the presidential and vice-presidential candidates of the major parties, following precedent established in the Eisenhower-Stevenson campaign.

Use and flow of intelligence by officials are illustrated by the following exchange between a congressman and Secretary of the Air Force Donald A. Quarles in 1957:

Mr. Whitten . . . Where do you get your figures on what Russia has? How are they fed up to you? I know with your multitude of duties you cannot bring them together . . .

Secretary Quarles . . . I get almost daily reports from our own Air Intelligence Office in the form of brief digests of information they have acquired or the intelligence community has acquired during the previous day. Then, of course, I see the Intelligence Digests and what we call the National Intelligence Estimates which are prepared by the whole intelligence community working as a team under the Chairmanship of the Director of the Central Intelligence Agency . . .

Mr. Whitten . . . do you, as Secretary, on occasion submit requests for specific information or things of that sort?

Secretary Quarles. Yes. I have done so. For example, we came to the view a year or a year and a half ago that our intelligence on guided missile work in Russia required a much more thorough study made of it . . . a very comprehensive report was prepared. Now you should qualify these reports this way. They bring together bits of information of very many different kinds and from very many different sources. Then they compile the best educated guess of what the evidence shows has been done or what capability they give the Soviets for doing things. Capability for doing things is, of course, different from a demonstration that they will do it or conclusion that they will do it. But, generally speaking, we take the view that we should, if possible, be prepared to meet what they are capable of presenting to us. That is, in a sense, the philosophy of these reports.[51]

This exchange between a member of Congress and a secretary of the air force reveals the constant availability if not the credibility of intelligence reports in the policy-making process. Intelligence estimates theoretically play a major role in determining the allocation of national resources to contend with the capabilities and probable intentions of potential enemies, as well as paving the way for creative or preventive diplomacy or for trying to shape the future in ways thought to be consonant with the national interest. In practice the estimate is sometimes inadequate, or, even more often, accurate but disregarded. The importance of the estimate, whatever its reception, makes clear the necessity for every step in the intelligence process to be performed with utmost skill and efficiency. It also suggests the need for a rationally structured organization for effective operation of the process. Today's organization for intelligence is based in part upon modern intelligence tradecraft and doctrines. But this structure also inevitably is influenced by possibly outmoded intellectual traditions and by the historical development of intelligence organizations and the intelligence function.

CHAPTER III

*United States
Intelligence:
Historical
Background*

Unlike Great Britain and the Soviet Union, America is a new-comer to institutionalized, permanent, worldwide intelligence activities. On the eve of World War II, what masqueraded as America's intelligence system was highly departmentalized, largely uncoordinated, and almost starved for funds. There was no central intelligence. In previous wars the armed services had greatly expanded intelligence staffs, had relied heavily upon civilian specialists, and at the end of hostilities had returned to a general neglect of the intelligence function. Prior to World War II, as General George C. Marshall once described the situation, our foreign intelligence was "little more than what a military attaché could learn at a dinner, more or less, over the coffee cups."[1]

Even though neglected as an important function of government by the United States, the concept of intelligence and of its importance to decision making or to the strategy of any operation, civil or military, is as old as government.

Intelligence: An Ancient Function

The Bible records that God instructed Moses to send what in effect were intelligence agents "to spy out the land of Canaan."[2] The net intelligence estimate from this forty-day mission, with Joshua and Caleb dissenting, was that the land, which God had chosen as the home of the Children of Israel, although abundant in milk, honey, and fruit was too well guarded by its inhabitants "men of great stature"—to be overtaken. Such timorous estimate invoked the anger and punishment of the Lord. In the sixth century B.C., Sun Tzu, a Chinese military theorist wrote, in his treatise *On the Art of War*, "What enables the wise sovereign and the good general to strike and conquer and achieve things beyond the reach of ordinary men, is foreknowledge." Sun Tzu explained that such knowledge is not available from the gods, from a study of history, or from calculations. It must be obtained from secret agents. Writing two thousand years ago, Sun Tzu categorized various kinds of agents, including what we now call "double agents" and "agents in place" (defectors). In his detailed views on an organized intelligence system, this early strategist recommended the use of all kinds of agents in an elaborate intelligence network. He discoursed also on the use of psychological warfare, counterespionage, deception, and other techniques. Sun Tzu's writings are said to be popular with Mao Tse-tung and standard reading for contemporary Chinese Communist tacticians.[3]

In the Mongol invasion of Europe during the thirteenth century, Subotai, a disciple of Genghis Khan, utilized the well-organized intelligence system of the Mongols in his spectacular advances westward. As one authority has noted, "Whereas Europe knew nothing about the Mongols, the latter were fully acquainted with European conditions, down to every detail, not excepting the family connexions of the rulers."[4] The pattern of history suggests that aggressive, expansionist Societies have the best organized intelligence systems. Foreknowledge is of primary importance to those who would seize the initiative in international affairs. It has been of equal importance to nations on the defensive, but often neglected by them.

The literature on intelligence is filled as much with complaints of its failures as with tales of its successful exploits. This is exemplified in the words which Shakespeare put into the mouth of King John: "O, where hath our intelligence been drunk? Where hath it slept?" With reference to King John's plaintive query, one observer has commented, "Knowing the two classic methods of Intelligence, he might well ask!"[5]

If spying is in fact an ancient activity, the "classic methods," as

49

suggested in the previous chapter, have become less and less useful, although they have by no means been completely abandoned. Intelligence has become a more scientific enterprise. Mechanical, automated "spies in the sky" threaten a mass of secret agents on the ground with technological unemployment. And as government bureaucracies have become more tightly organized and their personnel required to be more loyal to the state, if not more honorable, there is less information for sale to spies than in earlier times. The task of the intelligence agent has become increasingly difficult over the centuries. Spies themselves are perhaps a shade more reliable than in medieval days, when a Bavarian duke instructed his son, on the eve of a military expedition: "Whosoever wants to wage war well, must look out for good intelligence, much of it, and of various kind; but you must not trust them [the spies] and not tell them what you intend to do on the strength of their findings."[6] This was to suggest, perhaps wisely, that one's own spy in those times might with sufficient information easily become the opponent's. The development of a professional corps of American "spies" with what amounts to civil service status in the mid-twentieth century tends to eliminate this hazard. Yet the purveyors of secret information will perhaps always remain suspect. Even the "gentlemen spies" are by definition not true gentlemen; the "double agent" is still known to exist.

Library shelves bulge with memoirs and accounts, often a mixture of fact and fiction, of the activities of spies and counterspies over the past three centuries, particularly dealing with wartime exploits. Yet as a function of government, the gathering of foreign intelligence in the eighteenth and nineteenth centuries tended to be haphazard, with professional diplomats going one way (tending with some notable exceptions to shun spying) and military general staffs another (tending to give little attention to the diplomatic consequences of the work of commissioned spies). The conflict between diplomacy and espionage has continued to this day.[7]

One major exception to the haphazard nature of national intelligence systems in early times was the intelligence apparatus maintained during the reign of Queen Elizabeth in sixteenth-century England. By some accounts the present British Secret Intelligence Service can claim to be the oldest still in existence.*

* Further discussion of the modern British system will be found in Chapter VIII below.

Historical Background

The creation of an institutionalized and systematically organized intelligence service in modern times is widely credited to Frederick the Great. Under him, and with the later assistance of Wilhelm Stieber, the Prussians carefully developed an intelligence system as a necessary general staff function. It was operating with some efficiency and on a widespread basis in the late nineteenth century. Similar intelligence services were developed by other European nations, patterned on the Prussian military model. By the late 1800s, Europe had become a vast network of spies and counterspies. There were few hotels, restaurants, or similar places of recreation in major European cities that did not have secret agents, male and female, operating in disguise. As Roger Hilsman has described it: "The whole continent began to look like the stage of a comic opera with hundreds of secret agents dodging in and out of the scenery as they played the lucrative and, in peacetime, not-too-dangerous game of spy and counterspy."[8]

Such activities were apparently thought necessary to support a general staff system. Moreover, an accelerating military technology and the competitive war plans of continental powers required an increasing amount of information. Walter Millis has pointed out that some of the information which Captain Dreyfus was wrongfully accused of transmitting to the Germans was technological, dealing with the design of a new artillery recoil mechanism; another item pertained to France's War Plan XIII, at that time under development by the French general staff. As in the case of the Prussians, all the great powers began to develop elaborate intelligence systems.

American Neglect of Intelligence

The United States, on the other hand, pursuing a more aloof and independent foreign policy, relied chiefly upon its diplomatic agencies and military attaché system for the collection of whatever information seemed necessary regarding foreign nations. One such example was that of the United States Consul General in Havana in 1897-1898, General Fitzhugh Lee, who was praised by the captain of the Battleship *Maine* for his helpful "spying" activity.[9] It was through such open channels that most information was obtained, but there was no organization for coordinating information separately collected by the War, Navy, and State departments.

According to its own official history, the United States Army was "slow to recognize the importance of military intelligence and backward in its use in the solution of military problems."[10]

During the Civil War, Allan Pinkerton, a famous detective, was hired as chief of intelligence for General McClellan's Union Army. The internecine nature of the Civil War, with families and regions artificially divided, made espionage for both sides relatively easy. Counterespionage was correspondingly difficult. Even so, according to Allen Dulles,

No great battles were won or lost or evaded because of superior intelligence. Intelligence operations were limited for the most part to more or less localized and temporary targets. As one writer has put it, "There was probably more espionage in one year in any medieval Italian city than in the four-year War of Secession."[11]

Pinkerton, with his agents, was adept at ensnaring bank robbers and railway bandits, but possessed little competence in military intelligence. Consequently, his estimates of Confederate troop strength were greatly exaggerated—a fact which, coupled with General McClellan's pessimistic outlook, bolstered the excessive caution with which McClellan planned his Peninsula campaign. Pinkerton, who had been using the *nom de guerre* "Maj. E. J. Allen," was soon replaced by a more experienced intelligence officer, Colonel Lafayette C. Baker.[12] Baker later became a brigadier general and commanded a reorganized National Detective Police, one of the antecedents of today's Secret Service. Lincoln's assassination in 1865 casts doubt on the effectiveness of that unit's counterintelligence, though its espionage performance is said to have been an improvement over Pinkerton's. Meanwhile, within the Union Army a Bureau of Military Information had been created under the command of George H. Sharpe. Little is known of its performance, but it appears to have been relatively ineffective. Although the Confederacy supported many spies and counterspies, its intelligence service was even less well organized than that of the Union. Military men experienced in strategic intelligence were almost nonexistent at this stage of the nation's history, although the concept of intelligence was age-old, and military organizations, such as the Cavalry, often performed a combat intelligence function.

Not until the 1880s, probably in response to European military intelligence organizational development, were permanent intelligence units created in the United States Army and Navy. The army's Military Intelligence Division was established within the Adjutant General's Office. The navy's Office of Intelligence was created in the Bureau of Navigation. Military and naval attachés were also designated during this period and assigned to various foreign posts. When the general staff of the U. S. Army was created in 1903, military intelligence became "G-2"—the designation it still carries. Prior to the First World War, President Wilson's cabinet was reported to have demonstrated a "ludicrous preoccupation with a weird assortment of rumors,"[13] suggesting the absence of an intelligence system. Such a system might have prompted an effective attention to facts rather than to rumors. Decision makers were, obviously, simply misinformed on numerous occasions during this period.

World War I

When the United States became involved in World War I, Army Intelligence was a tiny section of the General Staff, consisting of only two officers and two clerks.[14] With reorganization, the Military Intelligence Division had grown into a staff of over 1200 officers and civilians at the time of the armistice. Its duties, however, ranged widely, including internal security and censorship. By the war's end the government was indeed intelligence-conscious, and twenty officer-specialists of Army Intelligence accompanied President Wilson to the Peace Conference as Versailles.[15]

The Military Intelligence Division of the General Staff evolved from the Bureau of Information in the Adjutant General's office. The duties of the division, as assigned in August 1918, were "to maintain estimates revised daily of the military situation, the economic situation, and of such other matters as the Chief of Staff may direct, and to collect, collate and disseminate military intelligence."[16] Collection of information remained the responsibility of the military attachés. A year after the war ended, 88 officers and 143 civilians were employed in the Military Intelligence Division of the army.[17] This number was rapidly cut back in the subsequent years of international retrenchment and isolation.

Intelligence clearly was neglected in the decades between the two world wars, but concepts of the proper function of intelligence were not wanting. Writing in 1920, a brigadier general who headed American wartime army intelligence, Marlborough Churchhill, expressed the fundamental concept:

National strategy must be based upon national policy. It is obvious that national policy must depend upon correct predictions concerning the international future, and that, after the national policy and strategy have been determined upon, war plans can never be satisfactory unless they are based on correct detailed information.[18]

But such a concept of intelligence was not adopted and vigorously pursued. Both army and navy intelligence hobbled along in the 1920s and 1930s, rarely attracting the most promising officers and receiving only meager congressional appropriations. Many congressmen tended to look upon the military or naval attaché as an officer being sent on a luxurious vacation at the expense of, and with no benefit to, the American taxpayer. Today, some veteran congressmen, perhaps as a matter of habit, still closely question military budget requests supporting the attaché system. Apparently they maintain a suspicion that money spent on attachés may be largely a waste.

World War II

As America entered World War II, this chronic lack of intelligence information in the War Department was, in the words of General Eisenhower "a shocking deficiency that impeded all constructive planning."[19] A basic requirement for the needed intelligence, a "far-flung organization of fact finders" was nonexistent. General Eisenhower further comments:

Our own feeble gesture in this direction was the maintenance of military attachés in most foreign capitals, and since public funds were not available to meet the unusual expenses of this type of duty, only officers with independent means could normally be detailed to these posts. Usually they were estimable, socially acceptable gentlemen; few knew the essentials of Intelligence work. Results were almost completely negative and the situation was not helped by the custom of making long service as a military attaché, rather than ability, the essential qualification for appointment as head of the Intelligence Division in the War Department.[20]

One consequence was the rather low esteem in which many commanders held military intelligence.* Sir John Slessor, former chief of the Royal Air Force, recounts an illustrative incident that took place at the time of the Allied planning for the invasion of North Africa. Intelligence estimates were, of course, an important consideration in the formation of such plans. Expert advice was required concerning the location of the enemy, his strength, and his likely reaction to alternate situations. This was the job of the intelligence staff. But, as Slessor recalls, some of the American officers on this joint planning effort "tended to take a robustly independent line in these matters—'to hell with the G2 guys—I don't give a damn what they say—that is what he'll [the enemy] do.'" As a consequence of this attitude, General Eisenhower found it necessary to issue an order that official intelligence estimates were to be accepted for planning.[21]

The Department of State, inherently a prime collector and user of political intelligence, also was poorly equipped to produce or cope with the volume and types of information required *circa* 1941. Dean Acheson, when Under-Secretary of State, testified before Congress in 1945 that until World War II the Department of State's "technique of gathering information differed only by reason of the typewriter and telegraph from the techniques which John Quincy Adams was using in St. Petersburg and Benjamin Franklin was using in Paris."[22] In 1909 the department had only four persons whose function was classified as "intelligence." By 1922 this figure had risen to a grand total of five, and by 1943 to no more than eighteen. In any one of these periods, of course, the great majority of State Department personnel were working in intelligence, very broadly construed.

It is commonplace to blame Congress and its inadequate appropriations for the sorry state of American strategic intelligence in the years between the two world wars. But the crux of the problem was the lack of recognition, within the State and War and Navy departments, of the importance in peacetime of coordinated "finished" national intelligence on foreign areas. A more fundamental cause of this neglect was the temper of the times—a period of isolation from world affairs, of governmental retrenchment, of America viewing

* Perhaps some commanders were persuaded by the dictum of Clausewitz that most of the information obtained in war is false, contradictory, or of doubtful validity.

itself as the world's moral bastion, and of a military policy of passive defense centered in the Western Hemisphere. Whatever the reasons, Congress in the 1920s normally appropriated less than $200,000 annually for army intelligence. Compare this with the army's 1958 budget request for $125,000,000 for the same purpose. In fiscal years 1934 and 1936 Congress expressly forbade the army to maintain more than thirty-two military attachés.[23]

A similar situation existed in the Navy. The Office of Naval Intelligence had in 1934 a permanent civilian force of only twenty, and only two officers and a clerk were assigned to twenty countries of Latin America.[24]

Comparing British and American military intelligence talent early in World War II, General Omar Bradley stated "the British easily outstripped their American colleagues."[25] Worse than that, commented General Bradley, misfits were sometimes assigned to intelligence. Recall, in this connection, the "Old Man's" advice to the young commander Melville Goodwin in Marquand's novel: "Put the prima donnas in Intelligence, but keep them out of Operations."[26]

In some segments of the military organization, the intelligence section became a dumping ground for officers unsuited to regular command assignments. This reveals much about the professional military attitudes in the past regarding an intelligence career. As General Bradley and others have recounted, the day was saved in wartime by the incorporation into intelligence units of numerous civilians with special knowledge or talents. The navy, with its predilection for general line (i.e., sea duty) officers, similarly was a discouraging place for ambitious officers to pursue an intelligence career.

The Impetus of Pearl Harbor

When a message that Pearl Harbor was under attack by Japanese planes reached Secretary of the Navy Frank Knox in Washington on Sunday afternoon, December 7, 1941, he exclaimed "My God, this can't be true. This [message] must mean the Philippines!" The Navy Secretary's reaction symbolizes the failure of strategic intelligence as America was plunged into World War II. The point, however, is not so much that intelligence was not available but that to political and military officials—even those in possession of suggestive intelligence—the attack was inconceivable. This was principally because it was expected elsewhere—in Thailand, Malaya, or the Philippines—even though the basic United States war plan, issued May 26, 1941, envisaged a possible surprise attack on the fleet in Hawaii. There were too many indicators that the Japanese were preparing to attack, but not at Pearl Harbor. Pearl Harbor is an intelligence lesson burned into the minds of planners of national strategy, general staffs, and responsible commanders in the field.

The Pearl Harbor surprise attack provided the stimulus for the development of a centralized intelligence community and a revitalization during and after the war of military intelligence personnel and the intelligence process. There is no need to review here the events leading up to Pearl Harbor nor to describe the attack itself. This has been done in 25,000 pages of official transcript of testimony and reports and in numerous books, the best of which is Roberta Wohlstetter's, *Pearl Harbor: Warning and Decision.* The reams of official testimony were produced by seven separate official inquiries and a postwar congressional investigation which itself turned out 39 volumes (15,000 pages) of hearings and a 573-page report.[27]

Some of the conclusions from this mass of testimony and reports will always be debated, but two facts now seem indisputable: one, that the Japanese achieved complete surprise in the attack;[28] and two, that the American information system, inadequate as it was, provided the major clues in advance of the attack but these were poorly interpreted and even more poorly communicated to those with a "need to know." If intelligence is foreknowledge, as previously stated, Pearl Harbor was a complete intelligence failure. It was a top-to-bottom failure of the intelligence system, but it was particularly a failure in intelligence interpretation, communication, and receptivity. Commanders—civilian and military—failed to utilize efficiently the intelligence available,[29] and it will be recalled that the navy's minesweeper *U.S.S. Condor* detected at 3:50 a.m. on December 7, and the destroyer *Ward* sank at 6:45 a.m. the same day, a submerged Japanese submarine in a forbidden zone near the Pearl Harbor entrance. But the *Ward*'s reports to higher commands were delayed and were still under discussion by various naval commands when the Japanese bombs began to drop. It is an

often told tale, also, that planes—the first Japanese attack force—
were detected by an army mobile radar unit at 7:02 a.m. as they
approached from the north. Such warnings again fell on unbeliev-
ing ears, and the radar trainees were told by a duty-officer to "forget
it."

The Pearl Harbor raid was for the Japanese in a limited sense a
brilliant success. In the long run, the attack, as it was carried out,
proved to have been strategically unwise, tactically incompetent,
and politically disastrous. There were better strategic targets at
Pearl than the ships. Permanent installations and oil tanks strangely
went unscathed. The Japanese made no attempt to knock out the
two Pacific Fleet aircraft carriers, which were at sea. In concentrating on Battleship Row, scant attention was paid to cruisers and
destroyers. Retrospectively, the choice of targets at Pearl, and
even the attack itself, was unwise. As more than one observer of
military affairs has remarked, "The loss of our battleships at Pearl
Harbor advanced U. S. naval warfare by a good ten years!"

But the Japanese did choose the battleships, and of the 94 ves-
sels of the United States Navy situated in the harbor, Japanese pilots
clearly knew which ones they wanted and where to find them. They
were well briefed not only about ship locations, but about the
Sunday morning habits and week-end liberty tradition of the American Navy. With complete surprise, and with informed precision, the
Japanese hit their chosen targets. After two hours of devastating
attack the navy had more than 2000 fatalities and 710 wounded.
Together the army and marine corps lost 327 killed and 433
wounded, and, in addition, some 70 civilians were killed. In the
course of the attack the battle force of the Pacific Fleet was wrecked
as well as about half the military planes on Oahu.

The voluminous testimony available on the Pearl Harbor episode
indicates that the not inconsiderable suggestive intelligence available prior to the Japanese attack was simply not believed. The im-
minence of war was widely felt, but both Japan's capabilities *and*
intentions were wrongly assessed. In the minds of many responsible
leaders, Hawaii was thought to be too far distant from Japan; the
Japanese Navy technically incapable of lauching such an attack;
Japanese military aviation insufficiently skilled for such an action;
and the risks of failure were believed to be too great for Japanese
war-making strategists.

The basic intelligence problem, then, as now, was only in part a matter of sufficient information. What mattered most were the pictures in the minds of responsible decision makers. The Secretary of the Navy's exclamation, "This can't be true," suggests the root of the matter.

Such an attitude goes a long way in explaining the Japanese success in achieving surprise. The problem was that from a great mass of warning signals, of "indicators," or "essential elements of information" with regard to what *might* happen, intelligence officials and decision makers, especially, selected out those expectations that were familiar, preconceived, or preferred rather than what, in objective reality, was likely or possible. In her definitive study, Roberta Wohlstetter demonstrates that "we failed to anticipate Pearl Harbor not for want of the relevant materials, but because of a plethora of irrelevant ones."[30] Developing this point, she utilizes the concept of "noise"—the mass of information which from hindsight is obviously useless or irrelevant but which cannot be easily sorted out as such by the contemporary analyst or decision maker. She notes the important difference "between having a signal available somewhere in a heap of irrelevancies, and perceiving it as a warning; and there is also a difference between perceiving it as a warning, and acting or getting action on it."[31]

In a later study comparing Pearl Harbor with the surprise emplacements of Russian missiles in Cuba in 1962, Mrs. Wohlstetter notes that in each case the intelligence system provided much information on the approaching crisis, but that this information was incomplete and ambiguous. No single, definitive signal was received that stated: "This is it." Instead, a conglomerate of signals—noise—was heard that tended to obfuscate the true signals. Who made the noise? Some of it was deliberately created by our adversary to mask his intentions; part was the result of chance. Some was created by the internal intelligence process itself. This is not to suggest, with respect to the Cuban missile crisis, that after twenty years little improvement could be seen in the intelligence warning system. But it does suggest, in Mrs. Wohlstetter's phrase, that "it is important to recognize that the difficulties facing intelligence collection and interpretation are intrinsic, and that the problem of warning is inseparable from the problem of decision."[32]

With the clairvoyance of hindsight it is always easy to be an armchair intelligence expert. Yet the intelligence lessons of Pearl Harbor are painfully clear, and the postwar development of a centralized intelligence community has been an attempt to reflect some of these lessons. Few question the necessity today of having a centralized system which guarantees, in theory at least, that properly evaluated, coordinated, and timely information is brought to the attention of all responsible officials. The concept of an intelligence system which serves—to use Henry L. Stimson's phrase—as a "sentinel on duty" at all times is now unanimously accepted in official Washington, although the product of the system has sometimes been disappointing.

Recognition of this concept, however, has not solved all the problems. For the warning function, it will be recalled, is only one of our intelligence requirements, and there remain questions of doctrine, organization, and personnel. These questions are all involved in facing the problem of balancing enemy capabilities with enemy intentions. When the Russians installed missiles in Cuba, the rapidity of the installation, wrote Roberta Wohlstetter, "was in effect a logistical surprise comparable to the technological surprise at the time of Pearl Harbor."[33] In December 1941 few believed that the Japanese had a *capability* for the Pearl Harbor attack. They had it. Even fewer, if any, were convinced that Japan had the *intention* of carrying out such an attack. The problem then, as now, was a tendency to create policy and plan actions based upon what potential enemies were likely to do, and this was too often defined in terms of what we would do if we were they, rather than in terms of their total capability. The fusing of capability and intention will always create a dilemma and will suggest the limitations of any intelligence system. Pearl Harbor was a tragic example of a classic intelligence problem. It was clear that at the least a better apparatus than existed in 1941 was required for intelligence assessments of such problems. During the war and in the postwar period, particularly, a beginning was made in applying the intelligence lessons of Pearl Harbor.

In the words of the 1955 Hoover Commission, "The CIA may well attribute its existence to the surprise attack on Pearl Harbor and to the postwar investigation into the part Intelligence or lack of Intelligence played in the failure of our military forces to receive adequate and prompt warning of the impending Japanese attack."[34]

With the sophistication gained from a dozen intervening years, the Hoover Commission task force in 1955 drew the same conclusion as others about the Pearl Harbor experience; namely, that information necessary to anticipate the attack was available to government agencies but that the breakdown came in its evaluation and dissemination. Thus appropriate decisions were left unmade, and timely instructions were not given to responsible commanders in the field.

Analysts of the Pearl Harbor episode have also cited interservice rivalries that prevented a full sharing of vital information, the lack of a high-level joint intelligence group, and the absence of a high-echelon organization for national estimates and an indications center. The latter deficiency was painfully evident on December 6, 1941, when raw intelligence reports—the intercepts in "Magic" (the broken Japanese code) of the Japanese ultimatum—were read but not properly evaluated, communicated, or acted upon. As previously suggested, there was no joint intelligence group or U. S. Intelligence Board to evaluate, analyze, synthesize, and promptly disseminate the available information. There was no "Watch Committee" or National Indications Center such as exists today, with trained sentinels perpetually scanning the globe. Nor did a National Security Council with its important secretariat exist to act in concert upon the basis of information known to some, but not all, high officials.[35]

The Beginnings of Central Intelligence

Five months before the Japanese attack, President Roosevelt had in fact moved to correct obvious national intelligence deficiencies. He summoned Colonel (later Major-General) William J. Donovan to draft a plan for a new intelligence service designed for the requirements of global war and patterned in large measure after British experience. "You will have to begin with nothing," he told Donovan. "We have no intelligence service."[36]

Donovan was a successful lawyer who had won the Medal of Honor in World War I. He was an imaginative, aggressive man who had traveled abroad extensively. So far as intelligence work went, he was an amateur, but in the American tradition of public service he seemed qualified to assemble what was to become the forerunner of CIA. In July 1940 Navy Secretary Frank Knox advised President

Roosevelt to send Donovan to England to study the British intelligence system. There he established important contacts, enabling the American President to be informed of how the British were organizing wartime intelligence. Donovan's most significant finding was that the British had created a central unit to coordinate intelligence activities and to process information for the Cabinet. Donovan became the architect of the American plan for an agency for centralized strategic information and operations.

On June 25, 1941, Colonel Donovan was appointed Coordinator of Information, with instructions to collect and analyze all strategic intelligence information and data and to furnish the results to the President and other interested agencies.[37] Amidst a maze of red tape, Donovan was attempting to organize and to ascertain the precise mission of his new agency when war came. In keeping with Roosevelt's administrative style, the relationship between Donovan's new unit and existing military intelligence services was initially vague. Originally, Donovan's unit was placed within the War Department, creating considerable confusion and adverse military and naval reaction. This resulted in an early change of status, in which Donovan reported directly to the President. Later, in June 1942, the Office of Strategic Services was officially created and placed under the Joint Chiefs of Staff. There is a widely told, perhaps apocryphal, story that strategic intelligence activities were considerably delayed on the eve of war because of an inability to find office space for new intelligence agencies.

With the formation of the Joint Chiefs of Staff in February 1942, it quickly became apparent that coordinated intelligence was needed if the JCS were to function effectively. Plans for combined interservice and interallied military operations, particularly with the British, necessitated the formation of a Joint Intelligence Committee (JIC) as an agency of the Joint Chiefs of Staff. Members of the JIC included representatives of the Office of Naval Intelligence, Military Intelligence Service (Army), Assistant Chief of Air Staff (Intelligence), Department of State, Office of Strategic Services (OSS), and the Foreign Economic Administration. This committee was the *ad hoc* response to the need for centralized intelligence in wartime, although most intelligence operations were performed by its constituent members. The Joint Intelligence Committee's role was to synthesize intelligence received from all sources for use by the Joint Staff and JCS. Much of its work in coordinating intelligence activities was carried on by specialized subcommittees. These included: Technical Industrial Intelligence, Topographical Studies, Joint Studies Publication, Archives, Weekly Summary Editorial Board, and Publications Review.

Under stimulus of the Joint Intelligence Committee, a government-wide effort was made to coordinate the strategic intelligence system in the field and various units in Washington. Joint Intelligence collection agencies, staffed from Army and Navy intelligence offices and with a heavy influx of civilian specialists in various fields, were set up in military theaters of operation. Their functions were to coordinate intelligence collection and dissemination and to maintain effective liaison with the field and with a Joint Intelligence Agency Reception center in Washington. Such joint collection groups were established in the Mediterranean, Africa–Middle East, India–Burma, and China theaters of operation. A more effective integration and dissemination of the resulting joint intelligence product was effected in 1943, when publication was started of the Joint Army-Navy Intelligence Studies (the JANIS series referred to earlier), which were encyclopedic volumes covering a vast field of intelligence on enemy capabilities, targets, terrain, and other factors.[38]

Jointly and individually, the wartime intelligence services, amidst some confusion, duplication, and much interagency conflict, sometimes measured up to the high standards set by the combat forces in the field. Some notable successes were the Navy's communications intelligence code-breaking performance at Midway Island, which led to the location and ultimate defeat of the Japanese Imperial Navy's carrier force; the thorough and skillfully executed deception plan before the Allied invasion of Normandy in June 1944, which kept German defense disastrously off balance; the generally excellent beach studies developed for the Pacific campaign; the identification of the German guided missile development center at Peenemünde; and the achievements of OSS described below. A notable individual performance was given by Allen Dulles, who became Director of Central Intelligence in 1953. Operating as OSS station chief from Bern, Switzerland, in the period of 1942-1945, he built up a combined political action and intelligence network employing hundreds of informants and operatives reaching into Germany, Hungary, Yugoslavia, Czechoslovakia, Bulgaria, Spain, Portugal, and North Africa.[39] One of his major achievements was to remove the German Army from the war in Italy by secret negotiations, which he described later in his book, *Secret Surrender*.[40] Dulles's wartime network is also credited with producing the first reports on the Nazi rocket experiments at Peenemünde and information about the V-2 "super-bomb" bases being set up for attacks against Great Britain.

But there were perhaps an equal number of intelligence breakdowns. Combat intelligence erred disastrously at the Battle of Savo Island (an Australian Air Force observer failed to inform the navy that Japanese cruisers were approaching) and at the Battle of the Bulge, the German surprise offensive in the Ardennes area in the winter of 1944. German ability to recuperate from Allied bombings of its industrial centers was underestimated.[41] Some strategic intelligence analysts are said to have overestimated the strength of the Japanese Manchurian forces in 1945, which aided the "get Russia into the war with Japan" advocates. In many cases, however, intelligence was blamed for what in fact may have been blunders or failures of judgment by military commanders in the field or by policy makers in Washington or London.[42] The Battle of the Bulge, for example, may have been such a case.

Intelligence supporters, using hindsight, claim that some Office of Naval Intelligence and Air Forces intelligence estimates suggested to the Pentagon and the White House early in 1945 that Japan, with her fleet and air force virtually immobilized for lack of oil, could not long survive. In fact, just as had been the case on the eve of the Pearl Harbor attack, there was no system for developing truly national composite estimates. Decision makers accordingly listened to some intelligence experts while turning a deaf ear to others, and finally decided that Russia should be brought into the war with Japan, that a large-scale invasion should be launched, and atomic bombs dropped at Hiroshima and Nagasaki. A majority of intelligence experts apparently believed that naval blockade and bombing could not alone produce unconditional surrender prior to the date set for invasion (March 1, 1946).[43] The wisdom of the decision to drop the first two atomic bombs will be endlessly debated, but the point is that a system for a truly composite intelligence estimate unfortunately did not exist.

Office of Strategic Services

The government's closest approach to a central intelligence system during World War II was the widely publicized, now almost legendary Office of Strategic Services. At least two legends are attached to OSS. One, to which its detractors adhere, pictures it as a catch-all group of scholars, socialites, Wall Street businessmen and lawyers, and adventurers, recruited to perform a variety of roles under the vague rubric, "strategic services." This legend suggests, without distinction among its various separate functions, that OSS generated more romantic activity than hard intelligence useful for strategic or operational decision.

The other legend, perhaps the more accurate, portrays an essentially amateur OSS as giving the United States, with its new world leadership responsibility, invaluable experience in meeting the variety of problems involved in operating a modern central intelligence system. In spite of its fumbles and the inevitable confusion surrounding any new Washington agency under amateur leadership in the wartime emergency, OSS, according to this legend, offered a constructive opportunity to a nation with little prior experience in the various functions which ended up within the OSS jurisdiction.

It is difficult to paint an accurate picture or make an objective evaluation of OSS because its official history to date remains unpublished and because most of the sources on its multifarious activities are ephemeral, contradictory, uncritical, or still under security classification. Moreover, there were many sides to OSS, from pure research to the wildest kind of secret operation. It seems clear, however, that the most publicized of the operations of OSS—of the cloak-and-dagger type—produced in many ways the least significant long-range results. This is not to underestimate the OSS role in and literally incalculable contribution to Allied victory, particularly in defeating the Axis Powers in North Africa, in aiding the French resistance movement in France and in Burma. Usually, however, the OSS role merely complemented the more traditional military function. Perhaps the melodramatic publicity given to the activities of OSS secret agents in the years following World War II is largely responsible for many of the prevailing myths concerning the nature of central intelligence.

Such myths have been perpetuated in new cold war forms in the

1960s by one of the leading phenomena of the period—the production and absorption of escapist literature, cinema and television plays depicting the work of secret agents. While commonly described as "spy" material, these mass appeal products normally have borne little true relevance to what properly may be called intelligence work.

The popular heroes of the wartime OSS—those who play the major roles in motion pictures and in television scripts about OSS— are the secret agents who worked behind enemy lines, or the secret operatives whose function was essentially sabotage or counterespionage. But perhaps the most significant work was done by those unheralded college professors, lawyers, and others who worked tirelessly in the research units, in the analysis of economic objectives, and in other operational analysis and technical groups within OSS. These groups contributed much information on which successful wartime operations were based, and developed techniques useful to contemporary intelligence research and analysis. Probably these analysts played a more significant role than the estimated 1,600 Americans who were infiltrated by OSS behind enemy-held territory.

This is not to suggest that the often heroic overseas espionage and political action work of OSS agents was not of value to a nation at war with a formidable adversary. The point is that the popular tendency to identify cloak-and-dagger activity as the principal and most important role of a central intelligence system has continued to distort the public concept of the nature and relative importance of various kinds of secret operations.

When the Joint Chiefs of Staff assumed responsibility, after 1942, for coordinating military intelligence, a function performed by the interservice Joint Staff and various JCS committees, Colonel Donovan abandoned further serious attempts to operate, as under his original mandate, an over-all government intelligence coordinating agency. His Office of Coordinator of Information soon was transformed into the OSS, which became a combined research, foreign espionage, and special operations agency. With the creation of OSS early in the war, the United States became engaged for the first time in intensive strategic intelligence research and extensive espionage and political action operations on a world-wide scale. OSS was the by-product of total war. Its purpose varied from the gathering, evaluating, and synthesizing of information about the capabilities and vulnerabilities of enemy nations, to the conduct of a wide variety of destructive paramilitary and subversive operations behind enemy lines.

One major effect of the presidential order creating the OSS on June 13, 1942, was to make it directly subordinate to the military direction of the war. The placing of OSS under the command of the Joint Chiefs of Staff not only made its administration easier, in terms of recruitment, supplies, and priorities in a war-tight economy. but also narrowed the scope of its activities. The direct supervision of OSS was the responsibility of the Joint Psychological Warfare Committee, of which Donovan was chairman. The Committee reviewed all the major matters pertaining to plans, logistics, research and development, and personnel. In matters pertaining to overseas military theaters of operations, the concurrence of the theater commander was required, but the ultimate authority was the Joint Psychological Warfare Advisory Committee, representing the various services and departments concerned.

Not unexpectedly, the Office of Strategic Services went through several reorganizations during the war, guided by the inevitable pragmatism of a new venture. The accompanying chart shows the structure of OSS when the war ended in August 1945.

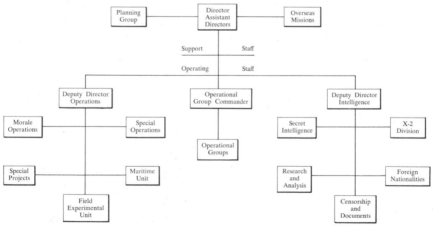

1. U. S. Office of Strategic Services, 1945. (Based on James G. Kellis, "The Development of U. S. National Intelligence, 1941-1961," 1963. Used with permission of the author.)

In the OSS structure the Planning Group was an interdepartmental unit comprised of representatives from the army, navy, and State

Department, as well as OSS. It prepared and reviewed strategic services plans, doctrine, budgets, personnel and logistical requirements. The Support Staff provided general administrative services, including a secretariat, security office, general counsel, research and development, and communications.

The most important of the three "operating staffs" was that headed by the Deputy Director for Intelligence. (In many ways, the postwar CIA's organization was similar to that of the OSS.) The Secret Intelligence division was responsible for overseas espionage, divided into four regional desks: Africa, Europe, Far East, and Middle East. Agents were stationed all over the globe, excepting Latin America, the special province of the Federal Bureau of Investigation. In addition to the regional desks, some functional bureaus were created, such as the Labor Desk, for secret contacts with foreign labor officials. In the course of the war, frictions developed between the Secret Intelligence division and other operating units, including the British intelligence services. This resulted from duplication of effort and self-defeating entanglements as one group tripped over the other's cloak and dagger.[44]

The X-2 Division was assigned the counterespionage mission. This was essentially a police function, its aim to protect the security of espionage agents. But this involved the penetration of enemy intelligence agencies which, when successful, was productive of important positive intelligence. Thus a sharp distinction was difficult to maintain between espionage and counterespionage. Many of the agents of X-2 came from the Bureau of Narcotics, where they were experienced in overseas covert operations. At war's end the X-2 branch numbered about 700 employees, at home and abroad.[45]

The Research and Analysis Division was the unit employing most of the large number of professional scholars who joined OSS. Essentially, this was the intelligence production unit of OSS, and it produced a wide range of reports from brief situation summaries to lengthy scholarly analyses. It was organized into geographic areas, each area having an economic, political, and geographical subunit. The main function of the Foreign Nationalities Division was to maintain contact with foreign nationality groups in the United States and with governments-in-exile elsewhere, particularly in London. Such contacts produced information, recruits, and advice on psychological warfare strategy. The Censorship and Documents division monitored selected enemy broadcasting stations, analyzed information gained from the Office of Censorship, and fabricated documents needed by secret agents, such as German or Italian identity cards, labor cards, travel permits, and the like.

Under the Deputy Director for Operations, a number of units were organized to plan, supervise, and direct the non-intelligence strategic operations. The Morale Division was charged with carrying out a variety of programs designed to weaken the enemy. These included attempts to incite resistance, to subvert morale, to spread false rumors, to circulate all forms of "black propaganda" (source concealed), and any activity "for the purpose of creating confusion, division and undermining the morale of the enemy."[46]

The Special Operations Division organized, supported, and directed resistance and illegal guerrilla groups in occupied countries, excepting the Southwest Pacific where the theater commander was operating his "own" guerrilla forces. While other divisions of OSS used foreign nationals for operations behind enemy lines, most of the persons in Special Operations were American citizens, recruited from the armed forces to perform "hazardous missions." Special Operations was divided into military theater desks, subdivided by country. Some 1600 operatives were sent behind enemy lines, but the division was responsible for attempting to aid and supply guerrilla and resistance movements numbering in the tens of thousands.

The Maritime Division was largely a training and development unit, instructing agents in the techniques of infiltrating enemy territory by small boats and submarines. The Special Projects and Field Experimental units were charged with developing all the secret weaponry and paraphernalia of the spy and counterspy. These small units were also charged with analyzing technical problems involved in determining what kinds of information were required to maintain surveillance on "secret weapons" under development by the Germans, such as rockets, jet engines, and atomic devices.

In the third grand organizational category were the Operational Groups, which were similar in some respects to the Special Operations groups, organized separately. Their primary responsibility was to support resistance and guerrilla movements, but in an importantly different way from Special Operations. The Operational Groups were units of "commandos," or "rangers," who participated in military operations in support of resistance movements. The groups fought as units, comprising some thirty to forty men, whereas the Special Operations units rarely exceeded three or four men, who were infiltrated to work with foreign nationals opposing the Axis powers.

These many-sided activities were organized and controlled from the Washington headquarters of OSS. But OSS maintained a number of regional headquarters overseas—in London, Chunking, New Delhi, Cairo, and Algiers—all located near the theater commands, thereby facilitating liaison.

Colonel Donovan's OSS blossomed and spread throughout Washington and the world in a manner described by some as resembling a Gilbert and Sullivan opera. When the war ended, approximately 13,000 OSS workers were engaged in some kind of work believed to be strategically important. OSS personnel comprised a hodge-podge of Americans believed to have some talent for the frontier-less game of strategic intelligence and special operations. OSS was, in fact, an assemblage of college professors and Hollywood stunt men, Wall Street bankers and Chicago bartenders, football players and missionaries. "There were men who did careful scholarly work; men who did sensationally dangerous work; and men who did absolutely nothing except travel around the world on a high priority at government expense."[47] An indication of the scope of OSS activity is seen in its budget estimate for the fiscal year 1945: 57 million dollars.

Undeniably, OSS bore the imprint of Colonel Donovan's personality. He has been described as "a mobile-unit of the first magnitude"; with the power to "visualize an oak when he saw an acorn"; a man who traveled fast, hatching new schemes at each stop, and surprising no one if, in effect, he "left one morning and returned the previous afternoon."[48] This explains in part the fact that OSS engaged in the widest variety of enterprises, calling for more diverse skills and personalities than any other American government organization that had previously existed. Donovan is supposed to have said frequently, "I always wanted to serve behind enemy lines." Apparently he derived vicarious pleasure in the large number of OSS agents infiltrated into enemy territory.

The OSS performed these many functions while ostensibly serving the Joint Chiefs of Staff in collecting and analyzing strategic intelligence and implementing specific special operations related to

Allied objectives in the war. To perform one of its major if less publicized functions, OSS built up an extensive, and in large part effective, research and analysis branch in Washington. This unit worked to supply policy makers and operators with essential facts and intelligence estimates.

The nucleus of OSS leadership was Colonel Donovan and his administrative assistants drawn largely from New York City law firms and financial institutions, and the so-called group of "100 professors" recruited early in the short life of the organization. The academicians brought the research techniques of scholars to bear upon the wartime requirement for strategic information. The roster of academic personnel who served OSS is long and distinguished. Their product was in many instances outstanding, and the techniques of analysis they developed valuable to the postwar intelligence system.

But, as previously suggested, OSS became more widely known for its special operations, a term covering espionage, counterintelligence in foreign nations, sabotage, "black propaganda (in which the true source is concealed), commando raids, guerrilla and partisan activity—in conjunction with such groups as the French maquis, Italian anti-Fascists, anti-Nazis within Germany, Kachins in Burma—and in various other forms of psychological warfare and underground operations. In essence, OSS assumed operational responsibility in a field previously ignored and scorned by many diplomats and military professionals. This was the field to be entered in later years by the U. S. Army's Special Forces, the "Green Berets."

As the war in Europe approached its end, the OSS was assigned the duty, performed by specially created units, to track down and apprehend war criminals, to recover art and other loot, and to trace the movement of funds that the Nazis were attempting to hide for possible later use.

Opinions on the effectiveness of its special operations in specific areas have varied and the evidence is sketchy.[49] OSS work was of prime importance in the invasion of North Africa. In Europe and the Middle East, OSS agents seem to have generally held the confidence of theater commanders to whom they were responsible. General Alexander M. Patch, commander of the U. S. Seventh Army, is said to have obtained from OSS agents some 60 per cent of the intelligence used for planning the invasion, with only a small force, of Southern France. General Eisenhower later applauded the close coordination between resistance groups and field operations.[50] In the Far East, with the exception of Burma, the quality of the agency's operations was more questionable, and apparently OSS activity was less successful. General Douglas MacArthur reportedly added to its difficulties in this area by placing stringent restrictions and controls upon OSS agents in his theater.[51] The principal reason for the exclusion of OSS from MacArthur's Southwest Pacific Theater was the existence of the Allied Intelligence Bureau, including Americans, Australians, New Zealanders, Dutch, and agents from the Philippines. Entry of OSS into that area was seen as raising serious organizational problems. In short, MacArthur had his own OSS. The OSS was also banned from operations in South America, a jealously guarded jurisdiction of the FBI's Special Intelligence Service (described below).

"Much balderdash has been written about the 'brilliance' of the work of OSS," writes Hanson W. Baldwin with reference to its special operations; "some of it was brilliant—particularly in Switzerland and some of the work in China and Southeast Asia—but much of it was inefficient, some of it was stupid, and for a considerable part of the war, we were dependent upon the British for much of our secret information."[52] Baldwin's view may represent much of the professional military attitude toward OSS, which patently was an unorthodox, nonprofessional organization. Considerable friction also developed among OSS agents and professional Foreign Service officers, perhaps contributing to icy relationships between American diplomatic and intelligence agents down to the present. The British Government, far more discreet about its secret services in war and peace, interestingly, has abetted and permitted publication of an authorative account of its Special Operations Executive (SOE), which was roughly equivalent to a major branch of OSS. SOE and OSS were, in effect, nearly unified in some of their London-based operations on the European Continent, particularly in occupied France.[53]

Until a detailed objective history of OSS is published—and at this writing none is known to be planned—it is possible to make only a general estimate of its value and significance to the evolution of a postwar central intelligence system.

Historical Background

The primary point to be made about the impact of OSS upon government intelligence is that it brought recognition that scholars and the best of scholarly techniques have a fundamental role in uncovering the facts required for national decision. In one sense OSS had, in this regard, the effect on national defense planning which the New Deal's acceptance of intellectuals in the 1930's had upon domestic government planning.

Creation of OSS also had its impact upon the academic community. For, as McGeorge Bundy has noted, "the first great center of area studies in the United States was not located in any university, but in Washington, during the Second World War, in the Office of Strategic Services. In very large measure the area study programs developed in American universities in the years after the war were manned, directed, or stimulated by graduates of the OSS—a remarkable institution, half cops-and-robbers and half faculty meeting."[54]

The recruitment of hundreds of academicians to staff the various OSS units in Washington and in the field had both a direct and indirect impact. The direct effect was the realization, at least by some persons, that scholarly analysis in many cases could be more rewarding than espionage. The indirect effect was that OSS competition provoked all the armed service intelligence organizations —Army, Navy, and Air Forces—to seek out the kind of academic talent employed by OSS. The net result: vastly improved armed service intelligence organizations.

Since many alumni of OSS today serve the intelligence community, either on a full-time basis or as consultants, the over-all intelligence experience gained in the four hectic wartime years remains valuable. Its value must, however, be balanced against the danger of a warlike, militaristic conception of the intelligence function derived from wartime experience. A fundamental lesson, at any rate, was learned by the fact that the government, in World War II, had to call upon individuals who essentially were amateurs in strategic intelligence. This produced the conviction that in the postwar central intelligence system, reliance would have to be placed upon men and women who are prepared to make this work a professional career and not a casual hobby.

Invaluable experience also was gained through OSS in intelligence procedures and methods of operation. Techniques of collection, either secretly from within the boundaries of foreign nations, or overtly from systematic analysis of nonsecret data, were tried and tested during the short existence of OSS. Important lessons were learned in an environment which cannot be duplicated today in Career Training Programs in the Virginia or Maryland countryside. The wartime experience also allowed the development and testing of techniques of evaluation of sources, interpretation of information, and synthesis of masses of data into an intelligence estimate useful to policy makers. And, finally, the existence of half-a-dozen major intelligence agencies during the war provided a laboratory for experiments in one of the most difficult of all problems—one which was, and remains, acute—the coordination of the government-wide intelligence effort.

The World War II operations of OSS also provided rewarding experience in the more technical aspects of central intelligence. The strategic requirement for the right kind of maps of areas around the globe resulted in the establishment of an OSS Map Division which produced thousands of essential maps in the period 1942-1945. Winston Churchill is said to have preferred OSS maps to all others during the war. At the Quebec Conference, the British Prime Minister reportedly called President Roosevelt to his room and, pointing to OSS maps on the wall, said, "See, I've got them too." At any rate, the contemporary, large-scale mapping program of the government rests in part upon the foundation hastily constructed by the OSS during the wartime emergency. Another technical field in which wartime OSS experience was of benefit was in the planning of strategic bombing targets. An OSS Economic Objectives Unit, stationed in London and working closely with Army Air Force operations analysts and British intelligence specialists, helped to work out optimum maturity targets for the selective bombing of ball-bearing, oil production, fighter-plane, and other vital facilities within the Nazi realm. Contemporary Strategic Air Command target systems, so important to American deterrence capability, owe much to the achievements of OSS personnel in World War II, and to the lessons learned from their mistakes. Still another technical field in which wartime experience contributed much was the always difficult communicating of secret information and the monitoring of secret messages of foreign nations. An elaborate world-wide radio network was operated by OSS during the war, contributing valuable skills to this specialized function.

Recognizing suddenly the need for thousands of intelligence agents as the war began, the United States was faced with the problem of recruitment and training. Although, as previously suggested, recruitment for the over-all OSS was done in a somewhat haphazard fashion, a serious effort was made to develop assessment and training techniques for candidates for overseas intelligence work, and particularly for those individuals selected for hazardous behind-the-lines missions in theaters of war. Psychiatrists and psychologists developed techniques for predicting the performance of intelligence agents in stressful situations. These assessment techniques provided the underpinning for some of the current intelligence personnel doctrine. The difficult task undertaken by OSS psychologists and psychiatrists of assessing the qualities of persons recruited by OSS and predicting their behavior on a variety of assignments is described in detail in the book *Assessment of Men*[55] by Henry A. Murray and others who led the program.

Finally, the wartime OSS experience brought the United States face to face with the still difficult problem of interallied intelligence cooperation. No organizations of government are more security-conscious than those whose business is intelligence. This innate characteristic of intelligence agents and agencies confronts allied governments in wartime with crucial problems. As previously suggested, the wartime experience in interallied intelligence was anything but smooth; yet, if nothing else, World War II acquainted the allies with the nature and magnitude of this problem, and the OSS experience, because of its multifarious intergovernmental activities, undoubtedly taught valuable lessons in how to cope with this continuing problem. Indeed, although the collective security concept is a cornerstone of the Western defense system, interallied sharing of intelligence information remains one of the more serious weaknesses of the Western alliance system. In sum, the American experience with OSS during the war, aside from the contribution made by OSS to allied victory, resulted in a net gain for the United States in knowledge of some of the basic requisites for a central intelligence system. For the range covered by OSS—research and analysis, espionage, and overseas political action—is covered also by the intelligence community in the contemporary environment.

Postwar Reorganization

At the end of World War II it was evident to those in the Executive Branch and in Congress that permanent changes were required in national intelligence organization. Wartime arrangements had been makeshift. In the words of former President Truman: "The war taught us this lesson—that we had to collect intelligence in a manner that would make the information available where it was needed and when it was wanted, in an intelligent and understandable form."[56]

When Mr. Truman became president in 1945 he was painfully aware of the imperfect coordination of national intelligence. Not a single official was responsible for national intelligence at the White House level. No truly national intelligence, in fact, existed, at least by present-day standards. Reports would flow across the President's desk on the same subject at different times from various agencies. These intelligence reports often contradicted each other.[57] The result was that the President had to act as his own intelligence evaluator, or, out of frustration with conflicting estimates, simply had to play his own hunches.

President Truman did not believe when the war ended that the Office of Strategic Services provided the answer to the problem of coordinating intelligence at the White House level. He was also under pressure from the armed services, the FBI, the Department of State, and the Bureau of the Budget. Another factor was undoubtedly Mr. Truman's own prejudice against cloak and dagger operations by the United States. He ordered the disbanding of OSS on October 1, 1945. To continue an international spying and secret operations organization in peacetime seemed to the President somehow un-American in the atmosphere of the immediate postwar period. This was the pre-cold war interlude when optimism flourished about the peacekeeping role of the United Nations, based upon the assumption of mutual cooperation between the United States and the Soviet Union. The President, however, was not without advice as to how to establish a permanent central intelligence service.

Historical Background

Centralization vs. Confederation

William J. Donovan, for one, had devised a detailed plan for a postwar centralized intelligence agency as early as 1944 and submitted it to President Roosevelt. Donovan called for removal of intelligence from control by the Joint Chiefs of Staff, suggesting that it be placed under presidential supervision. He expressed the view that the existing wartime arrangement was preventing the most effective use of information available to the government. Coordination of information—a truly central intelligence system—was needed to keep the President informed and to prevent overlapping and duplication. Donovan's view clearly stemmed from wartime frustrations and from ideas he developed for the best system for the postwar period. The Donovan plan was transmitted to the Joint Chiefs of Staff for review. There it came under the careful and critical scrutiny of professional military officers. The Navy studied the Donovan plan with particular care and with considerable skepticism and concluded that while there was much intelligence duplication to be eliminated and much better coordination to be effected, the degree of merger of intelligence services proposed by Donovan was not desirable. Too much centralization was considered not feasible because, in the words of the Eberstadt Report, "Each of these [armed services and civilian] departments requires operating intelligence peculiar to itself."[58] The navy's views on centralized intelligence were formulated largely by Rear Admiral Sidney W. Souers, then Deputy Director of Naval Intelligence. The navy proposed, in fact, a "Central Intelligence Agency" to coordinate foreign intelligence activities and to synthesize "departmental intelligence on the strategic and national policy level."[59]

This position, which in effect called for a confederation rather than complete centralization of intelligence, gained the general concurrence of the army. At the Department of State, Secretary James F. Byrnes reportedly maintained that his department should have predominant control over any national strategic intelligence agency.[60] This view was presumably based on the assumption that any kind of foreign operation in peacetime affects foreign relations and therefore should be under diplomatic supervision. Thus the State Department made a strong and logical bid, consistent with British intelligence practice, for control of secret intelligence operations.

77

In the midst of the controversy over the degree of centralization of intelligence, the OSS was rapidly being dissolved. Its highly skilled Research and Analysis sections and its Presentation section (intelligence briefing and reports) were transferred to the Department of State, later to become the Department's Bureau of Intelligence and Research. Espionage and other covert operations fell under the temporary jurisdiction of the army in an agency designated as the Strategic Services Unit (SSU) of the War Department. These secret agents were largely held in limbo to await a more permanent policy and operational directive. The SSU, comprising principally the Secret Intelligence Branch of OSS, the X-2 Branch, and Special Operations, was established as an autonomous agency under the direction of the Secretary of War. Thus the War Department came to have three somewhat disparate intelligence units: SSU, Military Intelligence, and the Counterintelligence Corps (CIC). The concept of a central intelligence system was initially lost in this immediate postwar shuffle.

The proposals for tight centralization and unification of intelligence, symbolized by the Donovan plan, and the federalization proposals embodied in the navy's position were the basis for lively debate in the 1945-1947 period. The question of how best to organize the national intelligence function was one of the many battles of the Potomac which ran concurrently with World War II and continued during the two years immediately following. Shadowing the debates was a fear in some quarters that an institutionalization of the wartime roles of the OSS would in effect amount to the establishment of an American secret apparatus that might prove to be incompatible with democratic values. The armed services were concerned lest their intelligence service—grown to considerable size during the war—be swallowed up by a centralized agency out of touch with the needs of the separate armed forces. The armed services also feared the establishment of intelligence units which would be partially under their jurisdiction but would also have the power to report directly to a centralized agency. Intelligence or counterintelligence which was not reported "through channels" was feared. In spite of such reservations the larger realization existed that a centralized system was badly needed to produce a truly national intelligence product, an effective warning system, and agreed-upon national estimates.

The postwar dispute over organization for national intelligence was a major side issue of the great debate over defense "unification." Pressures for greater centralization of the national establishment collided with organization concepts which placed great value on the principle of federation and of decentralization.

A powerful naval figure's view on centralized intelligence in 1945 is recounted in the Forrestal diaries. In March 1945 Secretary of the Navy James Forrestal asked Admiral Ernest J. King for his views on a proposed single, centralized intelligence agency. King replied that while such an arrangement was logical, it posed dangers. He feared a centralized intelligence agency that might acquire power beyond anything intended, and that might threaten our form of government.[61] This view coincided with the navy's strong opposition to the more extreme defense unification proposals during this period.

The armed services, particularly the navy, argued effectively for only limited centralization, and in the end the intelligence system which evolved was, like the national defense establishment, the product of compromise between the competing organizational concepts —centralization and decentralization. And, as in the case of most such compromises, it both left unsettled the issue of how much control was to be exercised by the central agency and opened the door for great duplication of effort. Such an issue has continually surrounded the Office of the Secretary of Defense since 1947; similarly, it has involved the role of the Director of Central Intelligence. In the latter case, however, considerably less public debate has been aired.

The Compromise

The referee in the postwar organization disputes turned out to be the Bureau of the Budget, which had on its staff administrative analysts specializing in the problems of intelligence organization. On January 22, 1946, President Truman issued an Executive Order —the result of much work by the Budget Bureau[62] and other agencies—establishing the Central Intelligence Group. This new group, forerunner of the CIA, operated under an Executive Council— the National Intelligence Authority—comprising secretaries of State, War, and Navy and the President's personal representative,

Admiral William D. Leahy. Rear Admiral Sidney W. Souers was named first Director of Central Intelligence, and he was succeeded six months later by Air Force General Hoyt S. Vandenberg. The Central Intelligence Group, representing a compromise of views held by the concerned governmental agencies, started out primarily as a holding company coordinating the work of existing departments. It was authorized, however, to perform services related to intelligence which the National Intelligence Authority determined could best be performed centrally. As a national intelligence collation group, it rendered intelligence service to the President and his cabinet, as well as to the cooperating departments.

Under this new organization the President began, in 1946, to receive a unified daily digest and summary of important international intelligence. As President Truman records in his *Memoirs*: "Here, at last, a co-ordinated method had been worked out, and a practical way had been found for keeping the President informed as to what was known and what was going on."[63]

Yet the intelligence millennium had not arrived, although President Truman was justifiably pleased with the progress made. Centralized intelligence was soon more substantially established and organized by congressional legislation under the National Security Act of 1947.*

Secretary of the Navy James V. Forrestal, who fought a hard and successful fight against the degree of defense unification advocated by many powerful persons in the 1945-1947 period, sounded a nearly unanimous note when he told a congressional committee considering defense unification:

We do need a central intelligence agency . . . we do need to have some machinery for collecting accurate information from the rest of the world, because . . . the speed, the tempo, and the fluidity of events in the world today very definitely require some central source here that is trying to evaluate those events for the various departments of government that are charged with our security.[64]

Both the National Intelligence Authority and the Central Intelligence Group were formally dissolved in the historic unification act by which Congress created a National Security Council, a semi-unified defense establishment, and the Central Intelligence Agency

---

* For a blueprint of a new organization for postwar central intelligence proposed by Allen Dulles, see Appendix A.

(CIA). Significantly, however, the principle of federation prevailed over the concept of tight centralization in shaping the structure of the intelligence community. The CIA was to be only one of several intelligence agencies of the federal government some of which, in the intervening two decades, would grow in size and scope that would rival the CIA. In trying to comprehend the problems of central intelligence, one needs to keep in mind that the growth of this multibillion dollar government industry is a phenomenon of the 1950s and 1960s. Most important to note, however, is that the CIA was established as an *intelligence* agency. There was no discussion, openly at least, of other "strategic services" it was to assume in later years.

CHAPTER IV

The Central Intelligence Agency: Basic Functions

When Congress created the CIA in 1947, the statutory language delegated intelligence (information) functions to the agency, and nothing more. No indication was given in the statute that the CIA would become a vehicle for foreign political action or clandestine political warfare. Probably no other organization of the federal government has taken such liberties in interpreting its legally assigned functions as has the CIA.

Today, all the world knows that the CIA was misnamed; almost from the start, it has been far more than an intelligence agency. Perhaps the two most significant influences on the agency were, first, that it was patterned after the wartime Office of Stragetic Services; and, second, that its birth coincided with the American declaration of cold war in 1947. Most persons did not know then that President Truman had seen to it, according to Allen Dulles, that the CIA was equipped to support the government's effort to meet Communist tactics of "coercion, subterfuge and political infiltration."[1] These terms Dulles has taken from the President's famous expression of the "Truman Doctrine," in which Mr. Truman asked Congress in 1947 to commit the United States "to help free peoples to maintain their free institutions and their national integrity against aggressive movements seeking to impose on them totalitarian regimes." So, while Pearl Harbor may be considered the father of the CIA, the Truman Doctrine certainly was its mother; the OSS was its hero model. If the United States was actively to defend "freedom" around the world, the nation would require a complete set of foreign policy instruments. Almost inevitably, given the state of the world in the mid-twentieth century and the nature of the competition, such instruments would quickly come to include not only a far-flung information-gathering apparatus but also an arm for secret political action.

Expansion of Functions

Congress, however, had not defined political action as a function of CIA. In 1947 Congressman Fred Busbey, as a member of a committee studying the National Security (Unification) bill, asked Secretary of the Navy James V. Forrestal: "I wonder if there is any foundation for the rumors that have come to me to the effect that through this Central Intelligence Agency they are contemplating operational activities."[2] The congressman received a vague reply. In the twenty-two years since its establishment, rumors have continued to circulate regarding the full range of CIA's activities. The agency's operations have expanded with the years to very wide dimensions, as have legends about its nature and functions. It is not possible to describe precisely the range of its contemporary activities, for according to its own stated policy "the Central Intelligence Agency does not confirm or deny published reports, whether true, false, favorable, or unfavorable to the Agency or its personnel. CIA does not publicly discuss its organization, its budget, or its personnel. Nor does its discuss its methods of operation or its sources of information."[3]

In contrast to whatever other successes it may have had, however, the CIA has patently been unsuccessful in maintaining effective secrecy regarding its organization, its methods, its personnel, and some of its sources. The agency has sometimes violated its own rules by giving "background" briefings to selected members of the press. Additionally, a series of events, particularly in recent years, has eaten away steadily at the secrecy curtain. The U-2 affair in

1960 and the attempted invasion of Cuba in 1961 opened the floodgates of publicity. The American press, particularly during that period, cast off the self-restraint regarding the agency, and the floodgates were never again fully closed, with far-reaching consequences.

In its earliest days the main office building housing CIA headquarters in Washington rather clumsily masqueraded behind a "cover" sign which read "Department of State Printing Office." Most taxi drivers knew its true identity and location. In its first ten years of existence, various divisions of the CIA sprawled all over Washington, occupying some thirty-odd buildings. Like most Washington agencies, it gradually spread out into the nation, establishing offices in more than a score of cities. But with the exception of a few generalized descriptive studies of CIA and some journalistic muckraking, the first ten years of its history were relatively quiet on the publicity front. In general, the public—including Congress and the press—knew little more about the agency than the CIA leadership wanted known.

In 1961, when the CIA moved its headquarters from the "Foggy Bottom" area of Washington out into the District of Columbia's suburbia, the move was symbolic of CIA's growing status and visibility in the Washington community. Strict internal secrecy procedures have continued. Office wastebaskets continue to be marked "Classified" and their contents carefully destroyed by security officers. Carbon paper and typewriter ribbons used by CIA stenographers are similarly destroyed. When the CIA took up housekeeping in its new sparkling and expensive Langley, Virginia, home, however, the size and importance of this agency became appreciably more evident; its anonymity had disappeared forever. Viewing its impressive office building in the Virginia countryside, one notes with some apprehension Parkinson's Law. Professor Parkinson has suggested, with as much validity as wit, that organizations tend to achieve architectural magnificence and comfort at a point when institutional effectiveness declines or signs of deterioration begin to appear.[4] CIA officials might have pondered Parkinson's Law as they moved from various temporary quarters into the new building. A former high official of CIA has been heard to say wistfully in more recent times that "maybe the agency should abandon the Langley headquarters and start all over in a *bordello* in Pittsburgh."

Deteriorating or not, the CIA for many years has been performing operational functions prescribed only generally by Congressional statute, and in more specific terms by National Security Council directives, which are, in turn, interpreted by the Director of Central Intelligence.

The National Security Act of 1947,[5] assigned to the CIA responsibility for coordinating, evaluating, and disseminating intelligence affecting national security. Like many other sections of the act, the central intelligence section was the product of compromise—in this case, between a loose coordinating committee system and a fully unified, monolithic intelligence organization.

CIA'S Statutory Functions

In the National Security Act of 1947 the CIA was assigned five specific functions, to be performed under the direction of the National Security Council. This unique status of CIA should be noted. In the formal structure it reports directly to the National Security Council, as an advisory agency to the President, who is chairman of NSC. CIA's statutory functions are as follows:

(1) To *advise the National Security Council* on intelligence matters of the government related to national security.

(2) To make recommendations to the National Security Council for *coordination of intelligence activities* of departments and agencies of government.

(3) To *correlate and evaluate* intelligence and provide for its appropriate dissemination within the government.

(4) To perform for the benefit of existing intelligence agencies such *additional services* as the NSC determines can be efficiently accomplished by a central organization.

(5) To perform *other functions and duties* relating to national security intelligence as the National Security Council may direct.

Such functions are prescribed in what is often called an *organic act,* in that the responsibilities and functions of the agency are defined only in a general way, with more precise assignment of functions left to presidential and NSC directives. But it is noteworthy that Congress intended that all of CIA's statutory basic functions should be related to or of benefit to the *intelligence* function. Only by seriously distorting the meaning of the term "intelligence" is it

85

possible to find statutory justification for the wide range of strategic services that CIA actually has come to perform. Such services can only be justified by stretching the meaning of the term, admittedly a common practice. This apparently has been done. By a more strict definition of intelligence, it can be argued that CIA performs functions, which over the years have cost billions of dollars, that have never been specifically authorized by Congress.

There are a number of significant *provisos* included in the statute establishing CIA:

(1) The CIA shall have no police, subpoena, law-enforcement powers or internal security functions. Here Congress intended to allay the fears of some Americans that a *Gestapo* or *KGB* would be created in the guise of central intelligence, and, incidentally, perhaps to quiet any FBI concern over the presence of a rival in the internal security field.

(2) It is made especially clear that CIA should not supersede most departmental intelligence functions, for the act states that the several departments shall "continue to collect, evaluate, correlate and disseminate departmental intelligence."

(3) The 1947 Act further gave the Director of Central Intelligence, subject to presidential and NSC recommendation and approval, the right to inspect the intelligence product of all government security agencies and specifies that these agencies will make their intelligence available to CIA for "correlation, evaluation and dissemination." One exception is the jealously guarded province of the FBI, the vast files of which may be approached only upon "written request."

The CIA is managed by a director and deputy director, both appointed by the President, subject to confirmation by the Senate. Commissioned officers of the armed services, whether in active or retired status, are eligible for either appointment. The two positions, however, may not be occupied simultaneously by officers of the armed services. Allen Dulles became the first civilian to be named director when appointed early in the first Eisenhower administration (1953).

A revision of the CIA statute in 1949 by the Central Intelligence Agency Act[6] was designed to improve CIA administration by strengthening the powers of the director. This new statute gave him virtually free rein to hire and fire without regard for Civil Service regulations.

The 1949 Act also exempts CIA from the provisions of any laws requiring publication or disclosure of the "organization, functions, names, official titles, salaries or numbers of personnel employed." The Bureau of the Budget is directed to make no reports to Congress on these matters.

Perhaps even more important, the Director of Central Intelligence can spend funds from his multimillion-dollar annual appropriation on his personal voucher. This may occur "for objects of a confidential, extraordinary, or emergency nature." This is truly an extraordinary power for the head of an Executive agency with thousands of employees and annual expenditures in the hundreds of millions of dollars.[7] The agency also is permitted to purchase or contract for "supplies or services" without advertising; to contract for "special research or instruction of agency personnel" at private universities; to make special travel allowances and "related expenses" for intelligence agents on overseas assignment; and to approve the entry of up to 100 aliens into the United States in the interest of foreign intelligence activities. An amendment to the Act in 1951 authorized the CIA to employ up to fifteen retired officers of the armed services, allowing such officers to receive either their retirement pay or CIA compensation. Several more recent amendments provide for other special "fringe benefits" for intelligence personnel. About one-half of the total funds expended by CIA is audited in routine fashion by the General Accounting Office. The remainder, including the "unvouchered funds," are considered to be so secret that they are audited by a special super-secure procedure established for this purpose. Intelligence officials insist, however, that such funds are audited just as stringently as more open ones.

CIA's Size and Role

It is popular sport for newspaper columnists and others to guess the size and annual expenditures of CIA. A reasonable estimate would put the number of its Washington employees at around 15,000, with some several thousand additional agents overseas or elsewhere outside Washington. A fair guess is that the total number of CIA employees is roughly 15 per cent of the total number of workers in the government intelligence community, broadly defined. Estimates of annual expenditures have been as high as five billions, but this would include all conceivable intelligence activities of the government. Direct expenditures by CIA between 1960 and 1967 probably amounted to between $500 and $750 millions of dollars annually. The most tangible source for estimating the number of CIA's Washington personnel is the CIA headquarters office building with a theoretical capacity initially estimated to be approximately 10,000 persons.[8]

While the general congressional mandate to the CIA is that it collect coordinate, evaluate, and disseminate intelligence affecting the national security, there is an even broader grant of authority in the assignment to it of "additional services" and "other functions" related to intelligence as the National Security Council may direct.

As previously noted, this cannot be read as an unqualified assignment of "other services." Congress clearly intended that the functions of the agency be related to information-gathering. The strategic services assigned to CIA, beginning in the Truman Administration, are a distortion of the intent of Congress. It can be argued, by adherence to rigorous semantic standards, that a substantial number of CIA's operations since 1947 have been performed outside the limits of its statutory mandate. This question will be further discussed later in this volume. Under broad grants of authority and the specific administrative latitude given the Director of Central Intelligence in other statutes, the CIA, operating under NSC directives, has expanded, nonetheless, into a mammoth governmental institution.

The CIA has become at once a central governing authority, a coordinator of strategic information, and a correlator of data gathered not only by its own wide-ranging overseas staff and its thousands of Washington intelligence analysts but also by the dozen or so departmental intelligence units. The total number of persons working within the intelligence community probably exceeds 100,000.

As earlier stated, CIA's operational functions are determined by NSC directives, which have seemed to be based upon the assumption that the congressional statute is a blank check. The fact that the Director of Central Intelligence has become a de facto member of the National Security Council, although by statute only an adviser to NSC, would seem to suggest that the scope of CIA functions and operations is to some extent self-determined.

The degree of self-determination would depend, of course, upon the degree of presidential interest in exerting control over the agency. The record suggests such interest has varied widely. Note President John F. Kennedy's comment, after the Bay of Pigs debacle in April 1961 had called the CIA problem sharply to his attention: "I have learned one thing from this [Cuban] business—that is, that we will have to deal with CIA. McNamara has dealt with Defense; Rusk has done a lot with State; but no one has dealt with CIA."[9] Of course the major national security department heads are *de jure* members of NSC and may be expected to protect the parochial interests of the Defense, State, and other departments, and the Director must also contend with the military services through the Chairman of the Joint Chiefs of Staff. Also, an NSC subcommittee, variously called the "Special Group," or "303 Group," exists to oversee the foreign political roles and missions of CIA, and a Presidential Board of Consultants maintains a broad, if sporadic, surveillance. Certainly the Congress has no voice as to how and where CIA is to function, other than having prohibited its engagement in domestic security activities.

As a matter of fact, the real operating constitution of the CIA is not so much the statutory authority given by Congress in 1947 and 1949, but a score or so of super-secret National Security Council Intelligence directives which only a few high government officials have ever seen. These directives, after accumulating for a dozen years, were "codified" in 1959, with the various intelligence and operational functions subdivided into such categories as: (a) general functions, (b) overt activities, (c) covert operations, (d) defectors, etc. It is reasonable to assume that many of these directives were drafted in the Intelligence Advisory Committee, renamed the U. S. Intelligence Board in 1960, of which the Director of Central Intelligence serves as chairman. It is very likely, therefore, that CIA's coordinating and operating role is compromised and horse-traded out in the Intelligence Board, on which sit high-ranking representatives of the major operating departmental and agency intelligence units.

Although the extent of its coordinating function and authority remains somewhat cloudy (for example, how far can the Director actually go in "meddling" in the intelligence process and substance of the various departments?), the CIA now clearly plays a role in national intelligence policy guidance both as a coordinator and as a conductor of extensive operations in the field.

The Coordinating Function

Sherman Kent in his classic, *Strategic Intelligence for American World Policy*, outlined his concept of the basic elements in CIA's coordinating function. These include (1) establishment of clear jurisdictions for the several departmental intelligence units, (2) the policing of these jurisdictional boundaries, (3) continuing evaluation of departmental intelligence standards, (4) assistance in raising departmental intelligence standards, (5) management of interdepartmental projects, and (6) setting of government standards for high-quality intelligence personnel.[10]

As for its operating function, the CIA Old Hand used to say that the agency has no *raison d'être* by and of itself, that it is essentially a gap-filler and "coordinator" of the old-line intelligence agencies. Yet CIA men would add, off the record of course, an important qualification—that there are certain things that can best be done centrally. This latter view, along with the pressures of technology, of two decades of cold war, and of the increasing requirements by decision makers for world-wide information that is well coordinated, nourished the CIA into a major bureaucracy in its own right. Another source of growing power for the CIA over the years is the military and diplomatic policy of rotation. This policy produces a military officer or diplomat who may serve only a year or two on an important interdepartmental committee. Meanwhile, the CIA representative serves on a more permanent basis and develops an expertise that often gives him more influence in deliberations. In the field, the CIA is believed to have as many persons overseas as the State Department. A former White House assistant at a very high level has stated that in a number of American embassies, CIA officers outnumbered those from the foreign service in the political sections. Often the principal CIA officer has been in the country longer than the ambassador, has had greater funds to expend, and apparently has exerted more influence than his diplomat colleague. Robert F. Kennedy once asserted "In some countries that I visited, the dominant U. S. figure was the representative of the CIA." According to Arthur Schlesinger, Jr., CIA in the 1950s "had acquired a power which, however beneficial its exercise often might be, blocked State Department control over the conduct of foreign affairs."[11] As the experience and competence of CIA personnel increase, so does its power and the relative importance of its role. The authority of CIA is exercised according to the shifting winds of personality and issue; inevitably a certain amount of interdepartmental conflict may be expected to be part of the day-to-day life of a government coordinating agency in Washington. As those who know Washington will confirm, one man's coordination is another man's dictatorship; one man's coordination may be yet another man's anarchy.

Like the office of the Secretary of Defense in another sector of the security organization, the office of Director of Central Intelligence has gradually increased its operating activities in many areas of the intelligence community. By means of directives, issued by the Director of Central Intelligence, details of which are negotiated within the interdepartmental U. S. Intelligence Board, jurisdictional boundaries in the community have been assigned.

Since the various operating departments and agencies are clearly authorized by statute to continue their own intelligence activities, how and where did CIA come into the operational picture? CIA has assumed responsibility for those functions of common concern to the intelligence community which must be centralized for economy and effectiveness. One of the most important of these is world-wide secret operations—the conduct of international "cloak-and-dagger" functions. By strict definition, as earlier noted, these have little connection with *intelligence* activities. Such operations have nonetheless become a centralized CIA function, taken over from the wartime activities of the OSS and the armed forces, and, in fact, initially employing a number of OSS veterans as career agents. The armed services conduct such operations only in combat areas in time of war. It is clear that if four or five agencies of the American government were attempting at the same time to run a covert political operation in and around Cairo, for example, they would, in the intelligence vernacular, quickly "blow each other's cover." Such a system could only lead to disaster; hence the need for centrally directed secret operations. Why such operations should come to reside under the CIA roof rather than be assigned to some other sector of government remains a moot question, to be discussed later.

In active military theaters during wartime, espionage and related intelligence operations are a legitimate responsibility of the military commanders. However, the question is likely to arise—as it did in World War II with the OSS—as to where military intelligence ends and civilian operations begin. The problem is even more complex when there is a military theater command in certain areas during a time of general peace, or even of limited war. The allegations that, prior to and during the Korean War, General MacArthur made it difficult for the CIA to operate within the Far East Command suggest the type of jurisdictional disputes in which CIA and the military can, and have, become involved.[12]

A dozen years later, in Vietnam, the problem of overlapping jurisdiction and conflicts among the military services, the State Department, and CIA over policy and its implementation resulted at one stage in the recall of the CIA Station Chief in Saigon because of a conflict with the American ambassador and military commanders. This was the first publicized illustration of the application of the new concept that the United States ambassador was to be "boss" of all American operations, other than strictly military, in his domain. In some areas, however, the ambassador's rule has been described as a "polite fiction."

Major issues of conflict today between the military services or State Department and CIA are likely to be resolved in Washington within the U. S. Intelligence Board, the National Security Council, or, if necessary, the President's office. Duplication, overlapping, and interservice conflict will likely remain a problem nonetheless under the present national security structure, in which the federation concept prevails. Perceptive students of public affairs visiting or working overseas often get the impression that CIA men and the intelligence agents of other government agencies are sometimes operating in uncoordinated fashion in every dark alley, behind every bush, and apparently often in each other's hair. In more recent years, increasing coordination has been effected by means of the "country team" concept, placing the American ambassador in charge of all operations by U. S. government personnel in a given country, as noted above. It has been particularly difficult to implement such a concept with respect to secret services, with their own "independent" budgetary sources and secret channels of communication. One is inclined to remain skeptical about the degree of control the diplomat may have—or in some cases even want to have—over the secret agent.

Another central function which has been assumed by CIA is that of monitoring foreign radio broadcasts and other forms of propaganda. Clearly it would be inefficient for various intelligence units of government to attempt to perform this function. Numerous other missions of the intelligence community involving collection, research, and analysis of nonsecret material, the operation of a central research library, and the like, are best performed by a centralized agency. In its survey of the intelligence activities of government, the 1955 Hoover Commission, for example, recommended that responsibility for procurement and collection of foreign publications and scientific intelligence be shifted from the State Department to CIA. Here, it was felt, was a function of common concern to the intelligence community that could best be performed centrally. It would not be unnatural, from a CIA point of view, at least, if more and more tasks of foreign intelligence were said to be most efficiently performed by the central organization. In fact, such centralization has increased over the years, even with the growth of a Defense Intelligence Agency and the National Security Agency.

Overseas Political Action

The "additional services" and "other functions" referred to in the CIA statute now cover a wide range and point to CIA as a major performer in international political operations. This is so, as noted above, in spite of the fact that one searches the statutes in vain to find reference to any mission other than that which is related to intelligence.

One journalistic account of CIA overseas activities, published when the agency was barely a year old but apparently written with some official help, contained the following description:

Though little is being said about it, CIA is known to be making wide use of the same spectacular techniques which OSS employed to rally resistance movements against Hitler. Both in front of and behind the Iron Curtain, CIA men are assisting democratic forces to resist Red excesses. Anti-communist political leaders, editors, labor-union chiefs, clergymen and others are getting CIA support in their struggles to retain or regain democracy. CIA men call this "building first columns."[13]

Even in those cases in which CIA "cover" has been "blown," there is little information verifiable by scholarly standards about how and to what extent the CIA has aided foreign rebellions and various resistance movements or has otherwise intervened in the political affairs of a given nation. One journalist pictures the CIA undercover agent moving "swiftly through foreign political back rooms, to rescue and revive a friendly government and a friendly people who were on the verge of being choked by Communist pressure."[14] A more recent description of the agency's functions comes in a detailed survey by the *New York Times* in 1966: "From wire-tapping to influencing elections, from bridge-blowing to armed invasions, in the dark and in the light, the Central Intelligence Agency has become a vital instrument of American policy and a major component of American government."[15] The survey goes on to note that CIA not only collects information but rebuts the adversary's propaganda. Against the Soviet Union alone it not only performs functions comparable to those of the Russian intelligence and political action arms but also imitates many of the methods performed by pro-Soviet Communist parties around the world. The CIA is known to have toppled foreign governments and replaced them with others; to have raised, trained, and supported small foreign armies, militias, and police organizations; to have planned, equipped, trained, and led an exile group in the invasion of Cuba; spied and counterspied by "all conceivable means"; established "instant air forces" and air lines; built radio stations; subsidized university research centers and radio stations; secretly backed the publication of books and articles, and established private businesses as "cover" for secret political operations.

Only speculation and rumor exist outside the inner sanctum of central intelligence regarding the exact details of this variety of CIA functions, but the compatibility of these many forms of covert political action with a more narrowly defined intelligence function is open to question.

In recent years the CIA has been blamed almost daily for actions in which there is no evidence that it actually played a role. To cite just a few examples, the agency has been accused of provoking a war between India and Pakistan, of supporting rightist army plots in Algeria against the government of France, of kidnapping Morrocan agents in Paris, of plotting the overthrow of Nkrumah in Ghana, and of an endless number of other acts which many at home and abroad seem ready to believe. Perhaps the most outlandish of all was the allegation that the CIA was involved in President Kennedy's assassination. Such credulity as exists for such wild charges stems in part from the fact that the CIA has been exposed as in fact having engaged in some bizarre operations. One example is the CIA plot to contaminate a shipment of Cuban sugar, bound for the Soviet Union, as it was stored in a bonded Puerto Rican customs warehouse. If one can believe a *New York Times* account of this episode, some 14,000 sacks of sugar were contaminated by a harmless but unpalatable chemical in pursuit of an over-all United States objective to disrupt the Cuban economy. President Kennedy was furious to learn that broad policy directives were being so implemented by the CIA. It was obvious to him that such an operation entailed risks and costs that clearly were greater than any gain to be made.[16] This and similar exposures clearly create an international willingness to believe almost anything about the CIA. And nearly every week the world press in recent years has contained some new allegation about a CIA operation which, even if false, falls upon believing ears at home and abroad.

The Forecasting Function

As a forecaster of impending events, CIA's record is uneven. The agency has been given credit for warning of a Communist attempt to supply the Red-dominated government of Guatemala with arms in May 1954. Foreknowledge enabled this scheme to be thwarted.

But foreknowledge has sometimes been lacking. The CIA was not blamed for failure to anticipate the possibility of the North Korean invasion in 1950 (the intelligence community thought invasion *improbable*), but, along with General MacArthur, has come in for considerable criticism for its handling of the Chinese Communist intervention estimates. This failure appears to have reflected an inability on the part of CIA to give sufficient weight to Chinese Communist warnings that United Nations crossings of the Thirty-eighth Parallel would compel Chinese intervention. In spite of the continuous barrage of propaganda warnings and the carefully monitored movement of troops into Manchuria, intelligence analysts and the policy makers failed to regard such threats seriously, and apparently neglected to read history as well, or they would have recognized the traditional Chinese fear of an enemy north of the narrow Korean waist. President Truman records in his *Memoirs*: "On October 20 [1950] the CIA delivered a memorandum to me which said that they had reports the Chinese Communists would move in far enough to safeguard the Suiho electric plant and other installations along the Yalu River which provided them with power."[17] Actually, the Chinese had begun crossing the Yalu four days earlier, with the apparent intention of throwing the United Nations forces out of Korea. Responsibility for the intelligence breakdown at this stage was shared by the entire intelligence community and was also due in part to poor liaison between General MacArthur and the Pentagon.[18]

Since then the CIA has been criticized for its failure to anticipate the speed of certain Soviet technological developments, as well as for an apparent failure to produce adequate forewarning of Soviet economic penetration into the Middle East and Southeast Asia. CIA similarly is blamed for failure to predict Egypt's moves in the Middle East crisis in the fall of 1956; is credited, on the other hand, with warning of an Israeli move in the Middle East, which led to the President's abortive warning to the Israeli premier in late October 1956, several days prior to the Sinai invasion, not to launch an attack.

Even more recently, the CIA's record has apparently been good in supplying accurate information about Soviet military developments and orders of battle, about Chinese Communist nuclear weapons progress, and in keeping top American officials informed about the capabilities of India, Israel, Egypt, and other nations to build nuclear weapons. Secret political reports from such turbulant areas as Indonesia, Algeria, Nigeria, the Congo, and Argentina are believed to have been of high quality.

But there are areas where the performance has not been so creditable. These include a failure to give adequate forewarning of the construction of the Berlin Wall in 1961, and of the rift between Syria and the United Arab Republic in the same year. Khrushchev's fall from power in the Soviet Union in 1964 came as a surprise to American intelligence. Similarly, reports from the Dominican Republic which served as the basis for American intervention there in 1965 are widely believed to have been dangerously misleading. Even more profoundly disastrous has been the misinformation that guided American policy in Southeast Asia through most of the 1960s.

As suggested earlier, the greatest failure since Pearl Harbor occurred in October 1962 with the surprise emplacement in Cuba of Soviet Russian medium-range ballistic missiles (with ranges up to 2200 miles). True, the intelligence community did identify such missiles before they became operational, but in fact offensive missiles capable of hitting major targets in the United States had been introduced into Cuba more than a month before their deployment on sites. They went undetected for several weeks although there had been intensive intelligence surveillance of Cuba for more than a year. It was not until mid-September that suspicions were aroused about the missiles. Subsequent photographic reconnaissance eventually produced conclusive evidence on October 14. The discovery was a shock not only to the intelligence community but to the entire country. Why this failure in forewarning by a highly organized intelligence system on which the United States had expended tens of billions of dollars since Pearl Harbor? A Senate Committee investigating the failure reached two conclusions: first, that the intelligence services paid too little attention to reports of Cuban refugees and exiles, who were regarded as biased and unreliable; second, that the failure resulted from the "predisposition of the intelligence community to the philosophical conviction that it would be incompatible with Soviet policy to introduce strategic missiles in Cuba."[19]

Yet to talk of intelligence failure is to assume a performance on the part of an intelligence system which may rarely be attainable. The "failure" is seen in retrospect. As the intelligence system attempts to fulfill its most challenging task—forewarning—it will often confront a set of "unknowables" the most basic of which may be that the decision maker whose behavior is being predicted may not himself be certain of his actions in all contingencies.

97

The Coordination Function and Its Limits

The suggestion by one authority in 1949 that CIA should have policing powers over the rest of the intelligence community in order to insure that each department operate effectively within its proper bailiwick has already been noted. It was felt that CIA should conduct "a continual survey of departmental intelligence" to see that it was up to standard and then be in a position to "diagnose and help correct" any trouble.[20] CIA has not in fact been given this kind of inspector-generalship. It does, however, exercise over-all responsibility for the National Intelligence Surveys, which are the encyclopedic compendia of intelligence on all major foreign powers and successors to JANIS. And since the Chairman of the Board of National Estimates is from CIA, the agency is in a position to exert influence over other intelligence agencies.

Sherman Kent's fear in 1949, incidentally, was that the CIA might not be a coordinator but would tend to enter the "substantive" field, that is, would become an active intelligence collector, collator, and evaluator. Kent warned of the danger that the agency might become "little more than a fifth major research and surveillance outfit"—a competitor separated from its consumers.[21] As a matter of fact, as we have seen, it has become as much an intelligence operator as a coordinator. Roger Hilsman wrote in 1956 that CIA "has undertaken both research and analysis functions and information-collecting functions, setting up a set of research and analysis suboffices for current intelligence and for economic intelligence and another set of information-collecting suboffices for covert collection, for intercepting foreign propaganda broadcasts, and so on."[22] Certainly, CIA today produces a large amount of intelligence "from scratch"; it has become not only a major producer of intelligence but an extensive operator around the globe. Kent served for many years as chairman of the Board of Estimates, and it is likely that his views regarding a very limited role for CIA changed when he became a leader of the intelligence community. But in his anonymous role his lips were sealed for two decades.

In fulfilling the functions assigned to it by the National Security Act of 1947—functions which have been broadly interpreted in directives of the National Security Council and specifically detailed in those of the Director of Central Intelligence—the CIA today is elaborately institutionalized for (a) *overseas operations*, which include the collection of secret as well as open information and backstage, always secret, political action;[23] (b) research, analysis, and other processes involved in strategic *intelligence production* in its domestic headquarters; and (c) *various support functions* for activities noted in (a) and (b). These are the basic operational activities of the Central Intelligence Agency. In addition, the agency attempts to coordinate the intelligence activities of other departments and agencies of the intelligence community.

The Importance of CIA Directorship

From the foregoing description of CIA's rather vaguely defined functions it is clear that the office of Director of Central Intelligence requires the best talent the nation can produce. Senator Richard B. Russell, for many years in the best position on Capitol Hill to observe the CIA, has declared that its directorship is second in importance only to the presidency. This is true not only because of the importance of the intelligence estimate, and of the fact that its production and effective communication are administrative tasks of the first order, but because a massive institution possessed of secret information and operating invisibly at home and abroad is a locus of power unchecked by the normal processes of democratic government. Thus the appointment of a Director of Central Intelligence ranks as one of the two or three most important choices a president of the United States may have to make.

An ideal Director of Central Intelligence would be a rare combination of administrative expert, imaginative scholar, courageous master spy, and a person of keen sensitivity to the political ideals of the American Republic. America's master spy also must be a master judge and politician, but not a political partisan, and should be possessed of an inner integrity and sense of common-law justice.

It is fair to say, as one observer has noted, that "more than any other individual, Allen Dulles is responsible for CIA as it exists today. In one way or another, he has been involved with the creation of the agency almost from its inception and . . . has put his personal stamp on it."[24] Of the agency's six directors in its first twenty years, Mr. Dulles had by far the greatest impact on the shape of this powerful new institution. Becoming its deputy director in 1951 and its director in 1953, he served the agency until November 1961 —the ten-year period of CIA's greatest and most significant growth. His predecessor was an army general, Walter Bedell Smith, who had been preceded by a navy admiral, Roscoe H. Hillenkoetter, CIA's first director. The agency has had a wide variety of individuals as directors—one might say it has had too many changes in leadership in its twenty years—but this may simply be the mark of an institution trying to establish its proper place in a complex world. Dulles was succeeded by John A. McCone, a man with no significant experience in intelligence work, although he had served as chairman of the Atomic Energy Commission. Prior to that he had been an aggressive and successful industrialist, principally in shipbuilding. McCone became director of the agency as part of a general restaffing at the upper echelons following the Bay of Pigs disaster, the greatest of all CIA's publicized failures. McCone's nomination encountered substantial and significant opposition in the Senate. In office he played an active role in policy making but was much less visible to the public than Dulles had been. McCone was succeeded in April 1965 by retired Admiral W. F. Raborn who, like McCone, was inexperienced in intelligence work but had an outstanding record as an administrator and builder in the navy's *Polaris* program. Raborn served little more than a year, and was succeeded by Richard M. Helms, who, in sharp contrast to Raborn, was an intelligence professional employed by CIA since the agency's creation in 1947.

Of the directorship Allen Dulles once stated, "If you haven't someone who can be trusted, or who gets results, you'd better throw him out and get somebody else."[25] Given CIA's importance to national security, the qualities required in a director, and the agency's immunity from popular surveillance and control, the same care that goes into the choice of a chief justice of the United States should always attend the choice of a Director of Central Intelligence. Whether such care has in fact been exercised is clearly debatable.

CHAPTER V

*The Intelligence
Community:
Other Principal
Members*

If the total foreign intelligence budget of the national government exceeds $4 billions annually, it follows that the CIA, expending considerably less than one fourth of that amount, is only one among several major intelligence units. In fact, a score of government agencies today are engaged in foreign intelligence work in one form or another.* But the principal members of the national intelligence community are the National Security Council and its staff adjunct, the Central Intelligence Agency; the Department of Defense, whose intelligence functions are performed by the Defense Intelligence Agency, the armed services, the Joint Staff, and the National Security Agency; the Department of State; the Atomic Energy Commission; and the Federal Bureau of Investigation.†

* Government organization, particularly for agencies directly involved in national security programs, is fluid. The structure described in the following pages was that found to exist in 1969. Minor structural changes are constant, and the majority of them remain under tight security classification.

† Also participating but without formal representation in the inteligence community are the United States Information Agency and the Agency for International Development. Each maintains numerous posts and missions around the globe and each is an intelligence producer and consumer.

As previously indicated, the CIA is today a major collector of foreign intelligence, particularly from secret sources and from the monitoring of foreign radio broadcasts. Even so, the brunt of the responsibility for data collection in many specialized fields lies within the Defense Department, the Department of State, the Atomic Energy Commission, the FBI, and the National Security Agency. The latter agency may exceed all others in the volume of raw data collected. As the 1955 Hoover Commission task force on intelligence activities noted: "Some of these agencies approach or exceed the operations of the CIA in functions and expenditures."[1] Except for the National Security Agency, the nation's ultra-secret, code-making, code-breaking, and communications-security organization, these agencies collect intelligence primarily associated with the nature of their operational role. But this is not to underestimate the value of their contributions to the production of national intelligence.

Armed Service Joint Intelligence

To maintain the interservice intelligence cooperation achieved in World War II, the armed services established the Joint Intelligence Committee on a permanent basis. Members of this committee were the Deputy Director for Intelligence representing the Joint Chiefs of Staff, who served as JIC chairman; the army's G-2 (Assistant Chief of Staff, Intelligence); the Director of Naval Intelligence, who also represented the U. S. Marine Corps; and the Director of Intelligence, United States Air Force. The Chairman of JIC also headed the Joint Intelligence Group, the working level intelligence body within the Joint Staff serving the Joint Chiefs of Staff.

Until 1961, coordination with the civilian side of the Department of Defense was maintained through the Defense Secretary's Assistant for Special Operations, who served as principal aide to the Secretary and Deputy Secretary on all matters pertaining to the national intelligence effort. The office of Assistant for Special Operations rather suddenly disappeared in the aftermath of the Bay of Pigs disaster in 1961. Another arrangement, never publicized, was made for a special assistant to the Defense Secretary to supervise these activities. He represented the Secretary on special interdepartmental intelligence boards and committees. The Secretary of

Defense is a statutory ex-officio member of the National Security Council, for which the CIA works. The Chairman of the Joint Chiefs of Staff also participates as an adviser in NSC meetings.

The Office of Special Operations, until it was abolished in 1961, had a director and a small staff, with an authorized total personnel of around twenty-five persons. The Director of Special Operations, who had the responsibility of advising the Secretary of Defense on national intelligence and counterintelligence, had an Assistant for Intelligence and an Assistant for Operations. The Office of Special Operations also housed the executive secretariat of two permanent National Security Council committees dealing with super-secret special operations for which the Department of Defense was executive agent. This structure was basically changed by the post-Bay of Pigs crisis and by the creation of the Defense Intelligence Agency.

The Defense Intelligence Agency

The newest major member of the intelligence community, the Defense Intelligence Agency, was established on August 1, 1961, by the Secretary of Defense and became operational in October of that year. The creation of DIA was a by-product of an increasing centralization in the Department of Defense, but its existence has ramifications beyond the Pentagon. The question of a more rationalized defense intelligence system had been under study for several years, having been initiated by the Eisenhower Administration. Recall that the armed services had strongly opposed the proposal advanced in the 1945-1947 period of a single, centralized intelligence agency. Each armed service has its own peculiar intelligence needs which it felt would not be adequately served by a completely centralized intelligence system. On the other hand, there had been much duplication and overlapping among the services during the 1947-1961 period. Furthermore, each service was inclined to use its own intelligence estimating system from time to time for "budgeteering" purposes. Thus the air force saw the development of a "bomber gap" and then a "missile gap" which never materialized. The navy was inclined to exaggerate Soviet naval power, and the army was often found estimating a number of Russian army divisions that existed only on paper. All of these activities tended to inflate budgetary requests and fundamentally to challenge the decision-making authority of the Secretary of Defense, particularly vis-à-vis Congress. Separate armed service intelligence units were not eliminated in 1961, but they lost representation in the highest councils of the intelligence community and many of their functions were taken over by DIA. The nature of the Joint Chiefs of Staff intelligence arm also was radically changed. The creation of DIA may be said both to have increased civilian control of military intelligence and to have created for the CIA a major competitor—whereas the separate armed service units had been minor competitors—in the intelligence community.

In describing the role of the new agency, the Secretary of Defense stated in 1962:

DIA reports to me through the Joint Chiefs of Staff and is under their immediate supervision. It already is integrating the current activities of the Joint Staff and the three military departments; it also has made possible the elimination of the Office of Special Operations on my own staff.[2]

The major objectives of DIA are to unify the over-all intelligence efforts in the Department of Defense; to make more effective the resources of the Defense Department for collection, production, and dissemination of intelligence; to improve the management of Defense intelligence resources; and to eliminate duplication among the services.

Control of DIA is assigned to a Director, a Deputy Director, and a Chief of Staff. They administer a headquarters establishment and a number of subordinate units, facilities, and activities specified by the Secretary of Defense through the Joint Chiefs of Staff (see Chart 2).

The agency carries out the following responsibilities:

1. Organizing, managing, and controlling all Defense Department intelligence resources allocated to DIA.

2. Reviewing, coordinating, and supervising those Defense intelligence functions retained by the separate armed services.

3. Obtaining the maximum economy and efficiency in the management of Defense intelligence resources, including those which can be integrated or coordinated with intelligence agencies outside the Defense Department.

4. Responding directly to priority requests made of DIA by the United States Intelligence Board, plus the meeting of intelligence

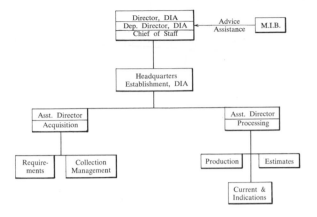

HEADQUARTERS ORGANIZATION—DIA

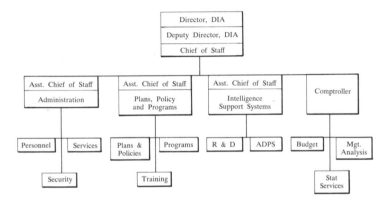

2. Defense Intelligence Agency Organization

requirements set by the major components of the Defense Department.[3]

In addition to these broad responsibilities, DIA was assigned the following "functions":

1. Produce all Defense Department intelligence estimates, information, and contributions to national estimates. These may contain any dissenting footnotes from various units within the Pentagon.

2. Set all Defense Department intelligence requirements and relative priorities; assign such requirements to the various Defense collection units; and request that outside intelligence agencies—such as CIA—fulfill specific information requirements.

3. Miscellaneous specific functions related to the above, such as:

establishment of a requirements registry; provide all Defense Department current intelligence; conduct any technical or counterintelligence assignments that may be assigned to the Defense Department; establish and maintain a Defense Indications Center; develop research and development requirements; develop training and career development programs in intelligence for Defense personnel; represent the Defense Department on the U. S. Intelligence Board and other committees; prepare a consolidated intelligence budget for all assigned activities; and perform numerous other management and service functions, including any new ones assigned by the Secretary of Defense or the Joint Chiefs of Staff.

By mid-1964 the basic part of intelligence reorganization had been completed in the Pentagon. The DIA budget had grown to $43 millions for 1965. Although DIA was for several years vigorously petitioning for its own new building, by 1965 most of the agency's personnel had been consolidated in the temporary buildings at Arlington Hall Station, the former home of the Army Security Agency, a predecessor of the National Security Agency. By 1969, DIA had still been unsuccessful in persuading Congress to appropriate funds for a new $25 million building. In the same year its direct budget had grown to about $72 millions and its total personnel to nearly 7000.

In addition to responsibilities and functions described above, the DIA in 1964-1965 came to be assigned new functions. These included:

1. the photographic intelligence functions previously performed at the Washington level by the separate armed services; the new responsibilities of DIA were to establish and operate facilities for military photographic processing, printing, interpretation, analysis and library intelligence services for the entire defense establishment;
2. the consolidation of intelligence dissemination facilities so that the DIA became the agency for communicating both raw and "finished" intelligence, from Defense and non-Defense sources, to the entire defense establishment and to authorized non-DOD and international organizations;
3. the management of all automated, data-handling projects and services of the Department of Defense, including plans for validation of information, assignment of data-handling tasks

and priorities, and the development of policies and program guidance for all Defense automated data processing for intelligence purposes. This program is decentralized at the operational level within the Departments of Army, Navy, and Air Force, and costs of operation are included in the service budgets;

4. a program of classified (secret) "extraordinary military activities."[4]

The rapid growth of the DIA's budget in its first half-dozen years of existence was a consequence of an ever-increasing centralization of intelligence responsibilities and functions, at the expense of the separate military departments. In mid-1965, for example, DIA took over responsibility for management of the military attaché system. A defense attaché system was created based upon a consolidation of the separate service attaché programs. Another reason for DIA's expanding budget was that, with the fulfillment of the various intelligence consolidation schemes outlined above, the size of the DIA staff in its numerous functional components grew considerably. And, finally, in the normal pattern of bureaucratic growth, the DIA came to have a number of new functions not previously performed by the separate armed services units. In the words of DIA's Director in 1966, Lt. Gen. Joseph F. Carroll:

. . . from the beginning, DIA has been charged with responsibilities in addition to those formerly performed by the military departments, and over the past four years [1962-1966], due to developments in world affairs, there has been a substantial and steady increase in the intelligence requirements levied upon DIA. Due to managerial improvements made possible through consolidation of intelligence resources, DIA has been able up until now to absorb in the 1961 level authorizations the substantial additional workload involved. However, this workload, particularly as it is associated with the situation in southeast Asia, has continued to increase to the point where additional resources are required to permit continuing responsiveness to growing intelligence needs.[5]

Like that of most other intelligence units, the performance of DIA is very difficult to evaluate from the outside. However, the agency came under heavy congressional criticism in 1968 when a House Defense Appropriations subcommittee found that information was being collected faster than it could be processed by DIA.

To congressmen it appeared that a glut of data may have been responsible for such crises as the seizure of the *Pueblo* in early 1968, the Israeli attack on a similar ship, the *Liberty*, in 1967, and the surprise Communist Tet offensive in Vietnam in 1968. Representative Jamie Whitten of Mississippi told DIA officers: "One could only conclude [after study of the situation] that the management of your intelligence assets is in a state of complete disarray." Creation of the DIA, it would appear, has not solved some classical intelligence problems.

Published information on the intelligence organization and function of each of the principal members of the intelligence community is, at best and perhaps inevitably, fragmentary. In the list of numerous histories of each of the armed services there are no unclassified works dealing in detail with intelligence. And when the armed services submit their annual budgets to Congress, testimony on the intelligence portion, with a few exceptions, has been off the record. For this reason only a very brief and sketchy description of the intelligence structure and function of the military intelligence services can be given here.

The Army

In congressional hearings on the Army's 1958 intelligence budget the Deputy Assistant Chief of Staff, Intelligence—Major General Robert H. Wienecke—was asked whether or not the Army could rely entirely upon CIA for information, thus eliminating the need for the Army's 125 million dollar intelligence apparatus. The general replied to the senator, "I think, sir, you will find their mission is a little different from ours. They get more into the field of political, economic, et cetera, whereas we try to deal mostly with military hardware."[6]

When asked how closely Army intelligence works with CIA the general replied "hand in glove." The Army's intelligence system makes major contributions to central intelligence; it is today a major intelligence bureaucracy in its own right.

Prior to World War II, Army intelligence, commonly referred to as "G-2," had been largely neglected (as indicated in an earlier chapter). During that war the army's intelligence staff was greatly expanded. By June 30, 1944, Army intelligence maintained in Washington approximately 1500 persons, including both military officers and civilians. Numerous organizational and administrative problems beset G-2 during this period. Rivalry and resentment pervaded the wartime intelligence community, particularly in the relationships between the army and the Office of Strategic Services and the growing army air forces, the intelligence staff of which rivaled in size army G-2. And the air arm rapidly gained a status virtually independent of the army. In this situation, inefficiency, overlapping of functional authority, and confusion were common.[7]

A major reorganization of Army intelligence occurred in 1944, following a study by a civilian-military board, headed by John J. McCloy, Assistant Secretary of War. The lack of modern intelligence doctrine in this period is perhaps best illustrated by the fact that in the survey conducted by the McCloy group, members were sent to study the organization and procedures of the *New York Times* and *Time* magazine. So little acquainted was the army with the requirements of a world-wide intelligence system that leading private news-gathering organizations were asked for help.

The 1944 reorganization of Army intelligence was aimed at eliminating organizational frictions and the administrative and functional hodgepodge. Included among the specific objectives of the new structure were the following: to separate policy activities that were distinctly intelligence from those that were operational; to organize better for specialized information on Germany and Japan, badly needed during the war; to institute better over-all administrative practices in the Military Intelligence Service.[8]

The chief feature of the new organization was the separation of the policy staff of G-2 from the operations staff of the Military Intelligence Service. The aim was to have G-2 restrict itself to intelligence policy and not become involved in the flow of intelligence information. The operating division—the Military Intelligence Service—had three main branches, the first headed by a Director of Information, the second by a Director of Intelligence, and the third under an executive for administration.[9]

In the postwar period, Army intelligence was no longer the neglected stepchild of the general staff, although it was still not a highly prestigious career branch of the army. In 1949 a Hoover Commission report stated that "G-2 in the Army has had seven chiefs in 7 years, some of them with no prior intelligence experience whatsoever."[10]

The rise of the United States to a position of world power and leadership immediately after World War II and the nation's extensive collective security and foreign aid programs, however, brought new importance to Army intelligence and particularly to the attaché program.

Army intelligence since the Korean War, with the importance of intelligence clearly apparent throughout the military defense community, has been well supplied with funds ($125 million for fiscal year 1958) and personnel, and its status has been elevated. And in the optimistic words of the Deputy Assistant Chief of Staff, G-2, in 1955, this branch of the service was "attracting some of the best officers in the Army."[11]

Army intelligence activities programed in the budget for fiscal year 1958 (the last year in which such figures were publicly available) were broken down into the categories and planned expenditures shown in the following table.[12]

	Millions of dollars
Army attaché system	2.5
Army centralized intelligence activity	3.0
Secret (classified activity)	27.0
Technical intelligence services	20.0
Continental and overseas field activities	7.0
Army Map Service	44.0
Installation support	15.0
Miscellaneous "small" projects	6.5

Army Intelligence Organization

Army intelligence includes a wide range of activities and organizations that are designed to furnish the intelligence and counterintelligence support the army needs to carry out its basic mission. The Assistant Chief of Staff for Intelligence (G-2) has general staff responsibility for all the intelligence and counterintelligence activities of the United States Army. This broad assignment includes, "planning, coordinating, and fulfilling the Army intelligence and counterintelligence requirements, and supervising Army intelligence and counterintelligence collection, production, and dissemination."[13]

The spectrum of army intelligence and counterintelligence activities ranges from the work of the army attaché in a United States embassy to the highly technical efforts of a communications and electronics specialist. In addition, each of the seven technical services of the army—chemical, engineers, ordnance, quartermaster, signal, transportation, and medical—has a specialized intelligence function, under general staff supervision. Army intelligence personnel are assigned to field and rear echelons both in overseas commands and continental armies.

The army attaché system, long a traditional source of foreign intelligence, operates in most of the countries with which the United States has diplomatic relations. Attachés serve as official representatives of the army chief of staff to the government of the country in which they are serving. They are also under the direct administrative control of the American ambassador or other chief of diplomatic mission, and act as his adviser on army matters. Once a prime target of isolationist-minded congressmen examining army budgets, the attaché system is now well recognized and is strongly supported. As indicated earlier, each of the services contributes personnel to a consolidated defense attaché system.

Army, navy, and air force try to maintain close coordination and liaison both in Washington and overseas in the operation of the attaché system. Unification of policy and function is effected wherever feasible. The communications function, for example, including cryptographic activities, is assigned to one of the services at each station; army and air force have a unified fiscal and disbursing arrangement; and joint photographic laboratories are maintained in many stations, as are other common facilities.

In June 1962 Army intelligence underwent the most significant organizational change in its history. At that time the Army Intelligence and Security Branch (AIS) was established. This was the first new basic branch to be added to the army since 1950. This reorganization combined into one branch the U.S. Army Intelligence Corps and the U.S. Army Security Agency. The purpose of this change was to attract competent and able persons into careers in intelligence and security. Prior to this time, officers who were

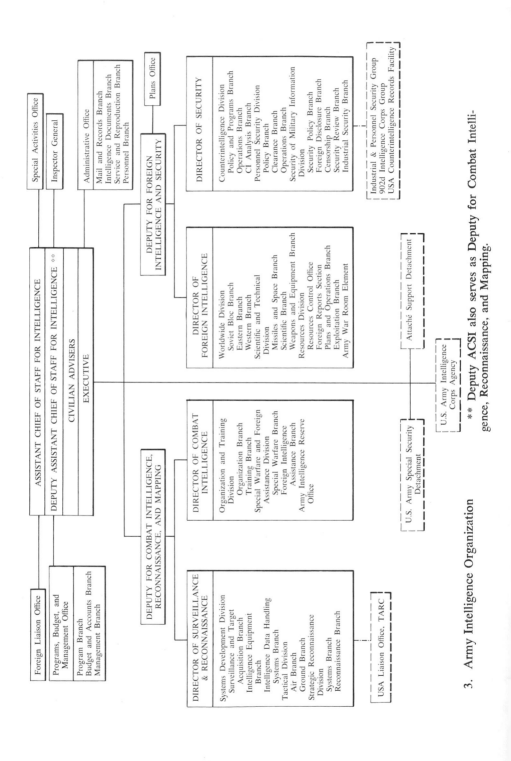

3. Army Intelligence Organization

** Deputy ACSI also serves as Deputy for Combat Intelligence, Reconnaissance, and Mapping.

actually involved in intelligence activities were assigned to any of the basic branches. For example, an officer would be assigned to the infantry and detailed to one or two intelligence assignments. Thus, intelligence offered little promise in career potential. As a consequence, most officers of high ambition were reluctant to take intelligence assignments. The creation of a new branch was designed, in part, to alleviate this problem. Obviously, if the army's intelligence functions were to be carried out with the required professionalism, the Intelligence Corps had to attract outstanding career officers.[14]

In 1966 the Army Intelligence Corps was changed to the Army Intelligence Command. This change carried with it the independence which any separate command of the U.S. Army enjoys. The Command comprises two major units, the Army Intelligence Command and the Army Security Agency.

Historically, one of G-2's best-known intelligence units was the Counter Intelligence Corps (CIC). While it is no longer officially known by that designation, unofficially what is now the Security division is still referred to as "the CIC." Its personnel are trained in investigative and security techniques and often in foreign languages. This unit, prior to 1942 called the Corps of Intelligence Police, is concerned with detection and prevention of attempts at treason, espionage, and sabotage, and the more mundane police problems such as gambling, prostitution, and black markets. A special counterintelligence training course is operated by the army. The counterintelligence division is the army counterpart of the civilian FBI and performs overseas many of the functions performed domestically by the FBI.

To illustrate the role of CIC in World War II, a few operations in which CIC participated can be cited. These include the capture of records of the Italian Secret Service and the German lists of Axis sympathizers during the North African landings in 1943; the seizure of German radar and wireless transmitter codes and the location of major mine fields during the landing on Sicily; and the responsibility for security of the now famous Manhattan Project, from its inception to the dropping of the first atomic bomb.

After World War II, in areas such as occupied Japan, where the United States Army maintained sizable troop deployments, CIC personnel were stationed in every prefecture and key town, where one of their functions was to monitor all local political, militant, or subversive activity and to keep General MacArthur's headquarters apprised of critical trends and developments. Since the war in Korea the CIC and its successor have performed a similar role for that country. Counterintelligence activities in the war in Vietnam are still largely unknown and classified. With the passage of time, however, some of these stories will become known and will be added to the exploits of the CIC of earlier days.

From a budget of $125 million for Army intelligence in 1958, $44 million were allocated to the world-wide army mapping and military surveys program conducted largely by the Army Map Service, Corps of Engineers, in conjunction with the Department of the Interior. This project, which also includes collecting the intelligence data required by the Corps of Engineers, provides for production and distribution of maps, map auxiliaries, geodetic data, terrain, topographic, and other similar intelligence studies required on a worldwide basis by the Department of Defense and others within the intelligence community. Requirements are established by the Army General Staff in coordination with the air force, the navy, and the Joint Chiefs of Staff. This operation is a vital part of the process leading to the production of the National Intelligence Surveys.

National Intelligence Surveys

A good example of the interdependence of agencies within the intelligence community is seen in the process by which these National Intelligence Surveys are produced. As previously indicated, each of the various technical services of the Army engages in specialized intelligence operations. Several hundred intelligence specialists, military and civilian, are constantly at work on the technical service level. An important part of their work is to provide basic material for the National Intelligence Surveys.

Let us take as an illustrative, though fictional, example, National Intelligence Survey No. 13, which, let us say, deals with Communist China.[15] Its content and format are determined by the National Intelligence Survey Committee, which is an important subcommittee within the Central Intelligence Agency, under the chairmanship of a CIA man with representatives from the various intelligence agencies of government. National Intelligence Survey No. 13 is divided into numerous sections, including, for example, separate sections on highways, telephone communications networks, railroads. Now, who prepares the basic material on mainland highways? This could conceivably be done by one of the many research branches of the CIA. In the intelligence community as presently constituted, however, the section of NIS No. 13—section No. 32—dealing with Chinese highways is compiled by the army's Transportation Corps; the section on telephone networks by the Signal Corps; and so on. Priorities and production schedules for various sections of the NIS come from the NIS Committee.

As soon as the section on Chinese highways is published, it becomes an item which the intelligence branch of the Army Transportation Corps must keep up to date. The basic material in the section would be the product of the Transportation Corps, with additional information supplied by other agencies of government—economic data from the CIA, political and cultural data from the Department of State, and so on.

Special Publications

Other technical service functions of Army intelligence include publication of the *Army Technical Intelligence Bulletin*, published every two months, containing current intelligence, as contrasted with the more general surveys; a "Class B Handbook," containing information on weapons and equipment of potential enemies; and the *Intelligence Review*, a document of current intelligence issued periodically and containing information on the latest foreign developments, particularly in the military establishments of Soviet Russia, and the countries of East Europe.

Army intelligence has progressed greatly since the lean prewar years, when military attachés were chosen only if they had independent means of support—usually a wealthy wife. Army G-2 is no longer an orphan of the army's general staff system. Its size and greater prestige reflect the realities of continuing East-West tensions and America's far-flung international commitments. With the rise of DIA, the role of G-2 in the national intelligence community has been redefined in more tactical terms, but it remains an important one.

In 1956 the Deputy Assistant Chief of Staff for Intelligence, Major General Robert A. Schow, was able, surprisingly, to testify that G-2 was "getting enough" funds to carry out its mission. Nevertheless, as Representative Daniel J. Flood noted at congressional hearings in 1957, G-2 was still only a two-star rank (major general) while the Chief of Research and Development, for example, wore the three stars of a lieutenant general. General Schow conceded to the congressman, in fact, that his own assignment to G-2 was, in terms of his prospects for future advancement, "almost the kiss of death."[16] The prestige or status to be gained from an intelligence career remains a serious question. Although the situation has improved, an intelligence assignment still is usually a transient one and is not considered a pathway to a successful military career in traditional values. It may be a fact of military life that the field command will always be more prestigious than an intelligence billet, a kind of intellectual pursuit.

Overlapping, and considerable and sometimes serious conflict between the army and other American intelligence agencies in the performance of world-wide intelligence operations, is still a problem. The army's comment on this in 1957 was given by its Deputy Assistant Chief of Staff, Intelligence (G-2). He told an inquisitive senator, "There may be a minor overlapping, sir, but we feel that a lap of small proportion is better than a gap."[17] A fundamental task of the intelligence community today is to see that such duplication remains "minor," not only between the army and the CIA, but among the various other intelligence agencies as well. The growing importance of DIA promises to mitigate this problem.

The Navy

American strategic design in the decades between the two world wars assigned the United States Navy to the first line of defense. Even so, naval, like army, intelligence was neglected. Not until after the Civil War was the intelligence function given attention beyond the bridge of a ship's commanding officer. The development of naval technology in foreign navies alerted the U.S. Navy to new intelligence requirements, and the Secretary of the Navy, in 1882, established an "Office of Intelligence" in the Bureau of Navigation. Its function was "to collect and record such naval information as may be useful to the Department in wartime as well as in peace."[18] Shortly thereafter, the Navy Department Library was combined with the Office of Intelligence. In the 1882-1888 period, naval attaché posts were created in London, Paris, and Rome. The war with Spain in 1898 was Naval Intelligence's baptism of fire and, given the general successes of naval operations, it may be assumed that it performed well. But, as in other branches of government, intelligence organization between wars was badly neglected. In the World War I experience, much of the required naval intelligence was supplied by the British Navy, giving a false sense of adequacy for the postwar years. Nonetheless, the Office of Naval Intelligence had by the 1920s taken a permanent form, with the nucleus for both positive and counterintelligence functions. But it was staffed for very modest coverage of world affairs. Convincing evidence of the neglect of the intelligence function between the two world wars was the government's call on the American public, in 1942, for snapshots and motion pictures of recent foreign travel. This was part of a desperate attempt, in preparation for the North African (Moroccan) landings, to fill the wide gap of information about beaches, sea approaches, and other data needed, particularly for night landings.

These kinds of data are currently provided in the National Intelligence Surveys, but it was all too scarce in the early days of World War II. According to Samuel Eliot Morison, "We dearly wanted, and never were able to obtain, photographs of the Barbary coastline taken from sea level just offshore, in order to enable our forces readily to identify beaches and other landmarks at night."[19]

The frustrations of an able naval intelligence officer in the interwar years are acutely revealed by Captain (later Rear Admiral) Ellis M. Zacharias throughout his book, *Secret Missions*.[20] Even after the declaration of war, in the period 1941-1945, the Office of Naval Intelligence had no less than seven directors. "Of the seven directors," Zacharias wrote, "only one was qualified by previous training, intellectual interest, and personal disposition to fill this particular job."[21] Only once in a while, he recounts, "chance

117

placed an officer at the top who tried, in the predeterminedly limited time at his disposal, to improve the office which was so haphazardly entrusted to his care."[22]

The rather restricted role played by the Office of Naval Intelligence on the eve of America's entry into World War II is revealed in the Pearl Harbor episode. The customary task of ONI was to gather intelligence about the potential enemy, but "it was not allowed to evaluate, much less to disseminate, the information so gathered."[23] Responsibility for evaluating intelligence data and predicting such things as the future movement of the Japanese Navy, and deciding to whom available information should be disclosed, was the responsibility of the war plans officer on the staff of the Chief of Naval Operations. This peculiar limitation on the role of the naval intelligence officer reflected, in part, the prevailing attitudes toward the prewar quality of the intelligence product. If the quality was in fact low, this was a result of official neglect.

Today the navy, like the army and air force, recognizes the crucial importance of high-quality intelligence, and in recent years has expanded the program for officer specialists. Consequently the navy now operates a well-staffed, highly trained service-wide intelligence organization. It forms a major cog in the machinery of the national intelligence community, although the advent of the Defense Intelligence Agency has changed the nature of the naval intelligence function, particularly in reducing the amount of general "reference" information gathered. Naval intelligence today concerns itself primarily with the informational needs of the Secretary of the Navy, the Chief of Naval Operations and the navy's technical bureaus. More than the other services, the navy has been reticent about disclosing the structure and functions of its intelligence system to the public, and no chart of naval intelligence organization can be procured. The following details, however, were available.

Navy Intelligence Organization

Center of naval intelligence activity is the Office of Naval Intelligence (ONI), within the Office of the Chief of Naval Operations. The Director of Naval Intelligence (DNI) is an Assistant Chief of Naval Operations who reports to the Vice Chief of Naval Operations and also is directly responsible to the Secretary of the Navy.

There is also an Assistant Chief of Naval Operations for Communications, under whom exists a Navy Security Group with cryptologic intelligence functions.

The mission of ONI is to meet the intelligence and counterintelligence requirements of the navy. This includes:

1. informing naval planners and policy makers of the war-making capabilities and intentions of foreign nations;
2. supplying the naval establishment with information needed for plans and operations;
3. warning of threats to the security of the naval establishment;
4. coordination of intelligence activities within the naval establishment and providing the naval contributions to the intelligence community of the government;*
5. development and recommendation of policies, to the Secretary of the Navy and the Chief of Naval Operations, on all matters pertinent to naval intelligence and the security of classified material.[24]

One of the major distinctions between ONI and the army's G-2 is that there is no semi-independent specialized unit such as CIC in the counterintelligence field; also, ONI agents conduct criminal investigations in the navy, a task performed by the provost marshal's office in the army.

The field organization for carrying out ONI's missions has three major components: (1) Naval District Intelligence officers, under the management control of ONI and operating in the United States and certain outlying areas; (2) intelligence organizations with the forces afloat, which are directly under unit commanders with over-all ONI supervision; and (3) naval attaché's, functioning under ONI direction as well as State Department and Defense Intelligence Agency supervision.

District intelligence officers operate primarily in counterintelligence and security fields. The District Intelligence Office (DIO) is directly responsible to the Naval District Commandant, with additional duty in some areas on the staff of the commander of the sea frontier of his district. Civilian agents usually are assigned to the district intelligence officers along with naval intelligence officers,

---

* The marine corps maintains a small intelligence staff in its headquarters, and intelligence officers are billeted throughout the corps. But these are concerned primarily with tactical, or operational, rather than national, intelligence.

and the former conduct security and major criminal investigations involving naval personnel or matériel.

With the forces afloat or in overseas bases, flag officers in command of each area, fleet, or task force have staff intelligence sections functioning primarily in the operational or tactical intelligence field. The intelligence officer who heads this staff section works not only for the unit commander, but also performs some collection missions for ONI.

Naval attachés, trained by ONI in intelligence and languages, collect naval intelligence for ONI as well as serve the diplomatic chief at the post to which they are assigned.

ONI not only is responsible for collecting intelligence on the navies of the world, with emphasis today on foreign submarine capabilities and deployments, but also has major collection responsibilities for beach, port, and harbor information. ONI has continued its World War II program of building up elaborate dossiers on the world's potential amphibious operations targets, and these dossiers are an important part of the National Intelligence Surveys.

Just as the Army Transportation Corps' intelligence experts supply basic data on Chinese and other foreign highway systems for the NIS, so ONI experts supply data to sections dealing with the Chinese and other foreign navies, with waterways, ports, and other elements of sea power. Thus Naval intelligence serves simultaneously the intelligence community and the specialized planning and operational needs of the navy.

The achievements of ONI in World War II, particularly in the operational intelligence fields, did much to raise the status of intelligence within the navy. Under the Military Personnel Act of 1947, provision is made for Intelligence Specialists in the Regular Navy, including flag rank billets in ONI. A feeling remains, however, that intelligence specialization may be a dead end for the ambitious career officer, a sentiment ONI works to overcome.

It may be noted, however, that many naval intelligence assignments, particularly with the forces afloat, are closely allied with operational training and experience so that the rotation of line officers with intelligence training, in and out of operational or combat intelligence billets, may in many cases be a desirable system.

Other Principal Members

The Air Force

Prior to and during World War II the U.S. Air Force was a branch of the army. Air intelligence consequently suffered even more heavily the fate of army and navy intelligence—inadequate support in funds, in personnel, and in organizational status. "When the war began," according to air historians, "the AAF probably was more deficient in its provision for intelligence than in any other phase of its activities."[25]

The low state of air intelligence in the 1930s is evidenced by a comment made years later by General Henry H. Arnold, wartime commander of the Army Air Forces. "I know now there were American journalists and ordinary travelers in Germany who knew more about the *Luftwaffe's* preparations than I, the Assitant Chief of the United States Army Air Corps."[26]

When he was appointed Chief of the Air Corps in 1938, General Arnold viewed air intelligence as the weakest link in the air organization. This is not to suggest that air intelligence was completely neglected. Military attachés, special foreign trips by air corps officers, and other sources produced data on foreign air power. But no formal air corps agency existed for the systematic evaluation of such information. An exception, the Air Corps Board, may be cited. This overworked group had many other duties, yet managed to incorporate intelligence data into field and technical manuals and handbooks for airmen. It was not until November 1940, however, that an Intelligence Division was created at the Chief of Air Corps staff level, from the redesignated Information Division. This division became A-2 (Assistant Chief of Staff, Intelligence) within the newly organized army air forces in June 1941, with a responsibility for both assessment and dissemination.[27]

Yet air intelligence during the war leaned heavily upon the more experienced British staffs and collection facilities. The air intelligence product in World War II has been judged little better than the product of a "sincere adolescent."[28] When the army air forces gained a semi-independent status, there were constant disagreements between A-2 and G-2, and considerable overlapping of function and jurisdiction. Responsibilities for air intelligence on Japan, for example, were parceled into artificial penny packets to the navy, the army, and the army air forces. Thus there was lack of centralized direction, authority, and control, and the quality of the intelligence product suffered.

In his report to the Secretary of War at the conclusion of World War II, General Arnold stated, "Our past concept of Intelligence was insufficient to cover the requirements of modern war." It was clear to the wartime air chief that, particularly for an air force, "detailed and moment-by-moment knowledge of all aspects of civilian and military activity within the territory of an enemy or a potential enemy is essential to sound planning in times of peace and war." Looking toward the future, Arnold noted that it would be "suicidally dangerous to depend upon reports of military attachés and routine or casual sources of information regarding foreign states."[29] These had been the principal sources of intelligence before the war but clearly were inadequate for the postwar era.

The need for adequate intelligence is particularly urgent today in the United States Air Force, whose deterrence mission depends upon the credibility of its power to carry the attack far into the enemy's interior should war come. Knowledge of a potential enemy's air power and of the most profitable targets is absolutely essential to the air force deterrence mission.[30] Furnishing this knowledge is an intelligence function. Thus the air force maintains an extensive intelligence organization, reorganized several times since World War II, and is one of the chief consumers of and contributors to the national intelligence product.

Air force intelligence activities, under a 1957 reorganization which was stimulated in part by the Hoover Commission study in 1955 and in part by later reforms, are headed by the Assistant Chief of Staff, Intelligence. On the civilian side, a small intelligence staff serves the Secretary of the Air Force, operating under his Special Assistant for Intelligence. This office reviews and evaluates all matters pertaining to air force intelligence—policies, plans, and programs.

Air Force Intelligence Organization

The Assistant Chief of Staff, Intelligence, is charged with the responsibility for planning, directing, and supervising air force intelligence policies and procedures. The air force intelligence system has a special responsibility to guard against technological, strategic, or tactical surprise. Put another way, it mounts guard against a surprise bomber or missile attack. This is very much the result of Pearl Harbor's impact upon the system. In official language, USAF intelligence also "provides support to major commands and certain other comparable organizations with intelligence responsibilities . . . which they cannot collect feasibly or economically." Translated, this means that the air force serves the Central Intelligence Agency, the National Security Agency, or the Defense Intelligence Agency, when this can best be done with the use of air force personnel and equipment. There have been times, however, when sharp disputes have developed between the CIA and the air force over who was to man and control reconnaissance aircraft such as the U-2.

The office of Assistant Chief of Staff, Intelligence, also 1) co-ordinates the collection of air intelligence as well as its production into reports and their dissemination; 2) monitors the world-wide targeting effort; 3) provides liaison between foreign military groups and the air force; supervises the Air Security (counterintelligence) Service and related activities; 4) controls the transmission of secret air force information to foreign governments; and 5) represents the air force on numerous intelligence community boards and committees.

These functions are performed by six major subunits under the Assistant Chief of Staff, Intelligence (see Chart 4). These are Special Advisory Group, Intelligence Data Handling Systems

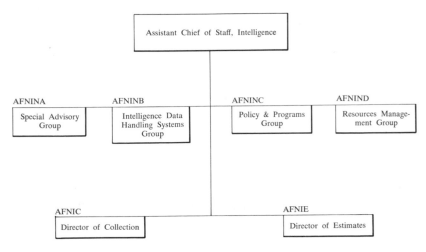

4. U. S. Air Force Intelligence Organization

Group, Policy and Programs Group, Resources Management Group, Director of Collection, and Director of Estimates.

The Special Advisory Group functions as the "brain trust" of air force intelligence. It tries to keep the air force abreast of technical, scientific, and strategic matters of prime concern to the air force. It is concerned with long-range planning, creative innovation, and representation of air force intelligence on air force and Defense Secretary committees concerned with the over-all intelligence requirements.

The Data-Handling Systems Group is primarily concerned with the growing question of what to do with the massive amount of raw data collected in the air force's world-wide intelligence net. It tries to keep ahead of data-handling requirements and is concerned also with research and development as well as with proper training in data-processing. The task of this group is to see that air force intelligence is properly organized, staffed, and equipped for modern data-processing, a formidable assignment in a fast-developing field.

The Policy and Programs Group provides staff support for the development of air force intelligence policy relevant to plans, programs, and staff actions of the Air Staff, major air commands, the Joint Chiefs of Staff, and other agencies. This group is also the focal point for liaison between air force intelligence and the Defense Intelligence Agency. It is concerned with such matters as what will be disclosed to the public about air force policy, equipment, and techniques. This group is also the focal point of Air Force concern for a wide range of intelligence policy matters, ranging from cartography, geodesy, photographic interpretation to the review, and defense of air force intelligence budgets.

The Resources Management Group has responsibility for all USAF intelligence matters pertaining to manpower organization, utilization of reservists, selection and utilization of personnel, administrative management, supply and services, and intelligence dissemination requirements. This is the group concerned with the selection of air attachés to serve within the world-wide defense attaché system. It maintains information on the availability of persons with particular intelligence skills; and it also controls the intelligence paper-work within the air force intelligence system, including the various intelligence publications, most of them restricted from public view.

The Directorate of Collection is the office primarily responsible for seeing that the air force leadership, including the Secretary of the Air Force and the Chief of Staff, is provided staff support in all matters concerning requirements and collection activities. The two main divisions of this directorate are the *Reconnaissance Division* (AFNICA) and the *Foreign Liaison Division* (AFNICB). The former is concerned with photography, airborne and ground-based signal intelligence, radar intelligence, infrared, and sonics. This division not only monitors operations in this highly productive intelligence field, but is charged with overseeing the development of the latest "spy-in-the-sky" equipment, some of it exotic. It is also concerned with the security of these operations as well as with cryptologic and cryptographic programs. In these matters it must work closely with units of the Central Intelligence Agency and National Security Agency.

The *Foreign Liaison Division* is concerned with making and implementing policies governing USAF relationship with foreign governments and their representatives. It plans and conducts official tours of foreign visitors, arranges for foreign visits by the Secretary of the Air Force and other high officials, and arranges for official accreditation of foreign attachés to the Department of the Air Force. The division controls the release of classified information to foreign governments, including information transmitted through foreign military aid agencies. It also serves as the tri-service coordinator for the Defense Intelligence Agency on requests for trips in the United States by military attachés from nations of East Europe.

The *Directorate of Estimates* provides the air force leadership with intelligence information regarding "threats to the security of the U.S., its forces and allies, as required for the accomplishment of the USAF mission." Thus this division serves air force intelligence needs, and its jurisdiction in this regard ends at the air force level; the DIA and CIA take over responsibility at the higher level. Inevitably this fine distinction leads to some overlapping—indeed, some duplication. His office is concerned with air force "inputs" into the national estimating process. Thus it maintains liaison with other intelligence agencies, working closely with the DIA, particularly its Intelligence Support and Indications Center, as well as its Production Center. It is the task of this division to serve the special intelligence needs of the air force leadership.

The Directorate of Estimates, which may be viewed as the culminating point of air force intelligence, is divided into a *Command Support Division* (AFNIEA) and an *Aerospace Intelligence Division* (AFNIEB). The former supplies the Air Staff with current intelligence in the form of briefings, estimates, studies and reports, as well as back-up graphics and training aid support for intelligence briefings and presentations. It is not only the point of contact with the DIA's Indications Center, but with the USAF Battle Staff, and various other special air force units. It is the primary channel for communicating air force intelligence to all segments of the service.

The Aerospace Intelligence Division is the air force action agency for national and joint intelligence estimates prepared under the supervision of the United States Intelligence Board and the Defense Intelligence Agency. While the Command Support Division concentrates on supporting air force leadership, the Aerospace Intelligence Division gives its attention to work with other elements of the intelligence community; its activities are more external than internal, although it does provide the Air Staff with threat assessments and estimates required for planning, weapons system development and deployment. But its chief emphasis is on representing the air force with the other services, the DIA, and the Central Intelligence Agency. It informs the DIA of air force requirements; assists air force witnesses in preparing testimony for congressional committees; and reviews intelligence contained in external air force papers. In a sense the division serves as the external affairs office for air force intelligence.

National Security Agency

Problems as old as intelligence itself are the secure communicating of secret information and the interception of such information transmitted by foreign governments or their espionage agents. A fundamental principle of classic intelligence doctrine is that the collection of secret information has little point if it cannot be secretly communicated to the user. Obversely, if you can intercept the secret communications of others, you have tapped a prime intelligence source. The use of professional code makers and code breakers is perhaps as old as diplomacy and espionage. What is new is man's electronic power in these activities.

Statesmen, diplomats, and soldiers since antiquity have employed various means of "magic" communication. Julius Caesar, for example, employed a regular cipher, consisting of a simple transposition of the alphabet, D standing for A, E for B, and so on. From the fourteenth century onward cryptography has become an established and highly refined practice, particularly in the diplomacy and espionage so artfully developed during the Renaissance by the Venetians. The Venetian Soro who died in 1544, has been called the father of scientific cipher.[31] The cryptogram remains a major factor today in international statecraft, in both intelligence and counterintelligence operations. An advancing computer technology has since World War II, along with an increasing number of American overseas commitments and activities, caused an enormous amount of attention to be given to techniques of making and breaking, communicating and intercepting, secret messages.

This is the principal business of the National Security Agency, a huge governmental intelligence apparatus, larger and more expensive than the CIA. Its structure and specific functions are secrets even more closely guarded than those of the Central Intelligence Agency. In his book, *The Craft of Intelligence*, Allen Dulles mentions NSA only twice in passing, with no description of its functions. Possibly some sightings of "flying saucers" in recent years can be attributed to electronic intelligence devices, American or foreign. The *Government Organization Manual* lists the organization and its two principal officers, but nothing more. Yet it is an agency with a $40 million building in Fort George Meade, Maryland, with at least 15,000 employees, and expending an annual budget of approximately a billion dollars. Very likely, NSA's role in decision making is greater than commonly assumed. Expressing his view of the agency, Senator Milton Young of North Dakota, a member of the highly select special Senate Subcommittee on the CIA, commented: "As far as foreign policy is concerned, I think the National Security Agency and the intelligence that it develops has far more to do with foreign policy than does the intelligence developed by the CIA."[32] The NSA specializes in communications intelligence, operating as a semiautonomous agency of the Department of Defense under the supervision of the Secretary of Defense.[33]

In addition to maintaining its own professional staff for technical operations, NSA collaborates closely with DIA and communications intelligence groups within the army, navy and air force.

Little published information is available on NSA structure and functions. One of its chief roles is the making and breaking of codes—the fascinating, challenging, and highly specialized profession of cryptanalysis. Dealing as its does with super-secret "communications security," with codes, ciphers, and electronic devices, NSA is today an almost anonymous agency of government. Only rarely is its name found even listed on the organizational charts of the United States government.

A brief but revealing glimpse into one aspect of the work of NSA was given when the government prosecuted one of NSA's employees, Joseph S. Petersen, Jr., in November 1954. He was indicted and prosecuted in connection with misuse of government documents dealing with the breaking of the Netherlands government codes, and of North Korean codes. Among other charges, he was accused of keeping in his apartment a document entitled "Chinese Telegraphic Code, SP-D, Second Edition, with Addenda and Errata."[34] It is clear from news accounts of this case that the euphemism "communications intelligence" refers more specifically to the age-old business of code making and code breaking. Obviously, then, NSA plays a major, if unobtrusive, role in the national intelligence community.

Details of the organization and functions of NSA were unexpectedly revealed in some apparently authentic detail when two of its employees, Bernon Mitchell and William H. Martin, defected to Russia in June 1960. Several months later, in a widely publicized press conference in Moscow, they issued a detailed statement, criticizing various specific American espionage operations and describing in considerable detail the organization and some of the operations of NSA. As employees of NSA, they had held top secret clearance on a "need to know" basis. In their September 6, 1960, Moscow statement, Mitchell and Martin commented on a number of matters about which they are unlikely to have had privileged knowledge in any substantial detail, suggesting that they were firmly in the hands of Soviet propagandists. Their employment in NSA for more than twelve years had undoubtedly been compartmented in highly specialized work. According to a congressional committee, "Mitchell and Martin did possess much knowledge, however, about the organization and operation of the supersensitive National Security Agency, and it was reasonable to presume that their disclosure to the U.S.S.R. of information about the NSA adversely affected the security of the United States."[35] Fears of what they may have known and disclosed to the Soviet intelligence service created shock, even panic, in American intelligence circles. According to one source: "Their revelations caused many nations to change keys and systems . . . the result was a partial dimout of United States communications intelligence—and probably of Soviet Russia's as well. Some NSA cryptanalysts went on double shifts, beginning the complex reconstruction of rotor wirings and lug and pin settings all over again."[36]

The NSA's secrecy is so tight, however, that apparently even a congressional investigating committee could only "presume" that Mitchell and Martin had made damaging disclosures. In its investigation the committee "did not attempt to learn the details of the organizational structure [of NSA] or the products of the Agency, feeling it had no need for knowledge in these areas."[37] So, details of NSA organization and functions are not only not known to the public; they are also outside the knowledge of those within government. Since July 1959, for example, the Civil Service Commission has been prohibited by act of Congress from analyzing NSA positions, even though this has been a major commission responsibility for most federal positions since 1949.

How, then, can one describe the organization, functions, and scope of operations of the National Security Agency? The fact is that this cannot be done in any verifiable way. One is forced to grant some credibility to the disclosures of turncoats Mitchell and Martin. The only published, unclassified source for corroboration are the personnel recruitment brochures issued by the National Security Agency and the Educational Testing Services and David Kahn's *The Code Breakers*. NSA has, however, advertised in the press for applicants for employment, claiming "unique and challenging career opportunities in communications, data handling and systems engineering."[38] The advertisement goes on to describe NSA as "a unique civilian organization within the defense establishment . . . responsible for developing 'secure' (i.e., invulnerable) communications systems to transmit and receive vital information." What does this mean in terms of its intelligence role? What are the major functions of so vast and expensive an agency?

These questions can only be answered in a general way, relying, regrettably, upon the disclosures of defectors and upon inferences to be drawn from the very limited information about the agency that has been officially released. In broadest terms NSA is charged with intercepting, "traffic analyzing," and cryptanalyzing the messages of all other nations, presumably friend as well as foe. Additionally, it is charged with maintaining the security of messages originating in the United States. It also functions to maintain order and coherence among the various cryptosystems of the CIA, the State Department, the FBI, the armed services, and other governmental agencies. According to its recruiting brochure, the NSA is "charged with responsibility for designing and developing secure/invulnerable communications and electronic data processing systems to transmit, receive, and analyze much of the Nation's most vital information." NSA is divided into five major divisions: Operations, Production, Research, Development Test and Evaluation, Communications Security, and Administration. The latter office is concerned with personnel, security, and the various administrative service needs of a major institution.

The *Operations Division* has charge of the field stations all over the globe for the intelligence motivated interception of foreign secret communications and other telltale electronic emissions. Thus NSA can be seen as using all known forms of techniques of electronic equipment for eavesdropping. Data gained are transmitted back to NSA headquarters between Washington and Baltimore for "production" into usable reports.

The principal function of the *Office of Production* (PROD, as it is called in NSA shop talk) is to receive all of the intercept materials from the operations division, break the codes if necessary, analyze radio traffic patterns, translate foreign language materials, and distill significant information from a mountain of data. Information may be sought according to "requirements" established by principal consumers; or it may be gained by induction from data empirically gathered and analyzed. The production division, by far the largest of all segments of NSA, with perhaps 7500 employees, is subdivided into numerous functional and geographic subdivisions, with some sections concentrating on diplomatic codes, others on military communications, according to various area and national subdivisions, and divided into Communist, non-Communist and allied sections. Indications are that America eavesdrops on allies and neutrals, as well as on her adversaries. As one writer has described its role, PROD's activities include "machines talking to machines—the self-interrogations of radars, the remote-control systems of guided missiles, the telemetry of artificial satellites, the IFF, or identification-friend-or-foe system."[39] Thus PROD is NSA's arm for the wide-ranging "ferreting" activities of American reconnaissance devices around the globe, picking up all possible electronic emissions for their potential intelligence value. These activities involve thousands of armed service personnel, supervised by NSA personnel. "Ferreting," recording, and other detection devices are located in planes, on ships, and at military installations overseas. The sensational case of the *U.S.S. Pueblo* is an example. That ship, seized by the North Koreans early in 1968, when it was on a mission to collect data on Russian naval operations in the Sea of Japan, was working for the National Security Agency.[40]

The *Office of Research and Development* centers its activities in the fields of cryptanalysis, the development of all forms of communicating and intercepting equipment and new forms of data transmission, handling, storage and retrieval.

The *Office of Communications Security* (COMSEC) is concerned primarily with maintaining security for United States secret communications. Other major nations, allies as well as adversaries, presumably operate communications agencies such as NSA. Thus the United States is in a constant battle to keep secret its own diplomatic and military communications. There is a constant need, consequently, for the design and redesign of cipher systems and hopefully invulnerable codes. NSA's original and principal concern is with codes and ciphers since this is the form of most secret communications. But with an accelerating communications technology, its functions have expanded greatly, and one now has the picture of the agency as the nation's great ear, listening to almost everything in a major effort to distill information from analysis of the world's man-made noises. Principal supporting units for the operating divisions are an Office of Personnel Services, Training Services, and Security Services.[41]

In addition to the divisions described above, NSA, operating under a director and deputy director, also maintains staffs at the top level for planning, for requirements, for budgeting, and for liaison with allied nations such as Great Britain, which operate a similar if much smaller communications facility. In recent years, NSA has actively and openly sought recruits from campuses all over the nation, seeking out particularly science majors and engineers. Anyone who can pass their stiff qualifying tests, however, may be considered, but they must also pass formidable security and psychological investigations. Each year NSA hires several hundred new college graduates, many of whom must of course undergo further training "on the job."

The National Security Agency occupies a huge establishment in Maryland, near the Baltimore-Washington Expressway, on the outskirts of Washington. It is a complex of buildings; the latest major one, completed in 1966, has a total of nearly 2,000,000 square feet, compared with CIA headquarters' 1,150,000 square feet. According to David Kahn, the NSA is "almost certainly the largest intelligence agency in the free world."[42] Its employees work primarily in Maryland but also staff its major branches overseas: NSA-Far East in Japan and NSA-Europe in Germany. NSA's budget—the figure is not disclosed—may be double that of the CIA. NSA also has links to a special Scientific Advisory Board and a Communications Research Division operated by a Pentagon subsidiary, the Institute for Defense Analysis. NSA cooperates in a major way with various North Atlantic Treaty Organization communications security units, which comprise an extensive NATO network. NSA also works in association with the communications security agencies of the armed services. The oldest of these is the Army Security Agency, which evolved out of cryptologic units of the American Expeditionary Force in World War I, through Herbert Yardley's famous "Black Chamber" and the Army's Signal Security Agency. The Air Force Security Service maintains a vast network in all parts of the globe, and the navy operates a communications security outfit within the Office of Naval Communications.

Times have changed indeed since the period in the late 1920s when the American cryptographic agency known as the "Black Chamber" under Col. Herbert O. Yardley was abolished. Upon becoming Secretary of State in 1929, Henry L. Stimson apparently thought it was immoral, at least in times which appeared to be profoundly peaceful, that an agency of the United States government should be reading "other persons' mail."[43] The Black Chamber had, for example, cracked the Japanese code during the Washington naval disarmament negotiations of 1921-1922. If gentlemen in the late 1920s considered "communications intelligence" as improper, gentlemen in the second half of the twentieth century either have changed their standards or have recognized the incompatibility between such high moral standards and the requirements of national security. At any rate, through the National Security Agency and related units, the American government is again engaged in what is euphemistically termed "communications intelligence" on a world-wide scale.

Much of the effort of spies and secret agents is devoted to attempts to obtain the keys to codes and ciphers of other nations. For this reason, cryptologic information is the most secret information any nation has. Within the United States intelligence system, code making and breaking equipment and documents are handled differently from other types of secret information. Top-secret security clearance, for example, does not permit holders automatically to see cryptologic material. When an automatic downgrading and declassification system for classified information was adopted in the early 1960s, cryptologic material was exempted. Even the presidential directive creating NSA is classified as security information.[44]

The National Security Agency is a symbol of the pervasiveness of technology. Because it chiefly involves machinery, it has managed to stay on politically neutral ground. It has been involved in few of the controversies over secret missions in an open society. But NSA is a huge, secret apparatus that bears watching, for it could become "Big Brother's" instrument for eavesdropping on an entire population if "1984" were ever to come in the Orwellian sense.

The Intelligence Establishment

The Department of State

By its very nature and function, the Department of State has always been involved in the foreign intelligence business. Its *raison d'être* has been to bring intelligence to bear upon the nation's foreign affairs. Diplomacy was once irreverently described as "spying in striped pants." As Professor McCamy has observed:

The practice of intelligence work in the conduct of United States foreign affairs . . . is as old as the practice of American diplomacy. It has not been called intelligence work, but it has been such. From our missions and other sources abroad we have tried to ascertain the effect of actions by other countries upon our own domestic affairs. Putting all the available information together we have decided policies and made plans of our own.[45]

Indeed, the State Department had its birth as a "Committee on Secret Correspondence," to supervise the relations of the American colonies with friendly European countries.

Latter-day State Department officials still regard their department as the center for the analysis and interpretation, if not the collection, of international information. In the words of Deputy Under Secretary of State Loy Henderson in 1957:

The Department of State and the Foreign Service represent the framework around which is assembled all of the activities of the U.S. in the foreign field. It is to the Department of State at home and the Foreign Service abroad that all agencies concerned with foreign affairs must turn for information with regard to international developments, for guidance with regard to policies, for advice . . . and for leadership in times of crisis.[46]

State has been specifically assigned, under intelligence directives from the National Security Council, the job of collecting, analyzing, and disseminating overt political, economic, cultural, and sociological intelligence for the community. In addition to serving departmental needs, State's intelligence experts make major contributions to the National Intelligence Surveys, to the National Intelligence Estimates, and to almost every major activity of the intelligence community. State's Director of Intelligence and Research is a key member of the U. S. Intelligence Board, and State's representatives are active members of the Watch Committee and numerous other interdepartmental groups within the community. The Director of "INR," as the intelligence division is called, holds the rank of Assistant Secretary of State.

A prime function of American diplomats and other foreign service officers has always been to send the background information for foreign policy. Yet, like the armed services, State prior to World War II was haphazardly organized for the evaluation, synthesis, and communication of all the information which flowed into Washington from foreign posts. There are those who insist that the department was haphazardly organized for any function. Collection of intelligence data in the field often was casually and inexpertly done. For many years there was, in fact, no separate and distinct intelligence function. One needs only to read the memoirs of pre-war secretaries of state to see how poorly informed they were on many aspects of foreign affairs. Little information that would meet current standards for intelligence collection and analysis was available, however great the activity of overseas agents.

The Department of State since World War II serves as a minor producer and major consumer within the new national intelligence community. But the intelligence function has been a major and bitterly fought issue of internal department organization during that time. The issue has centered upon the question whether research and intelligence should be organized as functionally independent, or amalgamated with, departmental policy offices. Put another way, should a functional or regional bureau of the department have its "own" intelligence specialists, or should there be a separate intelligence bureau within the department? A parallel issue has been the nature of the relationship between the Department of State and the CIA. The needs and objectives of these two agencies may be the same, but their methods must vary. One facet of the situation is that the CIA can dirty its hands in international espionage; the State Department must strive to keep its hands clean. Nevertheless, a rationalized organization would give diplomats the authority to veto operations by secret agents which might be too great a risk in terms of foreign policy aims.

On the eve of victory in World War II, in an atmosphere in which the need for centralized intelligence was widely recognized, it seemed as though the Department of State would become the focal point for coordinating national intelligence, and for providing leadership in government-wide intelligence functions, somewhat along the lines of British intelligence tradition, in which the Foreign Office surely, if secretly, guided all intelligence operations in peacetime. When President Truman abolished the OSS in the fall of 1945 and transferred its experienced intelligence analysts to the State Department, he wrote the Secretary of State on September 20, as follows:

I particularly desire that you take the lead in developing a comprehensive and coordinated foreign intelligence program for all Federal agencies concerned with that type of activity. This should be done through the creation of an interdepartmental group, heading up under the State Department.[47]

The proposal that the State Department should be the agency for coordinating interdepartmental intelligence was the advice President Truman had received from the Bureau of the Budget.[48] Accordingly, a Special Assistant to the Secretary of State for Research and Intelligence was appointed. He presided over an office which numbered some 1600 persons in 1945, including a large number of OSS alumni.

Within a few months after the creation of an enlarged intelligence unit within the State Department, the White House, under strong pressure from the chiefs of the armed services, reversed its opinion that intelligence was to be coordinated under State Department leadership. A major factor in this reversal was the opinion, strongly and widely held, that clandestine foreign operations should not be directed from the State Department but rather from an independent centralized agency. Accordingly, the National Intelligence Authority was created in January 1946, in which State served as a coequal member with the War and Navy departments and the President's military chief of staff. Its operating arm was designated the Central Intelligence Group, the forerunners of CIA, which was established by legislation in the following year. Consequently the number of intelligence personnel in the State Department was reduced to 936 with the transfer out in 1946 of the military segments of the former OSS operation. Twenty years later, State's intelligence bureau had been further reduced, by two-thirds, to a total of 323.

State Department Controversy

The new and refurbished State Department intelligence unit's activities were confined within the department, but here it was at once received as an unwelcome guest. After all, veteran State Department personnel seemed to feel, intelligence has been our province for all these years. Why, they asked, these interlopers? Veteran foreign service officers, largely centered in the traditional geographic "desks," greeted the newcomers with "suspicion and hostility," and "were unwilling either to admit the need for the new activity or to accept the new personnel as members of the State Department team."[49]

A bitter struggle ensued between those holding opposite points of view. At issue was the persistent question of the proper status of intelligence personnel. Should the intelligence function be performed by separate and semi-isolated units within the department? Or should such units, be amalgamated with the several policy and operating divisions—the geographic desks, for example? Since World War II, the organizational pendulum has swung widely. In 1957-1958, as a result of revolutionized personnel policies and of new intelligence leadership, new concepts were applied.

In April 1946 the proponents of decentralization temporarily won. Research units were decentralized as "self-contained nonoperating divisions to the four main geographic offices."[50] The intelligence chief, Alfred McCormack, resigned in protest. McCormack argued strongly for a "separation of the fact finder from the involvement in policies and objectives."[51] The structure was changed again when General George C. Marshall became Secretary of State in 1947. The intelligence research units were regrouped as a separate staff unit, as advocated by McCormack.

According to Roger Hilsman, a feeling persisted among officials of the State Department that professional diplomats, who rely on actual experience, are in a better position to evaluate foreign intelligence and predict the future course of events than research intelligence personnel, considered by some as "too academic." Hilsman reports, however, that there once was apparent consensus that there should be a unit within State which analyzes and presents "all the facts" to the policy men, since, if left to their own devices, the latter might only line up facts to fit preordained policy.[52]

State Department Intelligence Organization

In part because of the continuing controversy over how close to the geographical or functional policy-making "desk" the intelligence specialist should be placed and partly because of changing needs, the State Department's intelligence organization has gone through several major reorganizations since World War II. The other basic difficulty regarding intelligence specialists in the Department of State is the fact that most of the department's employees are involved to some degree in an intelligence function. The Secretary of State's staff, for example, labeled the Executive Secretariat, spends much of its time summarizing current information for the Secretary. For above all else, the Secretary's job is to keep informed of the current situation in world affairs, even if, as Dean Rusk once put it, "There is no such thing as a complete set of facts. You are always looking through the fog of the future."[53] The Secretary's staff, however, is not considered to be part of State's professional intelligence system. Many of the Secretary's staff assistants among the ranking officials of the department perform what in essence is intelligence work, even though they are not assigned to the Intelligence Bureau.

The office that deals exclusively with the intelligence function in a professional, specialized way is the Bureau of Intelligence and Research, commonly called "INR" (see Chart 5). Its principal function is to assist the policy makers in the State Department and the White House in both accurately appraising the current situation and "looking through the fog of the future."

Toward this end, the intelligence organization of the Department of State, in 1969, was organized as follows.

The Bureau of Intelligence and Research operates under a director whose rank, since 1963, has been elevated to that of an Assistant Secretary of State. The bureau has the double function of meeting the requirements of the intelligence community as specified by the National Security Council and the department's own research and intelligence needs. Congress was asked in 1963 to upgrade the office of director of the bureau to that of Assistant Secretary of State for reasons set forth by the Secretary of State:

In a rapidly changing world it is essential for sound policy making that adequate information be available regarding the current situation and the probable future consequences of potential alternative decisions.

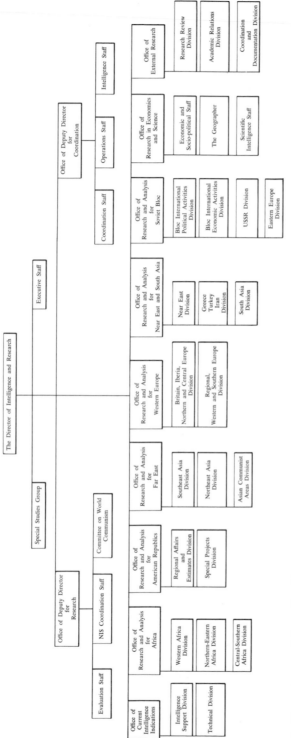

BUREAU OF INTELLIGENCE AND RESEARCH—INR

The Director of Intelligence and Research

Special Studies Group

Executive Staff

Office of Deputy Director for Research

Office of Deputy Director for Coordination

Evaluation Staff

NIS Coordination Staff

Committee on World Communism

Coordination Staff

Operations Staff

Intelligence Staff

Office of Current Intelligence Indications

Intelligence Support Division

Technical Division

Office of Research and Analysis for Africa

Western Africa Division

Northern-Eastern Africa Division

Central-Southern Africa Division

Office of Research and Analysis for American Republics

Regional Affairs and Estimates Division

Special Projects Division

Office of Research and Analysis for Far East

Southeast Asia Division

Northeast Asia Division

Asian Communist Areas Division

Office of Research and Analysis for Western Europe

Britain, Iberia, Northern and Central Europe Division

Regional, Western and Southern Europe Division

Office of Research and Analysis for Near East and South Asia

Near East Division

Greece Turkey Iran Division

South Asia Division

Office of Research and Analysis for Soviet Bloc

Bloc International Political Activities Division

Bloc International Economic Activities Division

USSR Division

Eastern Europe Division

Office of Research in Economics and Science

Economic and Socio-political Staff

The Geographer

Scientific Intelligence Staff

Office of External Research

Research Review Division

Academic Relations Division

Coordination and Documentation Division

5. Department of State Intelligence Organization

It is important to look ahead, to seek to anticipate problems or opportunities for American foreign policy, and to apply specialized skills to the task of improving the basic assumptions on which policy rests. For these reasons, the functions of the Bureau of Intelligence and Research are equivalent in importance to those of the geographic and functional bureaus, each of which is currently headed by an Assistant Secretary.[54]

It is the director's job to provide the White House and State Department with intelligence estimates and to develop and implement coordinated programs of "policy-relevant" research and analysis for the department and other agencies. This latter assignment was given greater emphasis in 1961 when Roger Hilsman was appointed director. A concerted move was made to increase the quantity and depth of "policy-oriented research," with greater emphasis than previously upon analysis of the probable consequences of alternative United States policies. With this aim in mind, the bureau greatly increased its program of contracted research by academic experts and institutions outside the government. Topics of such studies included "Latin American Political Parties," and "African Labor Organizations." During this period the bureau's staff also was expanded by more than 20 per cent. The bureau's program includes both the collection of information from foreign sources and the production of research studies and "spot intelligence" needed for taking and applying policy decisions. The director represents the State Department on the U. S. Intelligence Board and on other interdepartmental committees concerned with the intelligence function. The director is assisted by a deputy director. Hilsman's successor was Thomas L. Hughes, who was appointed in 1963 after having served as the bureau's deputy director since 1961. He served until 1969, when he was replaced by Ray S. Cline, former CIA official. Of some 350 employed in the bureau in 1966, about 10 per cent could be classed as "executive-administrative"; about 15 per cent were involved in "coordinating" activities; and about 8 percent were concerned with "external" functions. The remaining 67 per cent were "producers" of intelligence information in various forms.

The director is immediately assisted by a *Special Studies Group* and the *Executive Staff*. The former performs high-level policy-relevant analysis and research, making recommendations to the director regarding highly sensitive foreign policy matters. The way its functions are described in official literature leads one to guess that this small group may exercise policy surveillance over certain kinds of cloak-and-dagger activities.

The *Executive Staff* is the director's administrative arm, concerned with organization, budgets, personnel, and security. The staff coordinates and administers, for the director, the department's intelligence programs. Importantly, this staff also serves as a Communications Center in its administering of the mechanism for sending, receiving, and internally circulating intelligence documents. This Communications Center has been described as "the heart of the Bureau, for without the steady, quick, and well-directed flow of new information, work would at once come to a standstill—while without instant duplicating of the Bureau's own written reports, and timely delivery of them to the readers who can use them, its work would be in vain."[55] Its staff of about twenty handles several millions of documents annually.

There are separate staffs for research and for coordination in the *Office of the Deputy Director for Research* and the *Office of the Deputy Director for Coordination*. A separate *Coordination Staff* is mainly concerned with securing and transmitting new information. For example, it has the main responsibility for biographical data, and it is the central point for dealing with the CIA, DIA, NSA, and other intelligence agencies. It is also concerned with the overseas activities of American defense and other attachés. As another example of its work, the coordination staff briefs foreign service officers on the foreign intelligence needs of the State Department. Similarly, officers are interviewed or "debriefed" upon their return from foreign assignments. It is also the agency for communication between diplomats and other departments of American government.

The *Operations Staff* in the Office for Coordination works closely with policy officers of the department and of other major intelligence agencies. This is the group that, insofar as possible, attempts to keep the operations of other United States intelligence agencies overseas in line with American policy objectives. Finally, the *Intelligence Staff,* one of the newest units in the bureau, working under the Deputy Director for Coordination, concerns itself primarily with the management of highly sensitive intelligence information

141

that is communicated to a small inner circle of the highest national security officials. This unit is charged with the sometimes crucially important determination of who "needs to know" what kinds of highly classified information.

The *Office of the Deputy Director for Research* holds general responsibility for the efficient operation of the "production" side of the bureau. That is to say, the main function of the bureau— producing political, economic, and social analyses of foreign areas —is under the purview of this office, which is concerned with both the content and the exposition of the Bureau's written intelligence reports. This office coordinates all aspects of the bureau's research. Of particular importance outside of the Department is a subunit called the Office of External Research, which has operated the Policy Research Studies Programs, whereby the State Department seeks to hire on a temporary or consultant basis outside academic experts in special fields in order to provide the department with timely information required in policy planning. This office, through its staff and associated bureau units, is the focal point for outside private research on foreign areas and serves as a clearinghouse and coordinating center for contractual research in the social sciences on foreign areas.

The major producing area of INR is comprised of seven Offices of Research. Six of them are organized along standard geographic lines; West Europe, Africa, Latin America, U.S.S.R. and East Europe, Near East and South Asia, and Far East. The seventh office is called "functional," that is, it is concerned with such economic subjects as transportation, commodities, and population; scientific topics and political military questions; and problems of maps, territories, and boundaries. These offices are each further divided into several subregional or functional sections. There is very little of the "cloak-and-dagger" nature in State's intelligence system. Why, then, the label "intelligence" instead of simply "research and analysis"? The Deputy Director for Research, describing the intelligence functions of these offices in 1965, wrote:

The Offices of Research carry on all the operations familiar to any observer of an organization that produces finished intelligence. These operations can be regarded as traditional research in that the Offices accumulate information and evaluate, store, retrieve and reshape it. Their activity is at the same time called "intelligence" in the sense that it always deals with foreign situations, focuses on problems that are of immediate or prospective concern to the makers of policy, and points to the impact of developments abroad on U. S. interests. It is intelligence also in the sense of being usually estimative; its judgments are perforce based upon incomplete evidence, and it characteristically includes projections into the future.[56]

Finally, the Bureau operates an *Office of Current Intelligence Indications*. This office maintains continuous examination, twenty-four hours a day, of the world situation in light of the vast intake of information from the intelligence community. It is the task of this office, utilizing State Department as well as interdepartmental intelligence resources, to keep the top department leadership apprised of current situations, particularly in crisis areas, with special regard for diplomatic, political, or economic developments. Tangentially, State also operates an Operations Center, established in 1961 during the Cuban missile crisis to coordinate information from all sources. The "Op Center" is headed by a Watch Officer, whose mission is to keep top State officials advised during a crisis or warned of developing crises. The center is staffed by some forty-five State Department and five Defense Department officers who work on three eight-hour shifts.

The FBI

The Federal Bureau of Investigation is a major member of the national intelligence community, yet its direct role in the production of positive foreign intelligence is limited. This has not always been so. Today, however, the FBI, even though it assigns agents to major world capitals, operates largely as an agency for domestic counterintelligence. Its primary national security jurisdiction is investigating espionage, sabotage, treason, and other facets of internal security.

On the eve of America's entry into World War II there was concern about how the foreign intelligence vacuum would be filled by existing intelligence agencies of government. In subsequent presidential decisions a major sphere of action was carved out for the FBI. It was assigned responsibility for intelligence and counterintelligence in the Western Hemisphere, including Mexico, South America, Central America (except Panama), and the Caribbean. Other areas of the globe were the responsibility of the army and navy, according to agreements reached in Washington in 1940.[57]

143

The FBI's responsibility in the Western Hemisphere covered the collection of all "nonmilitary" intelligence; yet after the United States entered the war this assignment appeared somewhat vague. The result was considerable interagency dispute over jurisdiction. The subsequent creation of the Office of Strategic Services led to inevitable friction between the OSS and the FBI. This was reduced somewhat by attempts to define more precisely the FBI's role as that of collecting primarily civilian intelligence, but such distinctions are not always meaningful in a wartime atmosphere.

To perform its new intelligence role, the FBI quickly organized its Special Intelligence Service (SIS), whose agents were soon infiltrating south of the border under various guises. One went to South America as a soap salesman; another to open a stock brokerage business. Other SIS agents were attached to United States embassies or served in liaison posts with national and local police forces when the governments involved approved.[58] An SIS school to train such agents was operated during the war by the FBI. In the period of its operations between July 1, 1940, and March 31, 1947, the SIS identified, and in some cases succeeded in having arrested, hundreds of enemy espionage agents and propagandists, located some two dozen clandestine enemy radio stations, assisted in the seizure of huge amounts of contraband, and contributed in other ways to Allied security.[59]

In the discussion following World War II on the issue of central intelligence structure, the FBI quickly came forth with its plan to expand the SIS system on a world-wide basis. It would operate as the United States' "civilian" intelligence arm around the globe, leaving "military" intelligence to the armed services. This plan was shelved. As the Central Intelligence Group began to function on a world-wide basis in 1946, the FBI—apparently with some reluctance—withdrew from foreign intelligence operations, and the Special Intelligence Service was disbanded. So ended the FBI's direct participation in overseas intelligence operations.

The FBI's World War II operations in Latin America were essentially counterintelligence, but then, as now, this function often turns up information of value to positive intelligence. The nature of a foreign nation's espionage or sabotage attempts within one's own country will provide clues as to that nation's foreign intentions. The close link between counterintelligence and positive foreign intelligence necessitates efficient coordination between the FBI and the other intelligence and counterintelligence agencies of government. Coordination is provided now at the highest level of the intelligence community, where the FBI has a representative on the U. S. Intelligence Board, which is the "Board of Directors" of the intelligence community. In addition, the FBI director is a member of the Interdepartmental Intelligence Conference, which coordinates the investigation of all domestic espionage, counterespionage, sabotage, subversion, and other internal security matters.

Although the FBI relinquished overseas operations in 1946, the bureau still maintains overseas liaison agents with other security and intelligence agencies to insure a link between cases or leads which develop overseas but which come to rest in the continental United States. In the aftermath of the American intervention in the Dominican Republic crisis in 1965, there were reports that President Johnson had assigned FBI agents to certain missions on that island. If so—and the reports were never confirmed—such a mission was limited and temporary.

Atomic Energy Commission

On February 27, 1958, the Atomic Energy Commission issued the terse announcement that the Soviet Union on that date set off two large nuclear explosions, presumably hydrogen bombs at an Arctic testing site. Such announcements are the product of a worldwide monitoring system established by the commission for detecting nonpublicized foreign nuclear explosions.

In the period between 1949, when the first Soviet nuclear test was reported, and the end of February 1958, the AEC announced some thirty-one nuclear explosions as having been detonated by the Soviet Union. Not all Soviet atomic explosions are publicly announced by the commission, nor are full details given. But information about all such tests is quickly communicated within the intelligence community.

Such information is a basic requirement for officials responsible for national security plans and programs. For example, if the Soviets were known to be conducting certain types of nuclear tests, these might reveal the state of progress of hydrogen warheads for ballistic missiles or progress in developing defensive nuclear missiles.

The Atomic Energy Commission is therefore a consumer and producer of intelligence in the critical national security field of nuclear energy, and is accordingly represented on the U. S. Intelligence Board by its director, Division of Intelligence. The AEC is vitally interested in receiving data on foreign atomic energy or nuclear weapons developments and provides technical guidance to CIA and the intelligence agencies of the armed services in collecting these raw data. The AEC, in turn, becomes a producer of intelligence when it processes information on nuclear energy and develops estimates as to the atomic weapons capabilities of foreign powers. This processed intelligence is disseminated to the National Security Council, the armed forces, and others in the intelligence establishment.

The specific functions of the AEC Intelligence Division are to keep the AEC leadership informed on matters relating to atomic energy policy; in formal terms the division "formulates intelligence policy and coordinates intelligence operations." It sets the intelligence "requirements" of the AEC, which may be supplied by the various operating arms of the intelligence community. It represents the AEC in the interagency boards and committees concerned with foreign intelligence and it provides other intelligence agencies with technical information in the hope of assuring competency in the collection and evaluation of atomic energy intelligence.

The Task of the CIA

These, then, are the principal members of the intelligence establishment.[60] They participate jointly in intelligence policy planning through representation on the United States Intelligence Board. Each has its bureaucratic traditions, its unique organizational characteristics, its parochial requirements and outlook; thus each is a potential competitor with the others. Each is influenced to some extent by its own peculiar policies, its functional programs, and by its veteran personnel. It is the task of the Director of Central Intelligence, utilizing his influence in the various interdepartmental mechanisms, to create out of these diverse components a truly national estimate, useful to the national interest and not just to a particular bureaucratic preference. This is not an easy task.

CHAPTER VI

*Intelligence
End Product:
The National
Estimate*

The single most influential document in national security policy making, potentially at least, is the National Intelligence Estimate, commonly referred to as "NIE." Such estimates, according to Lyman Kirkpatrick, once CIA's Executive Director, "are perhaps the most important documents created in the intelligence mechanisms of our government . . . A national estimate is a statement of what is going to happen in any country, in any area, in any given situation, and as far as possible into the future."[1]

The significance of such an estimate is well illustrated by the example of the NIE prior to the 1962 Cuban missile crisis which predicted that the Soviet Union was not likely to apply a policy of such enormous risks as placing nuclear-tipped missiles in Cuba. Fortunately the world escaped from the worst consequences of such a bad guess. During the height of that 1962 crisis an estimate was hastily produced which warned that the Soviet Union might risk nuclear war rather than give in to President Kennedy's demand that the missiles be removed. Even more fortunate was the inaccuracy of that estimate.

What are these "estimates"? How are they produced? An illustrative answer is the case of the Soviet announcement on August 26, 1957, of the successful testing of an intercontinental ballistic missile. This was "intelligence" of a high order, publicly revealed by a nation known in the past to have used the broad public announcement as a propaganda weapon. What was the significance, the reliability, of this information? Asked about it in a press conference the following day, Secretary of State Dulles made the strange announcement that the reliability of the Soviet claim was "anybody's guess." He added, "The intelligence community is making a careful study of this statement."[2]

Behind the scenes, the intelligence community for some years had been charting as precisely as possible the course of Soviet missile progress.[3] Making use of radar and other detection devices and such information sources as espionage and reconnaissance aircraft, intelligence analysts working in CIA's Office of Scientific Intelligence, had tried, for example, to keep a running score of Soviet progress in missiles, as in all other significant developments in world affairs.

The reliability of the missile announcement may have been, in Secretary Dulles' opinion "anybody's guess." But the intelligence community for some time had been producing *national estimates* of Soviet missile capability that were at least well-educated guesses. Undoubtedly a revised estimate was transmitted to the Secretary of State and his fellow members of the National Security Council shortly after the Soviet announcement. Such estimates are the end product of the complex intelligence process and constitute one of the intelligence community's principal contributions to national policy making. More recently, with more sophisticated devices, including reconnaissance satellites in orbit, and a more expansive spy network on the ground, the system attempts to keep tab, for example, on the progress of Red Chinese nuclear-missile capability.

One of the chief criticisms of the intelligence community at the outbreak of the Korean War was that crucial intelligence was available from State, Defense, and CIA, but that these departments merely routed the raw intelligence around to the appropriate agencies without coming up with a joint national estimate. CIA, in particular, was criticized for failing to fulfill its duty "to correlate and evaluate intelligence relating to national security."[4]

The requirement that decision makers be provided with firm estimates as to future enemy capabilities or actions was recognized by the new Central Intelligence Director, General Walter Bedell Smith, who assumed office in 1950. A hard-driving administrator, General Smith was brought in to "beef up" central intelligence personnel, the process, and its product. He made an effort to use his office as a focal point for the national estimates. The CIA structure today is designed, in part, to produce these important building blocks of national security policy—the *National Estimates*. It should be noted, parenthetically, that "National Estimate" refers to an agreed-upon intelligence community estimate and not to an encyclopedic study, such as a National Intelligence Survey, of the characteristics of foreign nations. The National Estimate, a carefully evaluated intelligence report required by the President and NSC, is produced by a complex coordinating machinery capped by CIA and representing the entire national intelligence community.

Producing National Estimates

The procedure for the production of national estimates may be roughly described as follows: The President, the Director of Central Intelligence, some member of the NSC, or—perhaps more likely—the Assistant to the President for National Security Affairs will say, "I'm concerned about the situation in X nation. Let's have a national estimate on X. What's happening in X now, and what can be expected a year from now?" It can be seen at once that such questions pose problems of a different order of magnitude from the question "What are the current anti-aircraft defenses of X country?"

The next step in the fulfillment of this request is that terms of reference be defined by the Board of National Estimates. This board, a capstone agency in CIA, is composed of some dozen intelligence experts—former soldiers, diplomats, and scholars—who preside as a kind of planning general staff and intelligence super-council for the intelligence community. This group can initiate a study or, as is usually the case, act in response to a specific request from an intelligence consumer. The problem is defined, divided into feasible components, and then assigned to appropriate intelligence agencies—that is, military problems going to the Defense Intelligence Agency or to the intelligence unit of one of the armed services, and political matters to State, and other components to a CIA research division or some other intelligence organization—perhaps the Atomic Energy Commission's Division of Intelligence.

Resulting staff studies next pour into the Office of National Estimates, which maintains a small staff for integrating material received. An individual member of the Board will have been made responsible for the production of a particular estimate. The board may then put together a draft of either a *straight estimate*, one which attempts to assess a foreign nation's intentions or future policies with implicit assumptions as to future United States policy, or alternatively, *general assessments as to consequences of change in United States policy*. In either case the estimates attempt to consider the intelligence aspects only, staying as far as possible from policy recommendations or from estimates derived from viewing foreign-military affairs through policy-oriented glasses. In the latter alternative—the *general estimate*—the studies are not initiated by CIA or the intelligence community. They are developed only upon request from responsible policy makers. In this way the intelligence estimators try to avoid the danger of meddling with policy. They try to confine their attention to assessing the consequences of policy changes, either to the United States or to a foreign nation. Where assumptions as to probable or proposed United States policies are involved, these are furnished by persons concerned with policy per se—for example, the policy-planning staff of the Department of State.

The *straight estimate*, must be divided into two categories—the knowable and the unknowable. An estimate in the knowable category may involve past events or physical facts, such as the existence of an industrial complex, a railroad system, or an atomic reactor. Also in the potentially knowable category may be an estimate of Soviet long-range missile production or probable Chinese missile defense systems capabilities by a certain fixed date. In the unknowable category, as previously suggested, are predictions involving human intentions, which no one in any government can predict with certainty. These are of necessity relative terms, for even in the knowable category, disagreements frequently arise within the intelligence establishment about the interpretation of the same set of facts by different intelligence units. The system as presently designed attempts to resolve these conflicts so that decision makers will be saved from dilemma; but they are rarely saved from the necessity of an ultimate judgment in the most difficult decisions.

Intelligence estimates falling into the unknowable category are aptly illustrated by a remark by President Eisenhower in 1957 when a newsman inquired about the President's foreknowledge of the sudden removal from office of Soviet Defense Minister Marshal Zhukov. The following exchange occurred at the President's news conference:

Newsman (Chicago Daily News). Some weeks ago you expressed a view that Marshal Zhukov's position in the Soviet hierarchy seemed greatly strengthened. In the light of his apparent removal now, I wonder if you could tell us whether you are satisfied whether the intelligence estimates you received about that were adequate.

President Eisenhower. Well, of course, as I have, I think, warned each of you every time I have spoken about this subject, any effort to penetrate the Soviet mind, or at least the mind of the men in the Kremlin to determine their reasons for doing anything, is highly speculative, and that is all it is. I don't think that any intelligence system can give you a complete and positive answer on this . . . Marshal Zhukov seemed to come up from nowhere, almost, and now we don't know whether he is actually degraded, or whether there is some other move that is contemplated.[5]

Later Presidents have been similarly mystified by developments in the Soviet Union, China, and other areas where analysis must proceed with only fragments of required information.

A third type of estimate, the ultrasecret *net estimate*,* because of its policy ramifications, is handled by special machinery in the National Security Council system rather than by the Board of Estimates or the U. S. Intelligence Board. The intelligence community simply supplies the intelligence ingredient to this kind of estimate, the political or policy ingredient coming from other sources. A net estimate is the result of a highly secret calculation of a foreign nation's capability and probable intention (usually in the military sphere), with the capability and probable intentions of the

---

* The government has sometimes found it necessary to go outside of existing government institutions for some *net estimates*. Thus the Killian Committee in 1955 and the Gaither Committee in 1957 were called upon to render what, in effect, were net estimates on the future of atomic defensive and offensive capabilities.

United States as part of the equation. An example would be an estimate of this country's missile defense capability vis-à-vis the Soviet Union in 1975. Such an estimate, important to long-range planning, is at once the most difficult and most important kind of estimate to obtain. Yet, significantly, it is not handled by the normal CIA estimating system, because it involves important United States policy considerations. Rather, it is "war-gamed" among the major national security agencies—NSC, the Pentagon, Office of Preparedness, Joint Chiefs of Staff, and Atomic Energy Commission.

As the intelligence data for the *straight* or *general* estimate are evaluated, they may be compressed into a fifteen-page document. Such an integrated document is then referred back to the contributing agencies for appraisal and review, at which point dissents can be registered. By this process the product is further refined. How long does such a process take? An estimate on the Soviet missile industry may take four months. On the other hand, a new estimate on current Soviet long-range missile emplacements may take only four days. The machinery can produce either "crash" or long-term estimates. In the fall of 1956, CIA reportedly did "crash" estimates —which, it is claimed, later events proved correct—during the Suez crisis in the total elapsed time of as little as three and a half hours.

The U. S. Intelligence Board

The next step in the process is the submission of the estimate, with dissents, amendments, or revisions, to the U. S. Intelligence Board for final approval. It is within this group that the last-minute efforts are made to reconcile conflicting views. The important USIB serves, in effect, as a Board of Directors for the intelligence community. Not only is it the final forum for professional intelligence opinion in the construction of the important national estimates but it is within USIB that important managerial problems of the community—jurisdictional disputes, for example—are resolved. Under the chairmanship of the Director of Central Intelligence, the USIB is comprised of representatives from the CIA, the Department of State, the Defense Intelligence Agency, the National Security Agency, the Joint Staff, the Atomic Energy Commission, and the Federal Bureau of Investigation. The representatives of the latter two agencies confine their contributions to matters relating to atomic energy and internal security. Intelligence chiefs of the armed services attend as observers.

The accompanying chart gives an over-all view of the intelligence community in which the U. S. Intelligence Board is the "Supreme Court."

As a normal procedure, the Director of Central Intelligence sits down at least once a week with the USIB of which he is chairman, to review finished products. As Allen Dulles once explained, reports to the National Security Council usually take the form of agreed-upon national estimates, designed for use in decision making. But while unanimity is the general rule and the usual goal in producing the estimates, intelligence leaders are conscious of criticism for overprocessing information. Consequently, split reports are sometimes submitted to the NSC in preference to a watered-down, lowest-common-denominator agreement. Yet the danger always remains of an overly compromised estimate. For the intelligence community's concept of "finished intelligence" is that information which is transmitted to the President after agreement has been hammered out among various segments of the community.

As this process has been refined over two decades of experience, coordination and correlation of information are begun long before the data reach the Office of National Estimates or the USIB. Systems of communication and exchange, formal and informal, have developed at lower echelons in the community—for example, between State, DIA, and CIA—so that the process of national estimating can be said to begin whenever new data begin to flow into Washington.

But the National Estimate is not a routine survey turning up regularly, as it were, in a secret weekly magazine for the highest decision makers. There are, it is true, certain kinds of National Estimates produced on an annual basis. For example, a National Estimate might be made at regular intervals on the global dispersion of nuclear weapons. But normally the Estimate is an ad hoc preparation, developed at special request and dealing with a specific foreign development, whether it be a functional matter, such as disarmament prospects, or concerned with a particular country, such as predictions of the outcome and probable consequences of an election in India. In a crisis, a "SNIE"—Special National Intel-

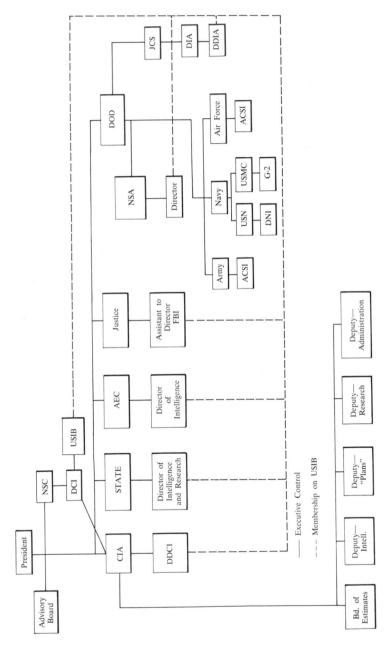

6. National Intelligence Establishment

ligence Estimate—can be produced in a matter of hours, as earlier indicated.

As a former Director of Central Intelligence summarized the process:

All aspects of every estimate get the fullest consideration, by the inter-agency working groups which begin the drafting, by the senior officers of long experience and proven competence in diverse fields of Government—and by the United States Intelligence Board. In the end, the National Intelligence Estimate is the report of the Director of Central Intelligence to the President and the National Security Council.[6]

Sir Winston Churchill offered an example out of World War II history of a danger in unanimous estimates. British intelligence, heavily sifted and compromised-down by the various agencies, failed to anticipate the Nazi attack upon Russia in June 1941. Churchill himself had concluded (so he recalls), however, on the basis of raw intelligence, and perhaps intuition, that a German attack was imminent but was being delayed by trouble in the Balkans. He so advised Stalin.[7] Churchill referred disparagingly to some intelligence estimates, calling them "this form of collective wisdom." Certainly there are pitfalls in lowest-common-denominator collective intelligence.

Collective or national intelligence represents nonetheless a great advance over the uncoordinated intelligence functions performed prior to reorganization of the intelligence community. Among the collateral benefits which are said to have accrued is a dampening of efforts on the part of the military to budgeteer through their own intelligence—that is, to magnify the Soviet Air Force or Soviet Navy in order to justify a larger United States Air Force or Navy budget.[8]

The Watch Committee and Indications Center

Another major unit of CIA, one closely associated with the Office of Estimates and the USIB, is the National Indications Center, a warning agency established in 1954. The Indications Center works under the guidance of the Watch Committee, a group subordinate to the USIB and representing each of the major intelligence agencies of the government. This mechanism, designed to prevent surprise, such as another Pearl Harbor, was described by Allen Dulles:

It works on a 24-hour basis. Anything coming in would go to our [CIA] watch officers, and to comparable officers in the Pentagon. If these officers felt that this intelligence showed up a critical situation, we would immediately call a meeting of the Intelligence Advisory Committee [USIB] . . . At any time of the day or night this Committee would sit down and go over any critical intelligence and make an immediate report to the President and National Security Council. The machinery is there to function, and unless there was a "human" failure, it would function.[9]

There may always be a need for a "crash estimate" which can test the efficacy of the Indications Center, the Board of Estimates, and the USIB. This was true, for example, on March 3, 1953, when information that Josef Stalin was dead flashed over the wires late in the evening to a teletype in CIA headquarters, then at 2430 "E" Street, N. W., and it soon became known that Georgi Malenkov would succeed Stalin.

What was the precise meaning of this change in the Soviet high command? How did Stalin's death affect American-Soviet relationships? Should the United States leaders be alerted to expect more aggressive moves, or a more conciliatory policy? Was there a chance of revolution in Russia? Informed answers to such questions were urgently needed by the President and National Security Council.

Allen Dulles, having been given raw intelligence by his CIA associates, quickly disseminated the known facts to key government leaders. His next step was to send orders to CIA agents and undercover operatives around the world. Requests were also sent to other agencies, asking information on what diplomatic or military moves to expect, information on troop movements, morale behind the Iron Curtain in Russia and her satellites, purges, arms shipments, and other data. The requirements sent out were based upon a now elaborate intelligence doctrine defining sets of "indicators." These are independent steps or actions by a foreign government and its agents overseas that, added together, signal an action about to be taken.

Dulles and his CIA colleagues, in conference with the Office of Estimates and the predecessor of the USIB, sifted through the reports, studied the background information on Malenkov and all other relevant data. Finally, when Dulles met with the President the next morning, he was prepared to give a summary which read like this: "Russia not prepared for war; an internal revolution unlikely;

no immediate foreign policy changes expected," and so forth. On the strength of such intelligence estimates, based upon the most careful analysis of the available "indicators," the President was able to issue a carefully prepared statement before noon on the day following Stalin's death.[10] When President Kennedy was shot on November 22, 1963, there was widespread official apprehension that the assassination was part of a larger scheme of attack upon the United States, including a surprise nuclear attack. The Watch Committee and Indications Center were soon able to ease such fears.

One of the most significant developments in national decision making since World War II is the refinement of a system of national estimates in various forms, including an "anti-Pearl Harbor" warning system. Only future history can tell how well it functions in all contingencies. It is true that such estimates still reflect the innate limitations of any forecast of the actions of human beings or governments, the shortcomings of any product which is the attainable consensus of an interdepartmental committee, and the gap between the real and the ideal in intelligence community spirit. Yet leaders of the intelligence community have expressed pride in the contemporary estimating mechanism and the closer ties which now exist between policy-making and intelligence estimates.

The Watch Committee institutionalizes the subspecialty of symptom-watching. This committee, as a standing group of USIB, makes certain that all available information within the intelligence community is shared among senior officials. Watch Committee reports are published, giving predictions of what is likely to happen "during the next few days"—particularly in times of crisis. Thus specialists in detecting "indicators" of hostile intent and in reading the globe for warning signs have come to occupy a central role in the system.

Leaders of the intelligence community now are assured that a community-produced estimate, granting its limitations, is available as a foundation for national decision making, even though the estimate may be disregarded or misinterpreted in the ultimate shaping of actual government policies, strategies, and programs. With policy makers, at least, intelligence credibility has increased tremendously and continues to grow. Intelligence leaders are encouraged by this; they feel that for every Churchill there are hundreds of policy makers whose "off the top of the head" guesses can prove to be seriouly wrong. Indeed, Winston Churchill, with all his self-esteemed intuition, was not always right, nor his intelligence advisers invariably wrong.

Yet with all the growing confidence in intelligence within the American governmental system, and with the increasing efficiency of the estimating mechanism, fundamental problems of perception and receptivity remain. Many responsible officials, in the last analysis, continue to serve as their own intelligence experts. Intelligence-by-committee still tends to suppress what at times may be the vitally significant dissent. Duplication, institutional rivalry, and jurisdictional jealousy continue to deposit sand in the gears. And the irresistible force of the National Intelligence Estimate collides on frequent occasions with such immovable objects as budgetary ceilings, partisan selfishness, or the omnipresent obstacle of unwillingness to believe unpleasant or unexpected information. These problems will be discussed in greater detail in later chapters.

CHAPTER VII

Surveillance by Congress

Writing in December 1963, President Truman expressed surprise that the CIA, first established in his administration, had become in later years far more than an intelligence agency. "I never had any thought," he wrote, "that when I set up the CIA it would be injected into peacetime cloak-and-dagger operations." Congress is entitled to an even greater surprise, for what legislators were asked to create in 1947—and what they thought they were creating—was an *intelligence* arm of the government. In so doing, however, Congress deliberately handed to the Director of Central Intelligence the authority to withhold information from the public, including Congress itself, at his discretion.

One result was that the CIA evolved into a multifunction agency, performing roles which Congress did not deliberately intend, and may not have been willing specifically to approve. An outstanding example is the CIA subsidies to the National Students Association, and numerous other private groups, first disclosed in early 1967. The granting of these subsidies was obviously motivated in part by the wish to spend government funds for foreign activities which Congress would not have approved.

159

Perpetual conflict amidst cooperation between Congress and the Executive is the inevitable consequence of the American system of government. The existence of a pervasive and highly secret CIA, expending hundreds of millions of dollars annually with only minimal legislative supervision expectedly has been a thorn in the side of many members of Congress, habitually jealous of legislative prerogatives under the American constitutional system. Efforts to regain a greater measure of congressional supervision of the intelligence establishment met with surprisingly little success in the first twenty years of CIA's existence, 1947-1967.

The Inevitable Executive-Legislative Conflict

Delineating precisely the respective roles of Congress and the Executive is a perplexing task under the American concept of the separation of powers. From the earliest days of the Republic, Congress and the Executive have been in constant struggle as a result of the deliberately imprecise constitutional division of powers. Often this conflict has involved a congressional desire for information which the Executive was unwilling to disclose.

Not only are roles and powers divided between Congress and the Executive; some of the important functions are also *shared* by both branches. This is particularly true in foreign and military policy determination, even though the Executive has an unequally heavy share of decision-making authority and responsibility.

Conflict is heightened when it comes to the question of the status of such a highly secret agency as Central Intelligence. Congress has by statute in effect given up, in the case of CIA, some of its normal and traditional controls over agencies of the executive branch. Yet, theoretically, constitutional control of Congress over CIA remains. With the burgeoning of the intelligence establishment in size and importance, the question has arisen significantly on several occasions during the past twenty years whether or not Congress should regain some measure of real control over intelligence activities.

This question has repeatedly come up, and not only in the legislative halls, where at intervals it has taken the form of concrete proposals in the shape of bills or resolutions. Additionally, a Hoover Commission study (1955) expressed concern about the absence of congressional and other outside surveillance of government intelligence activities. To the Hoover Commission, this lack of outside surveillance somewhat prophetically raised "the possibility of the growth of license and abuses of power where disclosure of costs, organization, personnel, and functions are precluded by law."

Congress and the CIA

The issue of closer congressional surveillance came to a head in the first instance in Senate action early in 1956. The specific point at issue was whether Congress was to establish a standing joint committee on the CIA, similar to the Joint Committee on Atomic Energy, to provide a fuller and continuing look at United States intelligence programs.

The CIA budget, as previously noted, is concealed within the budgets of various government departments, mainly that of the Defense Department. The average member of Congress has no more knowledge than the average citizen of the annual expenditures or of the size and scope of CIA operations. As members of CIA subcommittees of the Committees on Armed Services and Appropriations, a few congressional members receive occasional briefings on CIA's operations from the Director of Central Intelligence. As Allen Dulles once described the process, "I talk with them and give them a picture of the nature of the work we are doing, tell them about our personnel, and where the money goes."[1]

Dulles' successor, Admiral William F. Raborn, could say ten years later:

Ever since CIA was first established, the Director has been authorized and in fact directed to make complete disclosure of CIA activities to special subcommittees in both the Senate and House . . . When I say "complete disclosure," I mean complete and frequent. The CIA is completely responsive to their questions, no matter how sensitive. I have discussed matters with these special subcommittees which are so sensitive that only a small percentage of the personnel in CIA have access to them . . . In my first 12 weeks as Director I found that I was called to 17 meetings with these Congressional committees. Our legislative log for the year 1965 shows that the Director or his senior aides met a total of 34 times with the four special subcommittees.[2]

The congressional subcommittees are given what has apparently been considered to be adequate information, but this is not passed along to congressional colleagues.

CIA officials also present testimony to congressional committees seeking the latest intelligence estimates from the executive branch. In each case this testimony is presented in secret session, normally by the Director of Central Intelligence and his principal deputies. To other than the designated CIA standing congressional subcommittees, CIA activities, methods, and sources of information are never disclosed or discussed. CIA testimony provides the basis for legislative inquiries into national security, and intelligence estimates received are reflected in the subsequent questioning of other witnesses in open hearings and in the findings and reports of congressional committees. Although not made public, the testimony of the Director of Central Intelligence was, for example, of basic importance to the congressional inquiries of the Symington Senate (Armed Forces) Subcommittee's "Study of Airpower" in 1956, and the Johnson Senate (Armed Forces) Preparedness Subcommittee's probe in later years, of the defense program in 1957-1958, and in numerous hearings in later years particularly during the controversy over ballistic missile defense systems. An official description of CIA's normal relationship with Congress is described in Appendix B. But what is the extent of congressional knowledge of CIA's policy and operations?

A large and important agency of government, approaching in total personnel the size of the Department of State, and spending hundreds of millions of dollars annually, the CIA operates with only nominal legislative surveillance. Is such secrecy the inevitable by-product of modern defense requirements? Is the national intelligence community a proper domain for congressional exploration? Does the existing secrecy and sanctity alter significantly the legislative-executive balance of the American system of government? What are the consequences of such secrecy? What would be the consequences of wider congressional knowledge of intelligence activities? These and related questions were raised during the Senate debate in 1956 over the proposal to set up a joint committee on CIA, and again in 1966 in an attempt to broaden the representation on existing subcommittees.

Surveillance by Congress

The Mansfield Resolution of 1956

It is not surprising that members of the national legislature, who take seriously the constitutional provision that no money may be spent from the public treasury without congressional approval, should have become restless about the CIA's privileged position of secrecy. Such unrest has had various manifestations. One was in Senator Joseph McCarthy's characteristic statement in the Senate debate: "I have roughly 100 pages of documentation covering incompetence, inefficiency, waste and Communist infiltration in the CIA, which I am holding in the hope that a committee will be established so that I can turn the information over to it."[3] Another, more temperate, manifestation of unrest was in the Senate resolution to establish a joint Congressional committee on central intelligence, introduced in the Eighty-fourth Congress (1955) by Senator Mike Mansfield (D., Montana), with a total of 34 Republican and Democratic co-sponsors.[4] This was only one —though the most important—of a score of bills before Congress at that time with a similar purpose.[5]

The Mansfield resolution was reported favorably out of the Rules Committee on February 23, 1956, by a vote of 8 to 1, with Senator Carl Hayden (D., Arizona) dissenting.[6] The proposal would have established a joint committee to have legislative oversight of the CIA. It was to be composed of six members from each branch of Congress. The core of its membership would have been those senators and representatives already serving as CIA subcommittee members from the Appropriations and Armed Services Committees. The joint committee was to have a broad mandate to study (1) the activities of CIA; (2) problems relating to the gathering of intelligence affecting national security; and (3) coordination and utilization of intelligence by the various departments and agencies of government. All legislative proposals relating primarily to the CIA or to foreign intelligence would be referred to such a committee for consideration.

Senator Mansfield proposed further that the CIA keep the joint committee "fully and currently informed with respect to its activities." The committee, which was to have a permanent staff, would be authorized to hold hearings and to require, by subpoena or otherwise, attendance of witnesses and the production of books, papers, and documents. In other words, the committee as proposed was to assume the role of a regular joint congressional committee, with the power to investigate, advise, and report, and with a $250,000 budget for its first year.

Proponents of the measure asserted that it followed, in essence, a recommendation made to Congress by the 1955 Hoover Commission. The proposed committee was said to be analogous to the Joint Committee on Atomic Energy and, like it, "dedicated to the promotion of the public and legislative will in a sensitive agency imperative to our country's international survival."[7]

At the same time, the proposal was designed to preserve the continuity of existing congressional surveillance of CIA by limiting, if possible, membership on the proposed committee to those senators and representatives already privy to knowledge of CIA's operations. But surveillance was to occur on a more institutionalized scale, with all the trappings and power of a regular congressional committee, rather than the occasional meeting once or twice a year between CIA officials and members of armed services and appropriations subcommittees.

Arguments for a Joint Committee

The report of the Senate Committee on Rules and Administration on the Mansfield resolution described the background of the CIA and summarized the various studies and reports made of its operations. It then set forth the major arguments for the adoption of the proposal. These included the following:

(a) *Congressional surveillance has existed, since 1946, in the atomic energy field, an area equally as sensitive as foreign intelligence.* Most of the work of the Joint Committee on Atomic Energy, argued the Senate Rules Committee majority, "is of the highest security classification." Discussing its generally successful functioning in a sensitive area, the report concluded: "What is true of the Joint Committee on Atomic Energy can be true of a new joint committee organized to oversee the Central Intelligence Agency."[8]

(b) *A specialized joint committee would "promote new confidence between Congress and the CIA."* The new committee's staff would maintain "an effective check on the operations of CIA." A joint committee would provide a "forum for the registering of congressional doubts and complaints and the initiation of advisory and corrective action with respect to any errors which might be apparent." The effect would be to produce more constant liaison between Congress and CIA. Through all this, the report argued, "no classified or ill-advised revelations would be made."

(c) *Studies of CIA by ad hoc or temporary groups are not sufficient.* The fact that most reports of studies of CIA since its creation in 1947 have been highly secret has excluded Congress from details of CIA operations. The Senate report argued that "it is not enough that CIA be responsible alone to the White House or the National Security Council. Such responsibility should be shared with Congress in a more complete manner." It was argued that in our form of government—a system of checks and balances— it is essential that intelligence operations come under a more thorough congressional audit. Otherwise, the report states, "there will be no way of knowing what serious flaws in the Central Intelligence Agency may be covered by the curtain of secrecy in which it is shrouded."

(d) *A policy of "secrecy for the mere sake of secrecy" invites abuse and prevents Congress and the nation from "knowing whether we have a fine intelligence service or a very poor one."* The 1956 report acknowledged the importance of secrecy to any intelligence operation; yet the feeling was expressed that the veil of secrecy had been extended to cover too much from congressional scrutiny: "Secrecy now beclouds everything about CIA," the report complained, "its cost, its personnel, its efficiency, its failures, its successes. An aura of superiority has been built around it. It is freed from practically every ordinary form of congressional review. The CIA has unquestionably placed itself above other Government agencies."[9] In sum, the Senate Rules Committee majority felt that while secrecy is essential for certain facets of CIA operations, a wide area of its activities is proper ground for congressional review.

The sentiments expressed in the report on the Mansfield resolution were widely held in the Senate, as evidenced by the fact that more than one third of the membership was listed as co-sponsor of the resolution. At the same time some twenty-five similar resolu-

165

tions had been introduced in the House of Representatives up to 1956, indicating substantial congressional conviction that intelligence activities needed to be brought under closer surveillance.

Arguments against a Joint Committee

The dimensions of the debate were anticipated by the substance of the minority report submitted by Senator Hayden, who set forth the following counterarguments:

(a) *Existing surveillance by members of the Appropriations and Armed Services Committees is adequate.* Testimony was offered that CIA had demonstrated a willingness to keep these committees fully informed, and CIA officials had "candidly furnished the desired information and . . . responded to the specific complaints and criticisms . . . voiced in Congress and in the press."[10] Said Senator Hayden, "No information has been denied and all desired information has been candidly supplied."[11]

(b) *Functions of the CIA are essentially executive in character.* The agency serves the President, the National Security Council, and other departments in a staff capacity. "If CIA must have a 'watchdog' joint committee, why not have one for the FBI?"

(c) *CIA has been intensely, repeatedly, and adequately investigated by various special commissions.* Furthermore, the President, following recommendations of the 1955 Hoover Commission, had established a Board of Consultants on Foreign Intelligence Activities to advise him regularly and to report its findings at least twice a year. Senator Hayden suggested that Congress therefore let CIA get on with its work "without being watchdogged to death."[12]

(d) *The proposal to create a joint committee raised a constitutional issue of separation of powers between executive and legislative branches.* It was argued that since CIA undertakes activities only in accordance with National Security Council directives, any congressional action which seeks to interfere with or pry into this relationship "would tend to impinge upon the constitutional authority and responsibility of the President in the conduct of foreign affairs."

(e) *To compare CIA with the Atomic Energy Commission, or to use the atomic energy analogy, is invalid.* In size of operation, in impact upon the domestic economy, and in detailed legislative matters involved in atomic energy affairs, the atomic energy field is not comparable with intelligence. Atomic energy is a subject for general legislative consideration, unlike intelligence activities which were said to be "peculiarly the prerogative of the Executive and intimately associated with the conduct of the foreign relations of the country."[13]

These dissenting views, as presented by Senator Hayden, set the stage for the Senate debate on the issue. A key to the counter-argument was the notion expressed by Senator Richard Russell: "If there is one agency of the Government in which we must take some matters on faith without a constant examination of its methods and sources, I believe this agency is the Central Intelligence Agency."[14] The minority view was that Congress was generally informed, through its designated subcommittees of foreign intelligence activities. What Congress did not know about CIA activities, it was argued, was to be accepted "on faith." For, as Senator Hayden noted, "We must remember that the Central Intelligence Agency carries on its work outside the United States boundaries. Many of its agents are in constant physical danger."[15] About this work a few select members of Congress would be advised on a "need to know" and a "desire to know" basis.

Debate on the Senate Floor

The dimensions of the senatorial debate on the Mansfield resolution in April 1956 were forecast in the Senate report just described. The arguments pro and con listed above were decorated with the usual oratorical trappings, but few additional basic arguments were made in support of, or in opposition to, the proposal.

As a prime mover of the proposal, Senator Mansfield expressed fear that a creeping secrecy might produce a situation in which Congress would possess a decreasing amount of information about the performance of the intelligence community.[16] He felt that closer congressional surveillance would improve the product; that "Congressional guardians might be able to compel even swifter and surer reform than could an executive committee."[17]

Senator Mansfield made the further point in the debate that the development of CIA under tight executive control represented "arrogation of power on the part of the Executive and a diminution to that extent of the equality between the executive and the legislative."[18] Through its control of secret information vital to foreign policy making, Mansfield feared that CIA abetted the Executive's increasing domination over this field, to the exclusion of Congress.

On this latter point he was joined by the strongly stated arguments of Senator Wayne Morse, who expressed a suspicion that CIA "determines a great deal of policy . . . it has great influence in determining foreign policy."[19] Senator Morse's views embodied traditional American misgivings about maintaining an espionage system. He said that senators who were opposing the resolution were in effect "supporting a form of American police state system." Referring to an opponent in the debate, Senator Morse declared that "when he defends the present CIA system, he defends a spy system that is based upon a police state procedure."[20] He felt that all members of the Senate Committee on Foreign Relations and Armed Services ought to be informed about "the manner in which the American spy system functions."[21]

Senator Henry Dworshak (R., Idaho) although opposing the resolution, spoke up to recount that as a member of a defense appropriations subcommittee he had been unsuccessful in obtaining information from the Director of Central Intelligence. He had asked questions about the number of CIA employees and the amount of CIA expenditures and was told, emphatically, "This is classified information."[22] Yet even with thirty-five original supporters of the resolution, only a meager handful joined Mansfield and Morse in debate to support the measure. In light of later history it is interesting that Senator John F. Kennedy sided with Mansfield while Senator Lyndon B. Johnson opposed the proposed formation of a joint committee.

A bipartisan force of formidable size and prestige spoke out against the measure, with obviously powerful back-stopping from leaders of the Eisenhower Administration. Some of the members of the Senate with most prestige, Democratic as well as Republican, led by Senators Richard Russell and Leverett Saltonstall, echoed the arguments already summed up in the minority report of the Senate Rules Committee. Senator Russell, who like Saltonstall served on CIA subcommittees, declared that "although we have asked [Allen Dulles] very searching questions about some activities which it almost chills the marrow of a man to hear about, he has never failed to answer us forthrightly and frankly in response to any question we have asked him."[23] This view was seconded by Senator Saltonstall and others of the small interlocking group from the Armed Services and Appropriations committees who were at that time the Senate's chosen few to oversee CIA.

Although apparently getting all the information sought from CIA officials, it had been the practice of this select group to exercise self-restraint in asking questions. At least this is the inference from Senator Saltonstall's remark that "it is not a question of reluctance on the part of CIA officials to speak to us. Instead it is a question of our reluctance, if you will, to seek information and knowledge on subjects which I personally, as a Member of Congress and as a citizen, would rather not have."[24] During the 1950s, meetings with CIA officials (at which such questions went unasked) were held "once a year" in the case of the Senate Armed Services Subcommittee.[25] None of the members of these two CIA subcommittees voted for the Mansfield resolution.[26]

Most opponents of the measure made the point in the debate that secrecy is essential to intelligence operations and that a congressional joint committee would be incompatible with this required secrecy. As Senator Alben Barkley noted, "The activities of the CIA cover the entire world, and the CIA makes reports on the entire world situation."[27] As for the need for secrecy, Senator Barkley, who as Vice President sat for four years with the National Security Council, declared: "Some of the information gathered by the Central Intelligence Agency and laid before the National Security Council itself was so confidential and secret that the very portfolios in which it was contained were under lock and key."[28] The mystique of secrecy had profoundly impressed the Kentucky senator, who added, "I would lose my right arm before I would divulge it to anyone, even to members of my own family."[29]

It soon became clear in the Senate debate that the measure lacked adequate support for passage. Not only did Senator Barkley, as a former member of the National Security Council, lend weighty oratorical opposition, but he was joined by a former Secretary of the Air Force, Senator Stuart Symington. Also in opposition were the majority and minority leaders of the Senate, and high-ranking members—both Republican and Democratic—of the Armed Services and Appropriations Committees.

At its initiation the proposal had 35 supporters, but it was defeated by a vote of 59 to 27, with 10 Senators not voting.[30] Fourteen of the measure's co-sponsors, all Republicans but one, reversed their positions and voted against the measure. Obviously, a strong administration opposition to the measure had caused this contradictory performance. The 27 members who voted in favor of the resolution fell with a few exceptions into two general categories: liberal Democrats, most of whom had lesser seniority on Senate committees, and right-wing Republicans, who were generally associated with the camp of Senator Joseph McCarthy. Support for the measure therefore derived from two different attitudes.

One was the distaste of liberal Democrats for the "dirty business" of international spying and for the existence of a state apparatus for secret intelligence beyond congressional surveillance through regular committee procedures. A somewhat different attitude was reflected by the late Senator Joseph McCarthy and his associates, who perhaps expressed Midwestern resentment of the size and potential power of CIA, an agency engaged in an essentially intellectual process and seemingly led by an "Ivy League" assemblage of bright young men. The existence of CIA also was symbolic of America's new internationalism, which senators in this group, including for example, Senator William Langer of North Dakota, viewed with deep suspicion.

Opposition to the measure was made up of a group of "Eisenhower Republicans" of varying degree and of powerful Democratic senators, mostly southerners with high committee seniority. These men, some of whom were privy to bits of information about CIA, saw little need for a new joint committee. One astute observer of the Senate concluded that the measure was killed because the "Inner Club" of Senate patriarchs felt it had not been adequately consulted about the measure.[31]

As is often the case in congressional debate, some of the real and persuasive arguments for or against the measure remained below the surface. These arguments were the kind that are effective in the cloakrooms and corridors, but are not brought out in the public debate for any number of reasons. One such argument was that the establishment of wider congressional surveillance over CIA would be disturbing to the principal allies of the United States. Allied intelligence services work closely, though sometimes in an atmosphere of mutual suspicion, with United States intelligence agents in overseas operations, but apparently are wary of supplying the United States Congress with details of such operations. Intelligence units in allied nations enjoy immunity from detailed legislative supervision, though parliamentary government gives a direct responsibility to political leaders. Consequently, a more thorough check of CIA operations by Congress, it is held, would tend to inhibit vital and always difficult interallied intelligence cooperation and so dry up important sources for American government officials. This was not the kind of argument, however persuasive in the cloakrooms, that would swing great weight in the Senate debate, and thus it hardly came to the surface.

Of greater importance was the realization by senior members of the Senate that creating a joint committee on central intelligence would have the effect of slicing off a part of their jurisdictional authority. For example, the Committee on Foreign Relations oversees intelligence within the Department of State; the Armed Services Committee looks into intelligence activities in the armed forces; the Joint Committee on Atomic Energy oversees Atomic Energy Commission intelligence activities; and CIA is under the purview of a few senior members on Armed Services and Appropriations committees. Not surprisingly, then, senior members of the Senate opposed alteration in the fractured structure of Congress because that change would remove segments of the executive branch from their particular domain.

Opposition by Senate patriarchs made possible an effective alliance with the executive branch, particularly with the leadership of CIA, to whom the growth of a congressional committee intelligence staff long has been an anathema. Such a staff, it is feared, might turn out to be a haven for former CIA personnel whose mission in life might be to second-guess National Intelligence Estimates, or generally to harass executive intelligence agencies.

Whatever their motives, a sizable majority of members of a group traditionally jealous of congressional prerogative in the continuing legislative-executive struggle voted against a measure which seemed to promise at first glance to give them additional power. On this issue the Senate exercised restraint. Such restraint has been normal for the national legislature in the past only in wartime, in which large sums of money were blindly granted by Congress. Its World War II motto was said to be: "Trust in God and General Marshall." In the cold war atmosphere of 1956, the attitude seems to have been: "Trust in God and Allen Dulles."

The Issue Debated Again in 1966

Ten years later a similar issue came to a vote on the Senate floor. In the interim, each passing Congress had seen the introduction of proposals similar to that of Senator Mansfield. Between 1947 and 1967, for example, over two hundred resolutions had been introduced in the Senate, calling for stricter and more systematic congressional surveillance of the intelligence community. An even greater number of such proposals were made in the House. One of the most prominent and specific was an "investigation" of CIA proposed in 1963 by Representative (later Mayor) John Lindsay of New York. Lindsay proposed four major topics for congressional scrutiny: relations between the CIA and the Department of State; whether or not the CIA was the proper agency to perform secret political operations, distinct from intelligence gathering; personnel policies of the CIA; and the adequacy of the organization and process for evaluating "raw" intelligence. In other words, Lindsay was proposing a top-to-bottom study of the CIA, preliminary to the establishment of a permanent joint congressional committee on intelligence.[32] But as of 1969 the arrangement persists whereby small and highly select subcommittees of the House and Senate Armed Services and Appropriations committees are the only groups routinely privy to intelligence secrets.

In spite of strong resistance to the idea by CIA leadership and President Lyndon Johnson, the issue of more systematic congressional surveillance of CIA came to a head again in early 1966. This time the leader was not Mansfield but Senator Eugene McCarthy of Minnesota, who for some years had been critical in speeches and writing of the "invisible government" aspects of CIA, particularly after the 1961 Bay of Pigs episode. Indeed, he had led the fight in 1962 against the Senate confirmation of John

McCone, President Kennedy's choice as Director of Central Intelligence. Senator McCarthy's opposition to the McCone appointment was based upon what the senator regarded as unsatisfactory answers McCone had given the Senate Committee on Armed Services when it had been considering McCone's nomination. These questions had dealt with McCone's experience in intelligence work, his attitude toward the congressional role in foreign policy, and his noncommittal responses on various policy questions, including the proper limits of CIA action in foreign affairs.[33] In essence, McCone had replied that he did not regard the Director of Central Intelligence as being in a policy-making position and he planned to continue with existing methods for congressional relationship with CIA. Nonetheless, within governmental circles McCone had made clear his intention of becoming a "power" in the Kennedy administration, although, as it turned out, he "was restrained in his use of the power of CIA."[34]

By 1966 Eugene McCarthy was a member of the Senate Committee on Foreign Reliations. On the CIA issue he had found support from the committee's chairman, Senator J. William Fulbright, as well as from a number of other members, mostly Democrats. Early in 1966 McCarthy had proposed a Senate resolution calling for an investigation by the Foreign Relations Committee of American foreign intelligence activities. This was to be, in the words of Senate Resolution No. 210 "a full and complete study with respect to the effects of the operations and activities of the Central Intelligence Agency upon the foreign relations of the United States." The resolution called for a report by January 31, 1967, provided for a staff, and proposed expenditures of up to $150,000 for this purpose.

The duties of the proposed committee were:

. . . to keep itself fully and currently informed of the activities of the Central Intelligence Agency, the Bureau of Intelligence and Research of the Department of State, and other agencies of the Government insofar as the activities of such agencies relate to foreign intelligence or counter-intelligence. The committee's duties shall include, but not be limited to, review of intelligence and counter-intelligence activities and legislative oversight of the coordinating of such activities among the various agencies concerned.[35]

The proposal at once raised a jurisdictional issue with the

Senate Committee on Armed Services, which claimed full and exclusive jurisdiction over the CIA. That committee's chairman, Senator Richard B. Russell, was simultaneously chairman of the Senate's Combined Armed Services and Appropriation seven-man CIA subcommittee—the Senate's CIA "watchdog."

Senator McCarthy's resolution for a select committee was referred to the Foreign Relations Committee, where on May 17 it was approved, with amendments, by a vote of 14 to 5. Prior to committee approval, McCarthy had removed important provisions in the hope of making the measure palatable to the Senate establishment and more specifically to prevent its referral to the Senate Rules Committee, where he knew it would die. One change was to exempt the FBI's counterespionage activities from committee surveillance; another was to eliminate the hiring of a separate staff; and a third was to delete the proposed expenditures of up to $150,000 from Senate contingency funds. In effect, McCarthy's initial aim to set up a select Senate committee to investigate the intelligence community had become, by compromise, simply a proposal to enlarge the existing Senate CIA "watchdog" subcommittee by the addition of three members from the Foreign Relations Committee, which was not represented on Senator Russell's subcommittee. What originally had been a move to investigate the CIA had become a proposal to enlarge an existing committee.

Senator Russell had early made clear his opposition to this move. He let it be known that he would ask the Senate to refer the McCarthy resolution, strongly supported by Senator Fulbright, to the Senate Armed Services Committee, over which Russell presided, and which could be expected either to bury the resolution or to report unfavorably on it. Russell considered the McCarthy–Fulbright proposal a reflection on his stewardship of the existing CIA subcommittee and a challenge to his power. In bitter terms he characterized the resolution as an attempt to "muscle in" on the jurisdiction of the watchdog committee. The impression was also given that if the CIA surveillance mechanism were broadened to include the Foreign Relations Committee, the likelihood of leaks would be increased, endangering the lives of secret agents overseas or, in the intelligence vernacular, "blowing their cover."

In June the Senate leadership, under Senator Mansfield, made an effort to effect a backstage compromise so that the matter would

174

not be fought out in open debate on the Senate floor. Mansfield said that in such a debate, "fearful things would be said that would not help the agency or the Senate."[36] He was unsuccessul in achieving a compromise between Russell and his supporters and Fulbright and McCarthy and their less numerous supporters. President Johnson, who might have resolved the issue by instructing the Director of Central Intelligence to give information as fully to Foreign Relations Committee as he did to the Russell CIA subcommittee, remained aloof. Undoubtedly he could not disassociate the Fulbright–McCarthy criticisms of his Vietnam policy from the CIA issue. At any rate, he was in no mood to placate Fulbright. A floor debate on the issue was, in the circumstances, inevitable.

The central point in the Fulbright–McCarthy position was that the CIA plays an important role both in making and applying foreign policies and that the Senate Foreign Relations Committee ought therefore to be specifically represented in the Senate group created for legislative surveillance of the agency. The main point in Russell's argument was that, out of twenty years of tradition, the Senate Armed Services and the Appropriations committees were the only ones with proper jurisdiction. Any expansion of representation would jeopardize the security of information revealed to the "select seven" by CIA officials. Behind these arguments, it seems fair to say, were issues of personality and senatorial power; of cliques and Senate "club" intrigue; and some fundamental disagreements about the purpose of American foreign policy and the proper use of the intelligence apparatus in pursuit of policy objectives. The CIA, it should be noted, was willing to supply the Foreign Relations Committee with substantive intelligence information and had done so on numerous occasions. But it was adamantly unwilling to discuss "sources and methods" with the Fulbright Committee. For example, if Senator Fulbright wanted to know, as he did in 1966, whether "Fulbright awards" had ever been used as "cover" for CIA operations, the CIA leadership in 1966 was unwilling to discuss this or any other matter with him related to "sources and methods."

The then CIA Director, Admiral Raborn, had told Fulbright's committee that he would answer such questions for members of the President's Board of Consultants on Foreign Intelligence Activities—all nongovernmental "civilians"—or for Russell's intelligence subcommittee. He contended, however, that he had no authority to discuss such matters with the Foreign Relations Committee. In a later interview, Raborn explained his position:

I had authority to brief any congressional committee having a jurisdictional interest in substantive global intelligence. But discussion of CIA activities, methods, and sources is another matter . . . the National Security Act makes the Director of Central Intelligence exclusively responsible for protecting the security of the sources and methods of the entire intelligence community. I was authorized by the President and by National Security Council directives to discuss such matters only with the special subcommittees designated for this purpose, not with any others.[37]

Fulbright's argument was that CIA overseas activities, including the wide scope of its "sources and methods," had many ramifications for American foreign policy. To him, the Foreign Relations Committee had an obvious concern and jurisdiction because "the CIA plays a major role in the foreign policy decision-making process and . . . by its activities it is capable of exerting—and has exerted—a very substantial influence on our relations with other nations."[38] Another point that Fulbright stressed was his view that the National Security Council was no longer an effective body for maintaining surveillance over the CIA because, since the Eisenhower years, the Council no longer met regularly and because under Presidents Kennedy and Johnson "the formal National Security Council machinery in existence in earlier years has atrophied to the point of nonexistence."[39]

Another senator, Ernest Gruening of Alaska, observed that whether or not the CIA "makes" foreign policy, the agency certainly exerts major influence on the policy-making process. He cited the Bay of Pigs episode as a prime example.[40]

Senator McCarthy doubted that Congress was receiving information sufficient to allow its participation in the supervision of CIA. He was particularly nettled at Admiral Raborn's refusal to supply information to the Senate Foreign Relations Committee. He declared:

There was no offer to give the information if we went to the [CIA] building on the other side of the river. He [Admiral Raborn] said that he thought it was clear that he did not have the right to give it to us. What we propose to do is to make it clear that under the law the Director can give this kind of information to the members of our committee under the same conditions and terms that it is given to members of the Armed Services Committee and Appropriations Committee.[41]

The opponents of McCarthy's resolution took the position that the existing subcommittee had maintained adequate surveillance over the CIA. Members of the subcommittee contended that they could get all the information they needed, and more than they wanted, from the CIA. Senators Saltonstall, Stennis, Symington, and Young (R., North Dakota), all members of the watchdog subcommittee, made short statements against the resolution, stressing the adequacy of existing arrangements. As was the case in 1956, the strongest attack on the resolution was made by Senator Richard Russell, chairman of the existing Senate "watchdog" subcommittee. Even more than in 1956, Russell predicated his argument on the basis of personal prestige. He left no doubt that he regarded the resolutions as a personal affront: "Unless the committee of which I am chairman has been derelict in its duty, there is no justification whatever for any other committee 'muscling in' on the jurisdiction of the Armed Services Committee, insofar as it pertains to the Central Intelligence Agency."[42] Russell added that the press had unfairly criticized the CIA and his committee.

Senators Saltonstall and Stennis, both members of Russell's subcommittee, then took the floor to defend the chairman. Russell pointed out that, after the Bay of Pigs, President Kennedy had put the CIA in each foreign country directly under the control of the American Ambassador in that country. Russell contended that this arrangement had insured that the CIA would be under the control of the State Department in matters relating to foreign policy.

This was the crux of the Senate's debate on the McCarthy resolution. In a vote that was remarkably similar to that of 1956, the Senate voted by a margin of 61 to 28 to send the resolution to almost certain death in Russell's Armed Services Committee.[43] Thirty-four Senators had had the opportunity to vote on both the 1956 Mansfield resolution and the 1966 McCarthy resolution. Of the twenty-five who had voted against the Mansfield resolution, only three changed to support the McCarthy resolution—Aiken, Williams (Del.), and Case. Of the nine who voted for the Mansfield resolution, five changed and voted against the McCarthy resolution. Those who changed to opposition were Senators Jackson, Mundt, Pastore, Smith of Maine, and Smathers. There were only four who voted for both resolutions. They were Senators Fulbright, Gore, Mansfield, and Morse. In the 1966 vote, the members of the existing CIA subcommittee voted unanimously against the resolution. In the 1956 vote, only Senator Chavez from the existing subcommittee had been in favor of the resolution and he did not vote. After the 1956 vote, observers of the Senate said "the Establishment" had beaten the Mansfield resolution. After the 1966 vote, *Time* made the same observation:

The overt issue was the attempt by William Fulbright's Foreign Relations Committee to gain representation on the Senate's special CIA watchdog committee. The real question, however, was whether Fulbright would succeed in flouting Richard Russell, chairman both of the watchdog group and the powerful Armed Services Committee, and uncrowned king of the Senate's inner Establishment.[44]

Congress attempted to maintain some degree of control over the CIA by its actions in writing the assignment of functions into law. Congress in 1947 could not possibly have made a deliberate decision to authorize political action in the assignments of functions, because there was no information available to it that would have indicated that such activity was contemplated. The proposal presented to Congress in 1947 was essentially that the CIA would be an agency for the centralized gathering, evaluating, and disseminating of *information*. The additional growth and development of the agency has taken place with the de facto, rather than statutory, approval of Congress. Two resolutions—one in 1956, the other in 1966—designed to regain some degree of surveillance and control of the CIA were defeated because of the concentrated opposition of some of the most powerful members of the Senate. Power and prestige and access to classified information apparently have a reciprocal relation, one to the other. Personal factors of power and prestige were determinants of action rather than the more substantive issues raised by the defeated resolutions. Finally, the effect of the votes of a majority of the members of the Senate is to say that Congress—or at least the Senate—does have sufficient and adequate information about and control over the CIA.

But the Fulbright–McCarthy efforts were not without some ultimate impact. In January 1967 Senator Russell invited three members of the Senate Foreign Relations Committee, including Fulbright and Mansfield, to "attend all of the meetings [of the subcommittee]—at least for this session of Congress." It was a limited victory for the proponents of the McCarthy resolution.[45]

Senator Fulbright viewed the issue in the context of his advocacy of greater congressional participation in foreign policy making. He later wrote that "as part of a broader effort to redress the constitutional unbalance in foreign policy the C.I.A. should be brought under effective congressional oversight. The technical means by which this is accomplished is not of critical importance. What is wanted is the will and determination of Congress to place checks on the power of the intelligence establishment and to make it truly accountable."[46]

In 1967, even after the disclosures of CIA's secret subsidies to the National Students Association overseas programs and numerous other labor, education, and cultural organizations, Senate leaders doggedly expressed satisfaction with the existing degree of congressional surveillance. Senate Majority Leader Mansfield, Minority Leader Dirksen, Senator Richard Russell, and House Minority Leader Gerald Ford all were reported to be in agreement that "there is enough Congressional surveillance of the CIA."[47]

Senator Mansfield's position was of course the most surprising—an apparent complete about-face. In a television interview on "Face the Nation," March 14, 1967, Mansfield explained the basis of his satisfaction: first, the inclusion of three members of the Senate Foreign Relations Committee (of which he was one) on the special Senate CIA subcommittee, and, second, his confidence in the Director of CIA, Richard Helms, the first intelligence career professional to occupy that position in the twenty years of CIA's existence.

After twenty years, the issue of more systematic congressional surveillance of the central intelligence system remains as a dormant volcano. The Senate and House establishments are for the most part content with an arrangement of limited surveillance over the intelligence establishment. The wisdom of the leadership attitude, shared by the presidency and the CIA up to now, remains a moot question. The issue will be dealt with again in the concluding chapter.

CHAPTER VIII

The British Intelligence System

Of several secret intelligence system models in the modern world, certainly Great Britain's must be listed as one of the most important and one that influenced the American system in its formative years. Her Majesty's Secret Service, as an institution, has left its mark on the development of many other Western intelligence systems as well, and it has been glamorized over the years by an unending flow of fiction. Yet surprisingly little factual information about it has ever been made public.[1]

Although there are important organizational differences, Great Britain's Secret Intelligence Service (SIS) is roughly the functional equivalent of the United States Central Intelligence Agency. And while the CIA carries a seriously burdensome, if not entirely deserved, reputation as the juvenile delinquent of American foreign policy, its British counterpart established a reputation as the world's best secret service at the end of the First World War. For two decades after World War II it continued to retain a public image as the most prestigious of the world's secret services, but this reputation became seriously tarnished with the 1967 disclosures concerning its penetration by the Soviet secret service.

The prodigious amount of publicity in fictional form about the British Secret Service has, in the main, diverted attention from or concealed its true nature. The service has long been the home of the mythical secret agent. The most famous recent example was James Bond, Ian Fleming's creation, whose style with enemy agents, guns, automobiles, and women excited tens of millions. Bond's fame spawned numerous imitators. These included countless children begging their parents for the abundantly available toy equipment, allegedly that of the spy and counterspy, including female dolls with knives concealed in their shoes. But if fiction has painted a picture of daring adventure, never have so many been so misinformed by so few regarding the true nature of the Secret Service. The simple fact—not so simply explained—is that the British Secret Service has successfully maintained secrecy from the public, if not entirely from the Soviets, for its organization, its agents, and their operations.

The British have managed to adhere to the principle that, in the real world of secret intelligence, silence is the golden word. Of factual books about the contemporary British Secret Service, comparable to half a dozen available on CIA, there are none at all. The "cover" is rarely "blown" on a British secret operation. If this occurs, the British press, except in rare instances, prints few revealing details, in sharp contrast to the world-wide publicity attending numerous CIA misadventures.

How have the British so successfully managed this? How is the intelligence community organized in Britain? Is it under responsible political control? Under what circumstances may the British system of secrecy break down? Since the United States has to date suffered from severe management problems with the intelligence system, are there lessons the British can teach the United States?

These are questions not easily answered, and because of meager evidence, scholars have not raised them before. Along Whitehall and into Parliament Square, where this writer explored the subject, only a privileged few, even in the highest ranks of the government service, were found to possess detailed, trustworthy information about the organization and activities of the Secret

Service. Probably some knew more than they were willing to admit. Until his name was publicized in an American book, *The Espionage Establishment*, by two journalists, published late in 1967, few could have told you, if they dared, the name of "C," head of the Secret Service. The code name "C" is derived from the first head of the modern Secret Service, Captain Mansfield Cumming of the Royal Navy. Englishmen generally not only have been unaware of "C's" identity but for two decades after World War II possessed fewer authentic details about their own Secret Service than about the American CIA.

The few British officials with authoritative knowledge simply will not discuss the structure and functions of their Secret Service. British civil servants, to be sure, are reticent in discussing almost any aspect of the internal workings of British government. In the words of an astute British journalist, Anthony Howard, "The first and great commandment for all British civil servants—even those operating in the sphere of press relations—is 'least said, soonest mended.' "[2] The British government barely acknowledges the existence of a Secret Service. This proverbial rule dominates: "He that has a secret should not only hide it but hide that he has it to hide."

Official acknowledgment of a Secret Service does occur, quietly, once a year, when Parliament is sent estimated expenditures for the coming year for the government's "foreign and other secret services." The figure sent to Parliament for 1965-1966 was nine million pounds (about $25,000,000), a one-million-pound increase over 1964-1965. (Compare this with an estimated annual CIA expenditure of $660,000,000.) Officials in the Treasury Chambers in Great George Street, London, will admit only that the announced sum includes the annual funding for both the Security Service (commonly but incorrectly called MI-5) and the Secret Service, often referred to as MI-6. No other details are ever given to the public, the press, or even to Parliament. Officials flatly refuse to discuss the almost certain fact that the published expenditures for the Secret Services represent only part of the funds actually allocated under the cover of other budgetary items. Even so, the British Service undoubtedly costs a small part of the amount expended on its American counterpart.

British Intelligence

Historical Background

World Wars I and II placed great burdens on the intelligence services of all nations, particularly on the United Kingdom, whose economic lifelines are vulnerable targets to adversaries. Long before the development of mass-destruction weapons, however, Britain was engaged professionally in a secret war of wits. While the CIA is little more than twenty years old, the British Secret Service may be the western world's oldest, dating back at least to the sixteenth century. From Elizabethan times, a distinction developed between internal security (counterintelligence) and positive foreign intelligence functions. Elizabeth I's state secretary, Sir Francis Walsingham, is one of the most famous of all espionage chiefs. Walsingham recruited some of the best graduates of Oxford and Cambridge into his network, a practice that some of his successors continue, with questionable impact on the efficiency of the organization. If they were not the "best" academically, they generally had important connections as part of a social elite, an asset of doubtful utility for an agency trying to discover the objective realities of the outside world. Some who have thought that this kind of recruiting by the CIA is ultimately a mistake have raised similar questions, particularly in its early years, about the "Ivy League" background of CIA leaders.

England's successful defense against the Armada of Philip II of Spain resulted from Walsingham's foreknowledge of Spanish plans. Walsingham, whose motto was "Knowledge is never too dear," concerned himself not only with an extensive foreign espionage network but with the codes and ciphers needed for secret communications. As historian Garrett Mattingly has expressed it, "No power in Europe, not even the secretive Venetians, had a more efficient system of security and counter espionage, such that 'not a mouse could creep out of any ambassador's chamber but Mr. Secretary [Walsingham] would have one of his whiskers.' "[3]

Daniel Defoe was another major figure of the Secret Service. Defoe's reluctance to write about spying in his novels, despite his detailed knowledge of that secret world, helped to establish a tradition of reticence that continues to preserve today both the secrecy and good reputation of the Service.

The Secret Service has detractors as well as its more numerous admirers. Not all observers agree with Allen Dulles, who once told a Senate Committee: "The British system has behind it a long history of quiet, effective performance, based on highly trained personnel with years of service and great technical ability." One who did seem to agree, but possibly with tongue in cheek, was Ian Fleming, who served in British Naval Intelligence in World War II. Fleming is supposed to have given credence to the motto: "Never has so much been known by so many about so little." Yet Fleming glamorized the Secret Service beyond all recognition. Ironically, James Bond, popular images notwithstanding, is neither spy nor intelligence agent but a rather fuzzily defined counterintelligence operative. In London there is a widely believed, probably apocryphal notion that both the Security Service and Secret Service maintain special sections with the prime duty of inspiring Fleming-like fiction, aiming to terrify adversaries and mislead the public on the realities of secret operations, and to provide the absolute secrecy that intelligence professionals demand.

Among public detractors of the Secret Service is Malcolm Muggeridge, who served in British intelligence during World War II. With a prejudice presumably deriving from his own experiences, he turns sharply against the Service on occasion. "The Secret Service is itself a fantasy," he wrote in one instance. "The fantasy lies in taking it seriously, and imagining it to be capable of achieving worthwhile results."[4]

Another critic is Graham Greene. His novel, *Our Man in Havana*, pictures a Secret Service agent conspiring to obtain and send home plans of a monstrous secret weapon which turns out to be a design for a huge vacuum cleaner. The story ends in a flourish of bureaucratic self-deception when the agent, who so grandly fouled up the assignment, is summoned to London and reassigned to the training of other agents. A more subtle critic is John Le Carré (David Cornwell), whose more recent novels depict the sometimes pointless suffering and death involved in the pursuit of the "black arts" of espionage and secret intervention. Her Majesty's intelligence professionals have a low regard for Fleming's Bond, but think highly of the authenticity of Le Carré's characters, if not of the author's skepticism about the utility and morality of most secret operations.

Through nearly two decades of cold war the British Secret Service retained its reputation for skill and efficiency, an image protected by a high wall of secrecy. Such protection has shielded the actual, as opposed to the fictional, episodes in the modern history of the Service. Just the opposite is the British government's reputation for internal security and the protection of secret services from infiltration by adversary agents. On this score the *Sunday Times* of London, reflecting on how H. A. R. Philby, as a Russian agent, managed to infiltrate the Secret Service in 1940, characterized the leadership of SIS as "improbable" and referred to "its bizarre recruiting policies, its uneasy relations with the rest of the intelligence community."[5] During the early forties, the Secret Service was operating in a "moribund" atmosphere, in the judgment of Bruce Page and his co-authors writing in 1967. According to them, the Secret Service during World War II "escaped any basic reconstruction." It was superseded in many of its activities by the Secret Operations Executive, civilian-led and staffed during that war. One thing is clear: the Secret Service maintained its secrecy and its public image as an efficient, professional, discreet organization. What is less clear is whether this reputation was justified. Revelations in 1967 raised profound doubts on this score.

The Philby case is one of the most bizarre intelligence episodes of modern times, all the more so because it affected a service thought to be more immune than others to the kind of treachery suffered. A graduate of England's "best" schools, Philby lived the life of a double agent for nearly thirty years, narrowly escaping to the Soviet Union in 1963. He became a Soviet agent in 1933 with instructions to penetrate British intelligence. He did so with a success that ultimately afforded him access to the American CIA. Philby patently gave the Soviet intelligence system a secret view of many Western intelligence operations. For a period, he was in charge of Britain's counter-Soviet intelligence network, and at one stage in his career he seemed to be a likely choice to head Britain's Secret Intelligence Service. Whatever Western plans existed to subvert Communist governments after World War II may have been effectively defused with the knowledge supplied by Philby and his associates, who included Guy Burgess and Donald Maclean, officers in the Foreign Service.

The defection to Russia in 1951 of Burgess and Maclean first brought Philby under suspicion, ending his executive career but, incredibly, not his association with British intelligence. He maintained a connection with British espionage activities until he fled to Moscow in January 1963, became a Soviet citizen, and married the divorced wife of Donald Maclean. The Philby case was profoundly shocking to the intelligence establishment and raised basic questions about the British system of recruiting, organizing, and controlling secret agents. Aware of incipient deficiencies, British political leaders in the mid-1950s effected an unpublicized reorganization of British intelligence that corresponded to changes made in the American intelligence system after the outbreak of the Korean War.

Developments After World War II

Since World War II the total British "peacetime" intelligence effort, like that of the United States, has grown enormously, and the British "intelligence establishment" comprises a number of organizations with distinct missions. Britain has no exact organizational equivalent to the CIA, where there is a director of Central Intelligence who acts as the Chief Executive's principal intelligence adviser and coordinator of all of the government's foreign intelligence activities.

Of the various British groups with foreign intelligence functions, two major contemporary agencies are the Secret Intelligence Service (SIS) and the Security Service. There has always been considerable public confusion about these two separate agencies. Fictional accounts of British secret operations have compounded the confusion.

The Secret Intelligence Service has as its popular label, MI-6, a name dating back to its wartime military affiliations. Today, as it was under Elizabeth I, it is a civilian rather than military service, although it was headed in some crucial years of the 1930s and 1940s by "old soldier" types.

The Secret Service is mainly concerned with the information required in foreign policy-making that is unavailable through routine and overt intelligence channels. These overt sources would include Foreign Service officers, accredited military service attachés, and the Defense Intelligence Staff of the Ministry of Defense. The fact is, however, that like all other Foreign Offices, British embassies provide "cover" for secret agents. Thus, a consular official in any given foreign country may, in fact, be a secret operative. All the "gimmicks" of an espionage service, commonly labeled by diplomats as the "Department of Dirty Tricks," are employed by such agents, including, if infrequently, some of the methods and devices portrayed in popular fiction.

Like the CIA and any other major intelligence organization, the British Secret Service is organized into functional compartments. For example, one major section is devoted to the collection, evaluation, and analysis of intelligence information. Another major, if smaller, section is devoted to special operations, which may include dangerous espionage or underground foreign political action. No precise organizational details in this regard have ever been revealed. During World War II a unit called Special Operations Executive (SOE) was organized under separate political control for espionage and sabotage and, particularly, to further wartime anti-Axis resistance movements. This was closely affiliated with the American Office of Strategic Services (OSS), which had similar functions.

SOE was the product of the conviction held by a few British leaders that secret agents and other "behind-the-lines" forces could greatly aid in defeating Hitler, particularly in those subjugated nations, such as France, where the German occupation was most bitterly resisted. Moreover, early in the war British power to inflict major damage on Hitler's military forces was severely limited. Recruits were available, however, for underground resistance forces in occupied territories, provided they could be effectively mobilized and supplied. Prime Minister Churchill was particularly enthusiastic about the utility of fighting the enemy with underground forces. Some leaders in Britain—and Churchill did not discourage them— even dreamed of defeating Hitler by economic pressure, air bombardment of vital targets, and instigation of revolt by indigenous forces within occupied territories. An invasion by major Allied forces might be unnecessary.

After some spinning of wheels, Churchill appointed Sir Hugh Dalton to take charge of SOE on July 16, 1940. This was a new organization independent of existing intelligence, propaganda, and political warfare units. The SIS continued its separate existence. SOE's mission was, in Churchill's colorful phrase, "to set Europe ablaze." SOE's actual role having been defined initially in highly ambiguous terms, its function came to be to conduct espionage, sabotage, and—where feasible—guerilla warfare in Nazi-occupied areas.

By 1943 the field operations of SOE in Southern and Western Europe were placed under the control of General Eisenhower, as Supreme Commander in Europe, and the British intelligence unit became closely affiliated with the OSS, which carried out similar missions. In London the two organizations worked almost as one unit. British experience by 1943 could be exchanged for American supplies and additional manpower.

The value of SOE's contribution to Allied victory, like that of the OSS, is difficult to measure. There were failures as well as successes. By the time of the Normandy invasion in 1944, resistance groups, aided by OSS and SOE, were playing a major role in assuring ultimate victory for the Allies.[6] After World War II, SOE disappeared into Whitehall's darkest corner. Some of its functions are still performed under ultrasecret cover as a compartment of the Secret Service. This section can perform, upon assignment from the highest political authority, a wide array of strategic services. These would include "black" propaganda (in which the true source is concealed), various kinds of psychological warfare, and other forms of secret action in pursuit of the British national interest overseas. Secrecy for most of these functions, to date, has been nearly absolute. The government, in fact, only acknowledges their existence in a negative way by stating in Parliament, for example, that the "public interest" prohibits any discussion of the intelligence function. Until the breakdown in early 1967 regarding the publication of security information, the British press almost always cooperated.

Until the Government-Press furor of 1967 it was a rare occasion indeed when one saw newspaper mention of any part of the Secret Service. In January 1965 readers of the *Times* of London learned of an incident occurring in early 1957 involving the Service. At the height of the first Cyprus crisis, British agents in Athens managed to tap the telephone of the Greek prime minister, Mr. Karamanlis. Greek counterespionage discovered the tap, and it was disconnected after six weeks. The Greek foreign minister protested vigorously to the British ambassador in Athens, but the case was suppressed through mutual London–Athens agreement. The point is that, unlike what very likely would have happened had the CIA been involved, such revelations produced little apparent excitement in London in 1965 and no disclosures about the Service's structure and functions.

Chiefs of the Secret Service since World War II have included Major General Sir Stewart Menzies, an old Etonian former Guard's officer with close connections to the British social elite, including the Royal Family; Sir John Alexander Sinclair, a Royal Artillery officer and wartime chief of Army Intelligence; and the chief appointed in 1956, Sir Dick Goldsmith White, who attended American universities and whose name was not publicly known until widely published in late 1967 as a consequence of its disclosure in an American book. With this, most of the British press abandoned at least temporarily, the traditional principle of anonymity for the head of the Secret Intelligence Service.

Prior to these disclosures the name of "C" was deduced by this writer in London in 1965 without extraordinary difficulty. It was a matter of discrete inquiry among informed persons, the drawing of inferences, and the subtle confirmation from those who knew. The secrecy surrounding "C's" name was more a matter of convenience than of crucial security information; certainly the principal adversaries—the Communist intelligence network—knew his name. The British simply wished to divert attention—of the British public as much as of any adversary—from this office. British citizens at all levels seemed to accept this strict rule of anonymity without question.

The Security Service, commonly labeled "MI-5," attempts to protect British secrets from foreign spies and to prevent subversive action. The Security Service gained its commonly used military designation in the years preceding the First World War. At that time it was created as a fifth section of Military Intelligence in the War Office to deal with counterespionage. On the eve of World War II, MI-5 was led by Sir Vernon Kell, by then an elderly man. According to the *Sunday Times* of London, it was "an outfit whose principal occupation for the past twenty years [1919-1939] had been spasmodic tracking-down of the Bolshevik menace." Kell's men, according to the *Sunday Times* "were better suited for this than for the looming European war. They had been recruited almost exclusively from the Indian Police."[7] For nearly a century,

189

India had been one of Britain's major security problems, where, incidentally, the Russians had been a major adversary. Today the Security Service is staffed mainly by civilians, principally former armed service intelligence officers, lawyers, and former civilian police officials.

Head of the Security Service is the faceless "K." More recently he has come to be known as "the Director-General." The once popular code name "K" came from Kell, director of the Security Service from 1909 to 1940. Since the retirement in 1953 of Sir Percy Sillitoe, the colorful chief who seemed to enjoy publicity even as the head of the Security Service, the British press cooperated until late 1967 with the government's desire that the name of the Security Service's present chief never be published. This is not to conceal absolutely his identity—in London in 1965 it was possible for this writer to determine "K's" name also—but simply to implement the British principle that the leadership of the secret services should remain anonymous. Sillitoe, incidently, was succeeded by Sir Dick White, who subsequently, in a most unusual transfer, became head of SIS in 1956. A corresponding appointment in the United States would have been to name J. Edgar Hoover as head of the CIA. White was followed in MI-5 by Sir Henry Hollis, who in turn was succeeded, in 1966, by Sir Edward M. Furnival-Jones. Until 1967, these names were known to only a handful of people.

The Security Service, however, remains a silent branch, cooperating with—and sometimes in conflict with—the Secret Service at home and abroad, but specializing in counterespionage. Its overt domestic counterpart is "Special Branch" of Scotland Yard (the Metroplitan Police), which is responsibile to the Home Secretary and charged with making any necessary arrests. The Security Service makes no direct arrests.

The Security Service's cover was rudely ripped off in 1963 in the aftermath of the Profumo-Keeler scandal, when it was revealed that some confusion existed at the highest governmental levels as to who was responsible to whom in the Security Service. Prime Minister Harold Macmillan was late in receiving information that the Director-General of the Security Service had possessed knowledge for some time about Profumo's liaison with Christine Keeler. Lines of authority and communications subsequently had to be clarified.

British Intelligence

When he took office in October 1964, Prime Minister Wilson was not entirely satisfied with these arrangements. As a former civil servant himself, he perceived that effective control was largely in the hands of the permanent government. The Cabinet Secretariat and Civil Service serve the Prime Minister, but they are not his political allies. To assure that he would be properly informed about the Secret Services and that these agencies would also be firmly under responsible Cabinet supervision, he designated an old political ally, Colonel George Wigg, Labour M.P., as paymaster general. With this anachronistic and functionally meaningless title, Wigg's assignment was to keep the Security Services under surveillance, and particularly the "security" of Cabinet ministers under watch as the Prime Minister's alter ego. This did not seem to please Civil Service traditionalists, yet Prime Minister Wilson saw the need for a double watchdog to bark in the dark shadows of Whitehall.

In Great Britain the Prime Minister is ultimately responsible. In 1968 Harold Wilson's institutional watchdog for the Secret Service was Sir Burke Trend in his role as secretary of the Cabinet. For surveillance of the Security Service, the Prime Minister looked to Sir Laurence Helsby, as permanent head of the Civil Service. Another bureaucratic layer between the Prime Minister and the operations of the Security Service is the Home Secretary. For the Secret Service, this intermediate role is played by the Foreign Secretary.

Other principal units of the British intelligence system include:

A *Defense Intelligence Staff* that works within the Ministry of Defense. This staff replaced the Joint Intelligence Bureau, created at the end of World War II to make national estimates. Like its American counterpart (the Defense Intelligence Agency), British military intelligence has undergone an increasing amount of centralization in recent years. This process reached its peak in the summer of 1965 when separate army, navy, and air force intelligence directors were eliminated, and unified functional directors were appointed for an integrated military intelligence staff within the Defense Ministry. The chief purpose of this reorganization, as with the creation of the American DIA, was to stop the use of intelligence to back up the rival claims of the separate armed services to budget allocations. Also, as espionage becomes increasingly mechanized and automated, the military systems for collecting intelligence threaten to displace the human spy on the ground. Control of such expensive technological devices must be organized to promote the best economy and effectiveness. Thus, defense intelligence rises in importance.

Communications Intelligence, secret aspects of which once were called "magic," is concerned with codes and ciphers and various forms of electronic intelligence. It is sometimes called "GCHQ," from its wartime name, but more formally it is today the Government Communications Centre, comparable to the highly secret National Security Agency in the United States. As with the military, an accelerating technology gives ever-expanding importance and capabilities to communications intelligence in the contemporary setting.

Like the Secret Service, British code makers and breakers have always operated in the shadows, and under the general control of the Foreign Office. The success of the British in maintaining such secrecy over the years may be understood from the story of how the Admiralty tried to prosecute Sir Alfred Ewing, well-known engineer who died in 1935, for publicly describing intelligence activities of the 1914 war nearly ten years after it ended. This was revealed in the May 1965 issue of the *University of Edinburgh Journal*.

During World War I, Sir Alfred was in charge of "Room 40," the intelligence section responsible for deciphering enemy wireless messages. So successful was it that the German fleet made few movements that were not detected in advance by the Admiralty. Room 40 also intercepted a number of important political messages, including the famous Zimmerman telegram, in which Germany offered Mexico a conditional alliance against the United States, a major disclosure prompting American entry into the war.

On December 13, 1927, Sir Alfred, then principal of Edinburgh University, described Room 40 and some of its exploits in a speech to the Edinburgh Philosophical Institution. Shortly thereafter, the Admiralty prepared to prosecute Sir Alfred under the Official Secrets Act. Sir William James relates how he persuaded the First Sea Lord that such a prosecution would be extremely foolish since Room 40 was already well known. The Admiralty dropped its prosecution plans. Until recent years, historians trying to probe the story of past intelligence organization and procedures have encountered a familiar curtain of secrecy, particularly on any matter regarding codes and ciphers. A relaxation of rigid security on these subjects is now observable, however. The publication in 1968 of Donald McLachlan's *Room 39*[8] partially opened the door to a vast storehouse of secrets about British Naval Intelligence in World War II. The motives of the government in allowing such new disclosures were mixed but, like the new permissiveness regarding the supersecret Special Operations Executive in World War II, were influenced by the fact that the record would remain incomplete in the absence of any public knowledge of these significant activities. Historians will, nonetheless, continue to encounter serious obstacles to a fuller, less government-oriented account of the activities of the Secret Services.

The British "intelligence community" comprising the agencies already enumerated is under the general supervision of a Joint Intelligence Committee (JIC), a Cabinet defense subcommittee, comparable to the American President's "Special Group" created with the purpose of approving and supervising CIA operations, or the U. S. Intelligence Board that oversees the intelligence community. But the JIC also performs some of the functions of the Office of National Estimates of the CIA, for it is to this committee that the prime minister and government look for the best and final answer to the question: "What is this government's best information on . . . ?" Here are represented the major subdivisions of the various secret intelligence services. The JIC serves as a kind of board of directors for the intelligence and strategic services system. It processes the "national intelligence estimate" for top decision makers and supervises all strategic operations with political ramifications. Chairmanship of the JIC is held by a representative of the Foreign Office, usually the deputy permanent undersecretary. For several years, for example, Sir Patrick Dean, first as assistant, then as deputy Foreign Office undersecretary, was chairman, prior to his appointment as British ambassador to the United States.[9]

Traditions of Secrecy

British success in maintaining a high degree of secrecy from the public eye for their intelligence system is attributable to constitutional structure, Civil Service traditions, Official Secrets statutes, and a scheme agreed upon by government and press for a voluntary press censorship.

All foreign affairs were once under exclusive Crown jurisdiction. In British constitutional evolution, this has become, de facto, the prerogative of the monarch's ministers. Although English constitutional history highlights the gradual decrease in executive authority and the strengthening of Parliament, as the people's representatives, foreign relations have remained a crown-ministerial prerogative. Thus, the prime minister and cabinet have authority to conduct foreign affairs without reference to Parliament, although the government must sustain parliamentary confidence and must request and obtain from it the required funds. Executive authority includes the appointment of all foreign service agents, the making of treaties, and the formidable right to refuse information to Parliament on grounds of the public interest.

Invariably, this right has been asserted with regard to the Secret Service. Whenever questions are raised in Parliament about secret operations, the ministerial response invariably is that "an answer would not be in the public interest." This issue arose dramatically in 1956 when a retired British "frogman," Commander Lionel Crabb, was killed on an espionage mission to inspect the hull of a Soviet cruiser of new design. This ship was in a British harbor, having transported President Bulganin and Chairman Khrushchev for "tension-easing" talks with Prime Minister Anthony Eden and other British leaders. This affair set off an unprecedented parliamentary debate.

Opposition leader Hugh Gaitskell declared in Commons that in this case debate on the subject was proper. The government, he argued, had the right to withhold information only so long as four assumptions prevailed, namely, that (1) secret operations are "ultimately and effectively controlled by Ministers"; (2) such operations remain secret; (3) they "do not embarrass us in our international relations"; and (4) a feeling prevailed that the Secret Services were competent and efficient.[10] In this case the Opposition leader obviously was playing for partisan advantage. He pushed the Prime Minister hard on the point that he (Mr. Eden) had publicly disclaimed responsibility for the Crabb incident. Ministerial responsibility, Gaitskell argued, was a fundamental principle in

British democracy. "It is by this device," said Gaitskell, "that Parliament makes the Intelligence Service answerable to it." This was in response to the Prime Minister's statement to an astonished House of Commons: "While it is the practice of ministers to accept responsibility I think it necessary in the special circumstances in this case to make it clear that what was done was done without the authority or the knowledge of Her Majesty's Ministers. Appropriate disciplinary steps are being taken."[11] But Prime Minister Eden held fast to his refusal of the Opposition's request for information, stating bluntly that he was never prepared to discuss in the House of Commons the control, organization, or efficiency of the Secret Services. Such a tradition was doubly important in this case, he said, because of special diplomatic considerations. The British government has never varied from this principle, and although the British press, in somewhat exceptional behavior, gave rather full details of the Crabb episode, to this date there has been no official explanation of what actually happened. The Crabb episode was later described in the *Sunday Times* as "a hare-brained scheme from the start with not the slightest discernible advantage to offset the unimaginable political risks involved."[12] The episode produced some reform in SIS, the Prime Minister having been provoked into action by what he considered to be a personal affront. Mr. Eden thought he had issued orders against any "monkey business" during the visit of the Russian leaders. In some ways the Crabb affair was a Bay of Pigs in its impact on the intelligence system of Britain.

British civil servants, more so than their American counterparts, are expected to remain anonymous, impartial, and very secretive about the government's business. This is so even without the sanction of Official Secrets laws. If members of the House of Commons wish to penetrate this secrecy, they must attempt to do so through questions in Parliament. Ministers are held responsible for the actions of civil servants. Thus, strong executive control exists over the release of information. As to its effectiveness, Professor Brian Chapman, a leading commentator on British institutions, has observed: "The whole structure of British government is designed to protect the policy-making function of government from public scrutiny."[13] The suppression of information by the Civil Service is, Chapman argues, part of British governmental ideology. So the Secret Services stand, as it were, behind a double wall of secrecy, rarely penetrated by Parliament or press; it is a wall constructed by craftsmen with a mania for secrecy.

Also abetting secrecy is the existence of strong legal sanctions against disclosure. First, there is the general doctrine of privilege. All government information is the property of the Crown. Those receiving information from this source may not divulge it without Crown authorization. Bolstering this is the Public Records Act, requiring that a document classified as "secret" must remain so for fifty years unless declassified by appropriate authority. Second are the Official Secrets Acts which American intelligence leaders hold in envious regard. Said Allen Dulles, "The British through their Official Secrets Act and other related procedures have a better legal system in this particular field than do we and they are a country which prizes and protects the freedom of the press as do we."[14]

Official Secrets legislation was first enacted by Parliament in 1889. It followed the government's discovery that it could not sucessfully prosecute a Foreign Office temporary clerk, Charles Marvin, who conveyed to the *Globe*, a London newspaper, details of a secret treaty between England and Russia. An astonished government was even further amazed to discover that since no government document had been stolen—simply borrowed—Mr. Marvin had committed no crime in British law. The first Official Secrets Act was the result. Since 1889 the Official Secrets Act has been twice revised, each time becoming more heavily weighted against the accused. Scope of the law by administrative interpretation has been expanded to include possible prosecution of any unauthorized person—government employee or not—willingly coming into possession of official secrets or documents. It thus poses a threat to journalists. Many civil libertarians in England now feel that the Official Secrets laws are framed in terms so wide and loose as to go beyond the protection of national security. David Williams of Cambridge University, author of a 1965 book on official secrecy in Britain, *Not in the Public Interest*, declares: "Our knowledge of the workings of the central government nowadays is to a very large degree controlled by the Official Secrets Acts. Outsiders cannot look in."[15] Whatever their faults, Official Secrets statutes aid the Secret Service in remaining secret.

British Intelligence

The Role of the Press

Crucially important also are the attitudes and behavior of leaders of Britain's highly competitive press. Few subjects make better copy than stories of spies, counterspies, and secret operations. Patently, there has been no dearth of coverage in the British press about foreign spies and internal security scandals. How, then, can one explain press cooperation to maintain a cloak over the Secret Services? Beyond the deterrent effects of the Official Secrets legislation, the answer may be found in the working principles of the British press regarding national security, and in a formal cooperative system for voluntary censorship of security information.

As the editor of one of England's most prestigious newspapers told this writer in 1965: "In America the press operates on the principle of the public's *right to know* everything their government does. In England we are more inclined to follow the *need to know* principle." This more rigid principle suggests that the press will tend to take a government or civil service view on such issues rather than the independent, suspicious view that is more common among American journalists. Yet the same spokesman was quick to assert that if editors ever felt that the government's management of secrecy and security were jeopardizing the national interest, the press remained free to publish the forbidden "facts," or to work toward turning the government out of power. Events in 1967 described later in this chapter showed this to be in fact the operational principle. The British press generally accepts the assumption that the government's Secret Services, by definition, should remain secret. The American press, on the other hand, considers the CIA, for example, as fair game for any "scoop" that can be ferreted out. Reluctance to print whatever can be learned remains a rare occurrence in the American press. Most British press leaders, however, assume that the public, except in unusual circumstances, has no need to know.

The "D-Notice" System

But what about those gray zones of security where the press may be in doubt about whether or not to publish certain items of security information that may come its way in peacetime? In wartime a well-organized system of censorship, theoretically voluntary, has been the answer. In peacetime, a formal system has evolved for voluntary censorship: the Defense Notice system. Although not organized to its present degree until after 1945, this system has existed since 1912.

A "D-Notice" is a formal letter circulated confidentially to mass-media editors warning that certain items of information, normally protected by the Official Secrets Acts, but in danger of disclosure, should remain secret. The letter is signed by the Secretary of the Services, Press, and Broadcasting Committee—commonly called the D-Notice Committee—and is distributed to selected publications and other mass-communication outlets which could be expected to publish defense information. Represented on the Committee are four government and eleven press representatives from the major defense departments and the principal segments of the mass-communications media.

A proposed D-Notice normally will originate with one of the departments of government concerned with national security and may remain in effect for many years, or indefinitely. A draft is then discussed with the secretary of the committee, and, if deemed reasonable, is circulated among committee members. If approved, it is issued by the secretary in the committee's name. In emergencies the secretary may send out a notice on his own, providing that he has secured approval from at least three of the press members of the committee.

The secretary, normally a civil servant, is the linchpin of the system, serving the committee full-time and available to members of the press for advice at all hours. On some occasions a secretary undoubtedly gives "informal" advice for or against the publication of specific information. There were sixteen outstanding D-Notices as of June 1967.

While the D-Notice letters themselves have generally been considered confidential documents, two dealing with intelligence were published in the *Spectator* in 1967. One notice, dated 27 April 1956, asked newspapers to make no references to "secret intelligence or counter-intelligence methods and activities in or outside the UK." This would include any reference to intelligence personnel, either their identities or numbers, or to organizations, their location or methods of recruitment and training. An additional D-Notice, which, like the above, was a "standing request," asked the press to make no reference to "cyphering work carried out in Government communications establishments . . . Various methods used in the interception of foreign communications for secret intelligence purposes . . . [or] to the fact that on occasions it is necessary in the interest of defense for the services to intercept such communications."[16] The publication of these two D-Notices was unprecedented and was investigated by a Committee of Privy Counsellors. They determined that the *Spectator* had published them because its editors had concluded that the wording of the notices had become a major public issue and because the journal did not consider itself a part of the D-Notice system. In fact, its editors did not receive the D-Notices in question; nor were they on file in its offices.[17]

A D-Notice has no legal force; the press is, in theory, free at an editor's discretion to disregard it. Possible prosecution under the Official Secrets Acts, however, remains as a deterrent in the background. The government's aim is to make clear to editors what types of information or what specific items they should not publish. British editors defensively protest that the system is entirely voluntary, deny that the press is dominated by government on all security matters, and point out that D-Notices must be approved by press representatives prior to issuance.

General categories of information are covered by the notices, such as any discussion of secret intelligence organization, leadership, techniques, or sources of information. General prohibition also holds for most categories of atomic, chemical, and biological warfare information. Problems usually arise not with such categories but in specific instances. Being under no legal obligation to observe the notices, segments of the press have occasionally ignored a particular D-Notice.

An example is the case of George Blake, whose trial as a Communist spy began in London on April 24, 1961. On May 1 a D-Notice was distributed to editors requesting that they not print the report that Blake had been an agent of the British Secret Service. The notice explained that certain lives, presumably those of British agents, were endangered. On May 3 Blake was convicted after a mostly secret trial. But some disclosures leaked, and the press became restless.

A second D-Notice was issued after Blake's conviction, asking newspapers not to reprint stories appearing in the European press alleging that Blake had been a "double agent" working for both the British and Russian secret services and that he had exposed British agents in Berlin. The government seemed to fear that publication of such reports would tend to demoralize British intelligence agents and perhaps confirm information sought by the Russian intelligence service. Editors felt that in this case the government was trying to use the British press as a strategic ploy, and some rebelled by ignoring the D-Notice. (Moreover, editors are inclined to feel that the publication of information in the foreign press frees them from the D-Notices.) Even so, little was revealed in the Blake incident about British secret intelligence.

The system broke down in an even more serious way in February 1967 when the *Daily Express* published a sensationalized news account of what the British term "cable vetting." The story revealed how "thousands of private cables and telegrams sent out of Britain from the Post Office or from commercial cable companies are regularly being made available to the security authorities for scrutiny."[18] The procedure consisted of an initial sifting by an intelligence department of the Post Office; its "find" was sent along to the secret intelligence services for analysis of its potential intelligence content. It later became clear that the practice was by no means new, having been authorized by the Official Secrets Act of 1920, and that it involved in practice the setting aside of only a small percentage of total telegrams.

When the *Daily Express* disclosure was published, Prime Minister Harold Wilson accused the newspaper of ignoring the two D-Notices proscribing all mention in the press of intelligence sources, methods, and activities. Editors of the newspaper rejected the government's claim that D-Notices covered the information revealed, and a severe crisis developed in the relations between government and press. The Prime Minister appointed three privy counsellors to a committee of inquiry, under the chairmanship of Lord Radcliffe. This committee issued a 288-page report in June 1967.

The committee had been charged not only to examine the circumstances surrounding the publication of the *Daily Express* article but to consider what improvements might be made in the D-Notice system. The Report concluded that the *Daily Express* article had been generally accurate; that publication of the article did not amount to a breach of D-Notices; and that the *Daily Express* in its decision to publish the article was not acting with the deliberate purpose of evading or defying a D-Notice. The Report recommended no major change in the D-Notice system, although several suggested changes in its staffing and operations were made.[19]

The committee's finding was unacceptable to Prime Minister Wilson, who forthwith issued a White Paper on "The 'D' Notice System" with contrary conclusions. The government's argument was based upon the premise that national security was threatened by the *Daily Express* disclosure and so the publication of the "cable vetting" report was viewed "as a matter of the utmost gravity."[20] Indeed, the government's position was that the disclosure so damaged the national security that "the consequences . . . cannot even now be fully assessed."[21]

The essence of the White Paper's argument was that Colonel L. G. Lohan, as Secretary of the D-Notice Committee, failed to follow instructions or to try with sufficient diligence to stop publication of the story by the *Daily Express*, or to warn his superiors in time that the article was about to be published. The government's case rested upon the assumption that the article in question was covered by existing D-Notices, a view which the Radcliffe Report rejected.

The government further argued: (a) that the *Daily Express* article on "cable vetting" *was* misleading, although it could not "in the public interest" explain how; and (b) that defects had existed in the administration of the D-Notice system.

Involved here was an intermixture of partisan politics (with the *Daily Express* aiming to embarrass the government), a breakdown in the sensitive balance which must be maintained in any voluntary censorship scheme, and failure in the careful administration of the D-Notice system on the part of both government and press. The secretary of the D-Notice Committee, Colonel Lohan, was forced to resign. But the Prime Minister received a black eye from the press and perhaps from public opinion for his handling of the matter. The government had to set about to rebuild a working relationship with the press on security matters. In the process, the Prime Minister on two occasions summoned meetings with leading British publishers and editors. His general question to them was, "What kind of system do you want?" He found no consensus in their replies; some leading press "lords" were in fact antagonistic to the continuation of the D-Notice system of voluntary censorship.

In October 1967 a former director of Naval Intelligence, Vice-Admiral Sir Norman Denning, was appointed to succeed Colonel Lohan as secretary of the D-Notice Committee. Following the recommendations of the Radcliffe Report, a deputy was also named who was at the time of his appointment the Deputy Director of Public Relations of the Ministry of Defense. This would seem to suggest a closer government control over information, which some segments of the press would likely resist. On the other hand, Admiral Denning clearly set out to be more an advocate of the press than of the government in security matters, hoping to win the confidence of the press. But some old traditions had been broken in the course of the controversy which perhaps would never be repaired. By 1967 the changing nature of the cold war undeniably had affected the view of the press about security matters. The government was likely to have a more difficult time enforcing voluntary press censorship in the future, whoever the Secretary of the D-Notice Committee might be.

The British press nonetheless generally accepts the D-Notice system, regarding it more as a help than a hindrance. Cecil H. King, as head of the mass-circulation *Daily Mirror* group, argued that in the past some of the matters covered by the notices were "entirely petty, or so general as to be of no possible value to a foreign power. As a result, military equipment and policies openly written about on the Continent are frequently kept hidden from the British public." Such use of the system, King believed, "comforts only those who require secrecy as a cloak for their blunders." He would not abandon the system, but was wary of its misuse for political advantage.

Other leading figures in the British press display ambivalent feelings about the role of the press with respect to secret intelligence. On the one hand, they believe that the press should probe more deeply to keep the government alert to the question of efficient organization, performance, and responsible control. On the other hand, they accept the principle that a secret service ought to remain secret. Furthermore, some editors displayed fear of parliamentary and public criticism of the press for irresponsible behavior on national security matters. This seemed to deter them from probing. Finally, it remains difficult for the British press—in the setting described—to gain access to information that can be confirmed. The consequence is general press and public ignorance.

It is significant that little fault was found with the basic principles of the system, in spite of the 1967 uproar over the D-Notice. The system serves two purposes. In the words of a Government White Paper: "it protects the rights and privileges of a free press which, with the potent weapon at its command, must guard the public interest; and on the other it pays proper regard to national security."[22] The ultimate workability of the system rests on the government's good judgment on the one hand, and on the other, "the willingness of the Press to circumscribe its own freedom to publish, and it could not survive without the voluntary co-operation of the Press which understandably might be withheld if the machinery became too elaborate."[23] In late 1967 the system set off on a new path, with new leadership. But perhaps that year marked the end of an era of government-press relations. Superficially, at least, the British handling of security matters had seemed to turn in the direction of the American system.

Evaluation of the Secret Service

How good is the Secret Service? Since the system is, except in rare instances, protected from public view, one may only draw inferences from the conduct of British foreign policy. Undoubtedly, there have been Secret Service blunders as well as successes in terms of British foreign policy objectives. If one cannot argue, with evidence, that the Secret Service conforms to its image of professional efficiency, with greater confidence one can assert that the Secret Service, unlike the CIA, has not become a foreign policy boomerang often returning to embarrass and injure the government. Certainly Britain's world role and its foreign operations are considerably more limited today than those of the United States. American intelligence professionals will insist that the British lean heavily upon the CIA, thereby reducing sharply their own intelligence requirements. The Commonwealth system provides, also, a kind of built-in intelligence network. Therefore, the size of the British apparatus for secret operations is perhaps one twentieth that of the United States. But the quality of its professionals may be higher. The Secret Service has not acquired CIA's bad name among many intellectuals. Its recruitment of personnel from Oxford, Cambridge, and other major universities does not appear to suffer on this score. The general estimate, however, is that those graduates who opt for a secret service career are below the quality of those who join the Foreign Service. Nor has it, like the CIA, become at once a target for public ridicule and a source of genuine fear that it has come to be a "state within a state." The British, on the other hand, have a very poor reputation for internal security, which has come to reflect adversely upon the Secret Service. The fact that H. A. R. Philby held high office in SIS leaves an ugly scar on the Service's reputation.

Yet, in contrast to the CIA, one rarely hears the suggestion that the Secret Service operates on the basis of its "own" foreign policy; one hears no debates as to whether the Secret Service ought to be disbanded; and there are few who question whether the Secret Service is under responsible political control. This could be the consequence of secrecy. The British public has little basis for judgment on any of these questions. Leaders of the British press and of the senior Civil Service quietly argue that if the Secret Service were ever to be found operating "on its own" or irresponsibly, the traditional reticence and silence would be broken to assure that effective policy controls were reimposed upon the Service. Implicit in the argument is the assumption that the press may know far more about secret matters than it normally discloses to the public.

The British political system is not exportable to the United States. But out of several centuries of experience, the British do have something to teach about the proper management of the secret services. For one thing, they have avoided the American mistake of allowing its intelligence agency to become the center of international attention. Over the past twenty years, British intelligence professionals have boggled incredulously at a series of episodes: an American President publicly confessing that the United States spies on other countries by all possible means; that secret subsidies on a large scale were dispensed from 1952 to 1967 to college student associations, cultural groups, religious, labor, and press organizations in the United States for various overseas activities; a retired head of CIA publishing a book on *The Craft of Intelligence;* a major American university admitting that one of its major research centers for years was secretly supported by CIA funds; open press conferences held by the CIA; lengthy debates in the U.S. Congress over whether the CIA is properly controlled by responsible authority; and countless articles and books giving authentic details on almost every phase of American "secret" operations. While the world knows virtually nothing about the contemporary British Secret Services, the CIA is known to have overthrown governments and replaced them with new régimes; raised and trained armies and air forces; engineered an invasion of Cuba; established radio stations, schools, and airlines; secretly sponsored businesses, books, and magazines; created "private" foundations; and spied and counterspied around the globe. In this context, it ought to be added that the CIA has also been charged with countless acts it had never thought of committing—charges which millions have been willing to believe.

It is plausible to assume that the British have exercised far greater discretion in launching secret operations; presumably what has been done was done with greater skill, and generally on a much smaller scale. But of the fact that prescribed secrecy has been maintained, there is no doubt.

A striking feature of the British system contrasting with the American practice was, until American journalistic disclosures in 1967, the complete anonymity for the heads of the Secret Services. Citing the British pattern, some have argued that it would be wise for the head of CIA, and even of the FBI, to become virtually anonymous, instead of playing the role of major political figure in the Washington policy struggle. It may be argued that their invisibility would increase the danger of an "invisible government." On balance, however, anonymity would seem to be the wiser course, provided the American president forcefully asserts his leadership and control over the secret apparatus—a control that has been absent much of the time since 1947.

A D-Notice system, adapted to the American setting, is another possible, but more debatable, import. James V. Forrestal, as Secretary of Defense, tried to persuade leading editors and publishers to participate in a government-press cooperative scheme for voluntary security censorship. The press was unwilling, in 1948, to accept the implied restrictions. After the Bay of Pigs, President Kennedy called upon the press to accept "the self-discipline of combat conditions." In a private meeting with editors and publishers, Kennedy also was unsuccessful in demonstrating the need for government-press formal cooperation in security matters. On May 9, 1961, the President met with seven important newspaper executives and proposed that the press appoint a Washington representative who would be their adviser on national security. He would become privy to all the government's top security information and would advise publishers on questions concerning the advisability of publishing certain types of information. The publishers would retain their freedom to publish but would be better informed on the government's security rationale. The conference between the President and news executives was a "total failure . . . the delegation saw no merit in the President's approach."[24] President Kennedy seems to have chosen a poor time, just after the Bay of Pigs fiasco, to make such a proposal, but some form of American adaptation of the British D-Notice system could be of mutual government-press benefit. For many categories of information, government and press are natural enemies. There are some areas of security information, however, which might be managed, to the benefit of both press and government, more successfully than existing chaotic arrangements. For newspaper publishers are never likely to feel, as much as a president, the pressure of the fact that the nuclear age imposes new demands. As President Kennedy once put it: "The publishers have to understand that we're never more than a miscalculation away from war and there are things we're doing that we just can't talk about."[25]

Finally, the most important feature of the British system for possible import by the United States is a more meaningful application of the principle of effective Foreign Office control over all government foreign operations. This is a well-established British practice. Certainly there are sometimes friction and conflict between diplomats and secret agents, but the British follow the wise doctrine of the primacy of policy over the instruments of policy. Theoretically, the State Department at home and the American ambassador abroad control all foreign operations. This principle continues to be violated often, although American presidents in recent years have continued to strengthen the structural-legal authority of the State Department in the Washington national security community, as well as that of the ambassador in the field. The British, on the other hand, seem to have long since applied effectively this basic principle. Perhaps the British can teach us more than they have to date.

CHAPTER IX

*Problems of the
Intelligence
Bureaucracy*

Most general descriptions of decision making indicate that policy decisions involve the acquisition of knowledge and its manipulation within a framework of values, means, and objectives to decide courses of action. Soundness of policy—judged by its success in attaining objectives—often is shaped by the accuracy of information on which it is based. The quality of that segment of information labeled intelligence, as we have seen, is now determined in a complex process involving organization, doctrine, and perhaps most significantly, human beings.

This chapter will survey some of the generalized problems of intelligence organization and treat with the history of its evolutional reorganization insofar as information has come to the surface. Performance of the intelligence establishment will also be surveyed, particularly in its interrelationship with staffing and public surveillance. To put it another way, this chapter deals with some basic problems of the central intelligence bureaucracy.

A "pure" doctrine of intelligence demands that intelligence

officers "present the facts" and play no role in the actual policy choice. This is the opposite of a "pure" theory of decision making which insists that if "all the facts" are known, the optimum choice automatically becomes apparent.

If, in reality, having all the facts will not produce a decision automatically, certainly the more complete the decision maker's information the greater his choice. So it is crucially important to national policy decisions that a government which has undertaken global commitments have the most effective and efficient possible organization and personnel for intelligence collection, evaluation, and communication. And the product is inextricably related to the process. This process, in turn, is conditioned by organizational structure and individual personalities. While it is possible to draw a diagram of organizational jurisdictions and to discuss "models" of relationships between intelligence officers and policy makers, the lines of authority in the real world are much less distinct. For hierarchies and jurisdictional lines tend to evaporate in the presence of particular personalities and situations, and authority does not always convey influence or power. Thus it is a highly ambitious undertaking to attempt any analysis of the relationship between intelligence organization (largely secret in its details) and national security policy-making, a process no one has yet been able to describe adequately.

The inevitable result of any survey or analysis of the intelligence system itself will be a set of recommendations for improving its structure, the quality of its product, and the relationships within the intelligence system. Such, for example, were the basic recommendations of Hoover Commission task forces in 1949 and 1955.[1] It should be noted that several additional internal, secret studies have been made since 1955—including one in 1960; others after the Bay of Pigs in 1961; and a thorough "house" self-study during Admiral Raborn's tenure as Director of the CIA in 1965. But not since the 1955 Hoover Commission study has there been any public investigation of the intelligence establishment.

The ideal intelligence product, one which sets forth with 100 per cent accuracy the capabilities and intentions of foreign nations—allies or adversaries—will never be achieved. This is particularly true of attempts to make long-range predictions of what can and may happen two, three, or even five or ten years from now. Certainly a five- or ten-year projection of the strategic capabilities of the Soviet Union or Red China or Great Britain is a continuing requisite for United States security policy planning. Just as certainly, such projections will contain errors—sometimes major ones. The Central Intelligence Agency makes such projections, which must, because of their tentative nature, be continually revised. One may question whether it is even possible to make fully accurate long-range predictions of the American government's capabilities and intentions. Yet an advancing technology makes such predictions an increasing necessity. Accuracy in long-range forecasting is essential to the future security of the nation. In such fields as foreign economic policy, weapons development, and information (propaganda) activity, today's plans and programs will affect the nation's international status well into the future. The long-term requirements of other nations must also be predicted so that the United States may proceed with a coherent program of foreign economic and military aid, which in 1968 was dispensed to some seventy-five nations.

Effective Decision Making

Given a policy issue, ideally the first step in making important national decisions on plans and programs is a call for all the pertinent facts.[2] In the nuclear age, when, in spite of all long-range planning, crucial decisions affecting national security, may have to be made within a few hours—or even minutes—there are at least two basic requisites for making the right decision. First is the availability of all the pertinent data relating to that decision, though, in reality, urgent decisions reduce the likelihood that all the relevant information will be at hand. Second is a recognition on the part of the policy maker that such data are essential to his decision. This recognition, in turn, must be combined with a respect for the intelligence product—a respect to be earned. The best intelligence product in the world will never be a substitute for human judgment in the final casting of national policy. Yet more is to be expected in this age than a reliance by the policy maker upon personal bias, "hunch," or conditioned reflex. Too often in the past, public policy seems to have been made either in ignorance of—or disregard for—elementary facts. Yet it is fair to ask whether the basic facts *were* available and were in usable form. Certainly, prior to 1947, there was little institutional machinery for systematically providing the facts.

A corollary requisite for effective decision making, in addition to all the pertinent data and the policy maker's recognition of the need for it, is a continuing rapport between the producers of intelligence—the leaders of the intelligence community—and the consumers—the responsible decision makers. "All the pertinent data" will not necessarily be forthcoming if information needs have not been anticipated. Intelligence, like knowledge, knows no boundaries; yet clearly some discipline must be brought to the assembling of data. Guidelines must be established for the producer, through anticipation by the intelligence community of the information required, and through suggestions from the consumer of what he may need to know for policy decisions. Here lies an important distinction between the research and analysis function within the intelligence community and that carried on, say, within a university.

The exacting requirements for an effective intelligence system are not easily filled. There are basic problems of organization, personnel, and attitude which complicate the demanding burden placed upon the intelligence producer. Not only is delicately collected and skillfully evaluated intelligence required about the capabilities of more than a hundred and thirty-five separate foreign nations—friendly, neutral, and not friendly—but this information must be gathered through a score of agencies which are part of the massive modern American governmental bureaucracy, each jealous of its own domain. The activities of these agencies must be "coordinated," and the intelligence products amalgamated and fused into national estimates, either current or long-range. Getting these estimates to the right place at the right time within the bureaucracy is no easy task, and, assuming that the intelligence product is of high quality, getting it accepted as reliable and useful remains a problem. Finally, as the machinery for central intelligence itself expands into a complex bureaucratic maze, the problem of its direction, supervision, and control in keeping with the precepts of representative government remains acute. For if intelligence is to serve popular government, it cannot operate entirely on its own, free of surveillance by responsible political leaders, because it always threatens to be their master.

The Problem of Organization

The intelligence, like the military, function today is performed on an institutional basis, with semi-autonomy and confederation as its overriding principles. Most government agencies, whatever their function, have always had their intelligence staffs, whatever they have been called. The need felt after World War II for centralized intelligence, like that for military unification, clashed head-on with the fact that well-established organizations already existed for the performance of specialized functions. The Department of State, for example, had always considered itself to be the principal agency for the gathering of foreign political intelligence. And, in a sense, it always had been. Why then, should the central intelligence function not be centered within the department? In the first place, the precarious and dirty business of espionage and political action in foreign lands is not compatible with the protocol requirements of international diplomacy. Further, it would be administratively impracticable for one department, such as State, to attempt to coordinate the intelligence activities and products of its coequal departments and agencies of government.

The need for a supradepartmental agency resulted in the establishment and growth of the uniquely placed Central Intelligence Agency. Although the path of any coordinator of separate bureaucracies is a thorny one, CIA has the unique advantage of "working for" the National Security Council, which is to say for "the President in Council." Thus the agency is in an important sense very close to the President and sometimes in a position to utilize his authority and influence to get done the always difficult job of guidance and coordinating.

Prior to World War II, the President himself had to perform the last step in the national intelligence process—the fusion of conflicting estimates. Conflicting and confusing evaluations sometimes came to the presidential desk, before the establishment of a system for a coordinated national estimate.

Now this impossible burden has been eliminated in some degree from presidential shoulders and from those of his principal deputies. One of these, Secretary of Defense Robert S. McNamara, illustrated in 1968 his reliance on national estimates as follows:

The only true measure of the effectiveness of our "Assured Destruction" forces is their ability, even after absorbing a well-coordinated surprise first strike, to inflict unacceptable damage on the attacker . . . I would like to examine with you our latest analyses of how well our strategic forces can be expected to accomplish that mission: first against the "highest expected threat" projected in the latest National Intelligence Estimates and, second, against a Greater-Than Expected Threat . . .

The most severe threat we must consider in planning our "Assured Destruction" forces is a Soviet deployment of a substantial hard-target kill capability in the form of highly accurate small ICBMs or MIRVed large ICBMs, together with an extensive, effective ABM defense . . . these two actions could conceivably seriously degrade our "Assured Destruction" capability.

Again, I want to remind you that both of these threats are quantitatively far greater [under extreme assumptions] than those projected in the latest intelligence estimates. Moreover, we believe that the accuracy of Soviet ICBMs is still substantially inferior to that of our own missiles. Nevertheless, even though such a threat is extremely unlikely, we have taken account of the possibility in our longer-range force planning.[3]

A Secretary of Defense might become a prisoner of an intelligence estimating system, so the production of national estimates, with all its advantages, also has its dangers. It has been argued that intelligence systems are, after all, works of art, and whoever heard of a great work of art created by a committee? In compromising out differences of opinion on a difficult question—say, for example, the future capabilities of, and intended use for, Chinese nuclear weapons—it may be that the intelligence estimate will be so watered down by committee as to diminish its validity and usefulness. The intelligence community is aware of the danger arising from its important mission to produce "agreed-on" national estimates, and has worked out devices and procedures to cope with it. These include the use of dissenting footnotes or of language accurately revealing the uncompromised disagreements. This problem reflects the basic advantages and disadvantages of a federated intelligence system. A national estimate of the future capabilities of the Soviet Navy, for example, is not the product alone of Naval Intelligence, which might tend to exaggerate the threat, but has also traveled the rocky road of sharp questioning by the army, the air force, the CIA, and others. Joint estimates by several services tend to reduce the influence of parochial opinions and the tendency to "budgeteer" by use of narrowly conceived or partisan intelligence.

Consequences of Federation

The present federated intelligence structure fosters beneficial differences of opinion at the price of some duplication. The CIA's main activity is in those areas where the intelligence function is best performed by a central organization. It is not surprising that the agency came to believe that an increasing number of these activities could best be performed centrally. Thus the central organization grew steadily as it took on an increasing number of activities. CIA apparently could not escape the Washington malady of empire-building, although a conscious effort has been made to keep at modest size some important sections, such as the Office of National Estimates. Growth was curtailed in the early 1960s as the agency came increasingly into the public spotlight. Meanwhile, the various other departments, particularly DIA and NSA, to which specialized intelligence has seemed to be increasingly important, spurred on by the activities of the central organization, have greatly increased their intelligence-gathering.[4] Duplication is bound to increase, possibly in favor of an improved over-all intelligence product, but not necessarily so. For example, when the Nixon Administration began in 1969, serious inefficiencies characterized the management of Pentagon intelligence operations. By 1969 the world-wide defense intelligence activities cost an estimated two billion dollars annually, but were inadequately coordinated or controlled, resulting both in intelligence failures and overly dangerous espionage operations, such as the tragic and costly cases of the *U.S.S. Pueblo* and the EC-121, a Navy espionage aircraft. Lack of coordination between DIA and NSA is an especially acute problem, as is the relationship of each to the CIA. In the summer of 1969 an Assistant Secretary of Defense for Administration was charged by Secretary of Defense Melvin Laird with responsibility for improving the management of military intelligence. Barring some future operational tragedy, the public may never learn whether this has been accomplished.

The growth to its present size and importance of the Central Intelligence Agency also magnifies the basic organizational question: should intelligence be an increasingly separate province, divorced from policy making? Central intelligence today is regarded as a separate staff function, to be performed by specialists working full-time and separate from policy-making responsibility. It is assumed that the product of these specialists will be an input for policy making at the appropriate time and level. It is further assumed that the over-all intelligence function is logically decentralized into some twenty to thirty separate agencies of government, coordinated by a staff agency—the CIA—and the necessary national intelligence processed and approved by an interdepartmental committee, the U. S. Intelligence Board. It has become a very complex administrative structure, which, like much government organization, has evolved from departments and agencies existing in the past rather than from a functionally conceived design. It is a compromise between the needs of centralization and the requirements of institutions with separate and distinct roles. With all its advantages, it is a system difficult to operate, and there are plusses and minuses in its performance to date.

Intelligence Credibility

One of the most important problems of central intelligence is credibility of the intelligence product. Most of the users of intelligence, whether military commanders or top civilian decision makers, apparently regard intelligence with mixed feelings. Indeed, a variety of definitions exist as to what intelligence *is*. Consumers want enough pertinent facts to make the policy choice clear and are thankful for the help intelligence can give them. Yet they know they can never have all the facts. They suspect that somewhere along the line of intelligence production someone has made a guess. They assume the existence of an inevitable subjectivity in the selection process at every step, except for such "hard" data as photographs. But even most photographs have to be "interpreted." Moreover, users know from experience that the intelligence estimate has not always been correct; that, as a product of human judgment, it is fallible; and, since they are usually far removed from the source of data going into the intelligence estimate, their suspicions remain as to the derivation of the information. For the source, though graded and evaluated—that is, given a bureaucratic grade labeling—usually remains a mystery.

The element in the decision-making process with the label "Intelligence" must compete with the decision maker's bias, experience, and other "pictures in his mind." Each decision maker has various sources of information with which the intelligence product must compete. Let us assume that the final decision maker—the President or the Secretary of State—reads the daily and weekly press—the *Washington Post*, the *New York Times*, and *Newsweek*. These sources provide information, though with varying degrees of accuracy and bias, which competes in the mind of the decision maker with the papers which come to his desk labeled "Intelligence—TOP SECRET." The decision maker also encounters daily advisers, ambassadors, and military officers from the field, foreign visitors, and others, all bearing information of various kinds, and most of them attempting to influence the shape and color of his mind's pictures. For example, President Johnson is said to have studied domestic "issue polls" in the mid-1960s with as much care as he reviewed CIA reports on Vietnam.[5]

The growing band of professional intelligence experts in Washington, increasingly confident of their product, not unnaturally want to play a major role in the intellectual process by which decisions are made. They see their role to be that of supplying fact out of which enlightened policies evolve. They undoubtedly regard as half-baked much of the advice that reaches the ears of decision makers from nonintelligence sources. They recognize these outside threats. Thus the modern corps of intelligence experts can be heard speaking of the problems of "selling their product."

Intelligence professionals, incidentally, have sometimes been more successful in leading the enemy—in time of war—to believe fabricated intelligence than they have been in selling their legitimate product in the home office. During World War II, the British by an artfully devised and minutely planned scheme managed deliberately to mislead the Germans in a *ruse de guerre*

216

of spectacular success. After the battle for Tunisia, the Allies decided that the next step would be the invasion of Italy via Sicily. By causing to be washed ashore in Spain the body of a fictitious Royal Marine carrying letters containing "secret" military planning information, the Allies tricked the Germans (who were promptly informed by the Spaniards) into spreading their defense across Europe, even to the extent of removing warships from the Sicily area. This ruse paved the way for a relatively easy invasion of Sicily.[6]

Although the intelligence credit rose appreciably in the first twenty years of CIA's existence, the debit side of the ledger is not empty. Popular sentiment, as well as opinion in some policy-making circles, still reveals suspicion of, and a continuing ignorance about, the nature of the intelligence product.

Seasoned policy makers understand that intelligence estimates often are made in a form that is manipulatable in some degree. Errors are most likely to be made on the safe side, particularly when the military capabilities of a foreign power are being estimated by an armed service responsible for defending against them.

Skepticism of such estimates is sometimes displayed in the press. A *New York Times* dispatch from Washington on July 6, 1957, reported: "The United States Army suggested today that the Soviet Army was better equipped than itself to fight any type of war under any conceivable conditions." A few paragraphs later the article continued: "It has been recognized here that a good deal of the emphasis on Soviet capability is motivated by the United States military leaders' efforts to gain support for their own estimated requirements."[7] This news account demonstrates the skepticism of seasoned newsmen which turns out later to have been a healthy doubt. In the mid-1960s it became clear that the standard intelligence estimate of 175 Soviet Army divisions made in the 1950s had been a fixture long beyond the time when it had some basis in fact, if indeed it ever did.

Twelve years later, in 1969, one could easily find evidence that an "intelligence game" was still being played in policy debates. Again, the *New York Times:*

By stripping away some of the secrecy about SS-9, the large Soviet intercontinental ballistic missile, the Administration has apparently won the opening round in the Senate debate over a missile defense system . . . Never before had the Pentagon openly discussed the SS-9, and the fact that [Secretary of Defense] Laird chose to declassify intelligence information about the missile prompted Senator J. W. Fulbright, chairman of the Foreign Relations Committee, to complain that the Defense Secretary was indulging in the "technique of fear" to sell his Safeguard program.[8]

The Nixon Administration went on to "win" the antiballistic missile "Safeguard" debate in the Senate in 1969, and the intelligence estimates were pivotal factors in the "victory." One is bound to recall the "missile-gap" debates of the late 1950s or the "bomber-gap" debates of the late 1940s, when, in each case, decisions were made which later turned out to be based on exaggerated estimates. But the responsible decision maker must ultimately decide what kind of risk he is willing to take. The record of the past two decades indicates that decision makers tend to err on the "safe" side—a safety which may never be attained because it stimulates the arms race to ever higher levels. The main point, however, is that intelligence estimates rarely give the answers; decision makers must be expected to manipulate them in the context of other policy considerations.

Intelligence blunders or failures that result from manipulation often become public knowledge; intelligence successes usually go unnoticed. In either case, leaders of the intelligence establishment can say little, for either defense or bragging may have the effect of disclosing secret sources of information, or of projecting intelligence professionals into the political arena. Probably too much is expected of intelligence; yet the debit side of the ledger provides the basis for lingering skepticism in the face of those who would "sell the product" as always objective material.

Mistaken Estimates

Allen Dulles once commented, "Events which seem to defy analysis happen somewhere in the world every day. Few trends seem to follow a predictable course."[9] Mr. Dulles could have added that regrettably many important events during the years of CIA's existence have succeeded too often in defying analysis. Policy planners have rarely been armed with adequate foreknowledge; they have been continually confronted with surprises.

Problems of the Bureaucracy

The relationship between intelligence on the resources of a potential enemy and estimates of our own capabilities or intentions must be finely balanced. President Truman, in his *Memoirs*, rebukes General MacArthur for "estimating" in October 1950 that the Chinese would not intervene in Korea. This estimate, which proved totally wrong, was not based on poor intelligence as to Chinese capabilities—these were well known.[10] The wrong guess was made with regard to Chinese *intentions*, and MacArthur later maintained that his misinterpretation of Chinese intentions was largely due to his misreading of our own. MacArthur stated that his estimate was based on an assumption that *we* would "massively retaliate" in the event of Chinese intervention. He reasoned that the Communists would be working on the same assumption regarding United States intentions, and thus would not intervene. MacArthur's assumption and Washington's defense planning, however, were not the same. If nothing else, this incident points up the fact that intelligence estimates of this sort cannot be made in a vacuum. A closer link was required between national intelligence and United States policy, but the ultimate fusion of all factors—including value judgments as well as pure intelligence—should take place beyond the boundaries of the intelligence community.

Another example of intelligence failure was the German counterattack on the Western Front in December 1944, commonly called the Battle of the Bulge. As mentioned earlier, Allied commanders were surprised; they lacked foreknowledge of the attack. Here a basic intelligence problem is well illustrated in one observer's analysis of the episode.

The function of an Intelligence Officer is first to collect, then to evaluate, and finally to disseminate to other levels of command, information of the enemy. Through a process of over-specialization, which often seems to pervade our life, Intelligence Officers seemed to operate in a vacuum, charged with describing enemy intentions without consideration to our plans. Because our actions so directly affect theirs, it is difficult to say what the Germans may do if we do not first say what we intend to do, but this is exactly what our Intelligence Officers were doing throughout their combat career. For example, to discuss German intentions in the Ardennes without analyzing the weakness of our positions there, our present and pending attacks elsewhere, is to overlook the true situation.[11]

Postwar study indicates that Hitler had taken extraordinary security precautions prior to this attack. Plans were known only to
the highest military commanders, and lower-level commanders
were not informed of the plans until two days before the attack.
This made the surprise attack, in the words of one authority
"impossible for United States intelligence to predict unless there
had been a penetration of the German High Command in the
west, which there hadn't!"[12]

Intelligence analysts, clearly, cannot be blind to their own government's policy and intentions in constructing estimates, whether
they work at the tactical, or the highest strategic, level. Yet the
parallel danger remains that policy preferences may color the intelligence estimate. That is to say, if an intelligence analyst is committed to—even enthusiastic about—his own government's plans,
this could color his estimate of the enemy's capabilities and intentions. A finely balanced mechanism for relating policy and intelligence will help in meeting such dangers.

The initial phases of the Korean conflict also presented an
interesting intelligence problem. Mr. Truman claimed that the
United States knew "this was one of the places where the Soviet-
controlled Communist world might choose to attack," but, he
added, this was true of many other places on the periphery and
we could not be strong everywhere.[13] The failure was not so much
due to faulty intelligence as to an inability of the policy planners
to prepare for the eventuality of a limited war in Korea. Having
ruled Korea outside of the defensive perimeter in the event of all-
out war with Russia, there had been little consideration given in
Washington or Tokyo to providing for defense of South Korea
against limited war or outside aggression. Such intelligence predictions as there were—and they were ambiguous—fell on deaf ears.
But intelligence must finally be related to policy and, if the policy
guidance to intelligence analysts is absent, the intelligence may be
aimless.

Great Expectations

Historical evidence preponderantly suggests that the future will
be replete with surprises and will sometimes outwit all predictions.
If this is so, often too much is expected of intelligence. Many de-

cisions and events in world affairs, for both Communist and non-Communist states, occur on an ad hoc basis, without direct relation to patterns of enemy capability or intention. This presents an intelligence problem even more frequently faced by the Communists, who may fail to anticipate a United States move because we ourselves often act at the eleventh hour with little regard for capabilities or previously avowed intentions: witness both American and Chinese interventions in Korea in 1950, the Soviet emplacement of missiles in Cuba in 1962, and the United States intervention in the Dominican Republic in 1965.

The existence of an effective collection network capped by a coordinated and efficient estimating mechanism provides no guarantee that the right policies automatically will emerge. In fact, many national policies are made with a seemingly willful disregard for intelligence. Domestic considerations often are given more attention than careful intelligence estimates. The best estimate, moreover, can never be a substitute for responsible political judgment. Even the best possible intelligence community cannot compensate for military weakness, or leadership failure, or lack of national will to take necessary action. What it can do is attempt to insure that policy blunders are not made because known information has been wrongly evaluated or improperly disseminated. Often a policy maker comes to his job, or to a policy choice, with some "big pictures" in his mind, or with basic assumptions about the world situation. Sometimes these pictures will be judged by intelligence professionals to be basically wrong or grossly inaccurate. A contest may begin between the policy maker, who *tends* to seek information confirming his assumptions, and the intelligence officer, armed with the "facts" but chary of intruding into policy-making. Thus one often finds tension between a biased policy maker and an objectively informed intelligence officer, or an intelligence officer with a different set of biases.

For all its lingering deficiencies, the intelligence community has taken giant steps in the years since 1948, when Hanson Baldwin wrote that intelligence, our "first line of defense . . . is today one of the weakest links in our national security."[14] In today's nervous, polycentric world of many rival nations existing under a nuclear umbrella, there is less room than before for intelligence error. If being the first line of defense seems to be a great expectation for central intelligence, it must be remembered that the price of failure may be disaster.

The Personnel Problem

The greater the recognition of the importance of accurate intelligence, the less difficult the problem of securing well-qualified personnel for the various intelligence tasks. This problem within the military services has already been mentioned. It seems almost unnecessary to say, as did the 1955 Hoover Commission, that "the effectiveness of our national intelligence effort is measured to a large degree by the character and ability of the personnel, both military and civilian, engaged in this work."[15]

Serious problems remain, however, in the procurement and retention of the highly qualified persons needed to staff the multifarious intelligence positions. First there is the problem of the "career" secret agent who serves overseas. With the nation's global interests and commitments, it is thought to be necessary to have secret agents operating, or trying to operate, all over the globe. These persons must possess a unique combination of skills and be unusually motivated. They must be willing to serve their government in this anonymous and occasionally dangerous capacity—in what Harold Nicholson has called "the most boring and dangerous of all human occupations." They are expected to possess a keen intellect and sensitive judgment. They often must have in addition, special linguistic skills, sometimes in the most remote languages. The CIA maintains an assessment and training program for its overseas operatives, who require special indoctrination, area knowledge, language and communications skills, and special espionage paraphernalia. This program, like the activities of American secret agents overseas, inevitably is shrouded in secrecy.[16] But presumably a nation as large as the United States can supply the required number of individuals willing to become members of what is now a professional career service of overseas secret agents.

A second problem is the procurement, training, and retaining of qualified intelligence analysts for the domestic activities of CIA, largely centered in Washington. Even on the domestic front, service with CIA requires special motivations and qualifications. The 1955 Hoover Commission referred to some of CIA's problems in the personnel management field, including the need for improving the prestige of the civilian analyst, developing career incentives, and exercising greater flexibility in the recruitment of specially qualified individuals.[17] In the CIA's early days, employment with that agency was not highly regarded in many of the academic faculties training Ph.D.'s. A standard quip, when employment opportunities were being discussed, was the sarcastically downgrading comment: "Well, there's always the CIA." In some circles prejudice remains—indeed has grown—as a result of disclosures about CIA's subsidies to private organizations in the United States and the agency's various foreign interventions.

The only information openly available about the CIA's recruiting policies and programs is contained in the literature used by the agency in college recruitment. From this, one may learn that the CIA seeks qualified candidates from all divisions of the social sciences, physical sciences, and some technological fields. The agency recruits both "generalists" and "specialists." At each stage of the intelligence cycle, from the setting of requirements through collection, evaluation, and communication, scientists, technicians, and even engineers, are needed. For example, in the art and science of photogammetry—the increasingly important task of photointerpretation—geologists, geodesists, foresters, architectural and civil engineers, and many other kinds of specialists are required. Or a physical or biological scientist may be needed for the purpose of surveying foreign scientific literature.

According to a recruiting brochure, "the CIA scientist enjoys a congenial, stimulating and educational environment in which to further his professional interest . . . In many scientific and technical study areas, and in other research fields, advanced academic studies are sponsored by the Agency." The CIA maintains various "career fields" within its organization, including presumably intelligence production, science, economics, photo-interpretation, language skills, and others. When employed by the agency an appointee is assigned to one of the career services, in which he receives training and becomes eligible to advance to various levels in a career system. Not infrequently an individual is transferred from one career service to another, depending upon his own desires and the needs of the agency.

Few applicants are chosen for the "plans and operations" career service, in which one is trained as a secret agent for overseas duty. For the most part an employee of the CIA is as "safe" in his work —whether stationed in Washington or overseas—as the average employee of the State Department, U. S. Information Agency, or the Agency for International Development. All three of these agencies, in fact, are used as CIA "covers" in overseas assignments.

Each of the agency's various career services is presided over by a board of senior specialists who decide regarding promotion, assignment, and training for members within that service. In each service there are opportunities for overseas assignment for limited periods, unless one is a member of the career branch in which overseas duty is a permanent expectation.

Employment with CIA is much the same as Civil Service employment, with similar "fringe benefits." Salaries follow the Civil Service scale, ranging roughly (in 1969) from $7,600 to $15,800 at entry. In recruiting, the agency lists "academic fields of particular interest to CIA," and in the 1960s, these have included chemical engineering, physics, mathematics, cartography, geology, geography, economics (various specialties), accounting, public administration, library science, English, political science (various specialties, especially international politics), journalism, law, and psychology.

Recruiting literature refers to the agency's search for graduate students and college seniors as well as to those employed in other fields who "want to build new careers in intelligence." The system provides appointees with a year or two of "basic training" prior to their permanent transfer to one of CIA's career services. Even after such transfer, the agency stresses "on-the-job" training, and formal training programs exist well into mid-career. The agency operates elaborate foreign language "laboratories" which are used for both on- and off-the-job language training. Pay incentive awards are offered for language proficiency. Professional training in other fields is made available to selected employees, not only within the agency but in other government agencies or private educational institutions. In recent years two universities in the Washington area have been conducting evening programs of graduate and undergraduate study at CIA headquarters in Langley, Virginia. Other universities are said to "cooperate" with the CIA in its various training programs, but details are not disclosed.

In recent years CIA recruiting has looked increasingly to graduate students, although the agency continues to seek college seniors. According to its recruiting brochures in 1965, "a high percentage of the CIA organization is made up of men and women who have obtained their master's degrees from graduate schools, and many have their doctorates. More than 500 colleges, universities, and graduate schools have contributed to the present (1965) staff of the CIA." This would seem to be an answer to the standard charge over the years that CIA was strongly biased toward the "Ivy League"—a charge that used to be made against the Foreign Service corps. This charge has some validity with respect to CIA's top civilian leadership in its first twenty years. No detailed facts have been made available as to the agency's rank and file. It would be interesting to see a breakdown of male and female employees, college affiliation, and ethnic composition of its current personnel.

In the early period of CIA's development, large numbers of employees were hired without adequate attention to their qualifications for exacting work. Many of these were persons retiring from the armed services. Under the directorship of General Walter Bedell Smith between 1950 and 1953, a vigorous weeding out of unqualified personnel took place. As noted elsewhere, the precise number of CIA employees is a tightly guarded secret. Total employment by the agency has fluctuated over its first twenty years; the number of personnel was greatly expanded at the time of the Korean War and again in the late 1950s, with the advent of new space and photographic technology. Personnel strength is believed to have remained at about the same level between 1960 and 1968. Budgetary ceilings imposed in the mid-1960s have caused agency officials privately to complain. Indeed, substantial cuts in the operational side have reduced CIA's overseas personnel.

An additional personnel problem exists which threatens the future effectiveness of the agency. Since CIA is essentially an organization of specialists, the problem has arisen of providing administrators from within the organization. Those who tend to be promoted to top positions usually are the area or technical specialists, often with little administrative bent. Since the agency innately tends to be compartmentalized into isolated groups of specialists, this problem is compounded when those without administrative talent are promoted to head their section or division. This is a common problem on the Washington administrative scene, but par-

ticularly acute within CIA, perhaps the largest repository of intellectuals in the federal government.

Another serious problem is that persons needed for much of the
work of intelligence analysis, such as the trained economist, historian, or political scientist, still regard work with CIA as too in-
hibiting to be attractive as a career. Security restrictions and the
requirement of almost complete anonymity in CIA work continue
to be major obstacles to the recruitment of the most desirable personnel. Undoubtedly many otherwise qualified persons simply do
not care to work for an agency where lie detector tests are routine.
To be willing to work for CIA, one must follow a career in which
much of the work cannot be discussed with colleagues in other
branches of the agency, let alone with wife or husband or with those
in other sectors of government. This problem, aggravated by the
fact that CIA houses both "clean" and "dirty" operations, will always be difficult to surmount, barring a radical restructuring of
organization and functions. In recent years the agency has liberal-
ized somewhat its policy on the research and analysis side. There is
less secrecy concerning the identity of specific CIA personnel, and
some specialists with the agency are now permitted to publish in
the open and to participate in university seminars. Security, nonetheless, is a dominating presence in all of the agency's work; from
their earliest contact, employees are inculcated with a concern for
security. Any employee who is insufficiently "security-conscious" is
unlikely to make progress in the agency, even if he is permitted to
remain in its employment.

Overseeing the Intelligence Establishment

The burgeoning of the intelligence establishment, both in size
and importance has left unresolved the question of who should
oversee the intelligence community, particularly far-flung operations of CIA. The agency's freedom from congressional and other
outside surveillance led a Hoover Commission task force in 1955
to express a sentiment others have felt—that "there is always a
danger that such freedom from restraints could inspire laxity and
abuses which might prove costly to the American people."[18] This
apprehension led to the move in Congress (described in Chapter

VII), still unsuccessful as of this writing, to establish a joint congressional committee on intelligence.

As a neophyte engaged in a highly controversial activity, CIA has not, however, been left to enjoy merely the limited scrutiny of the National Security Council, the Bureau of the Budget, and a handful of congressmen. As already noted, two broad investigations were made in 1949 and 1955 by Hoover Commission task forces. In 1951, 1954, 1960, 1961, 1963, and again in 1966, additional surveys were conducted, often at the request of the White House, and detailed findings were reported confidentially to the President.

Early in CIA's history, the 1949 Hoover Commission's Committee on National Security Organization made an assessment of CIA after it had been operating less than two years. It found that unsatisfactory relationships existed between CIA and other intelligence agencies of the government—particularly Army Intelligence, the Federal Bureau of Investigation and the Atomic Energy Commission. It noted other defects:

Too many disparate intelligence estimates have been made by the individual departmental intelligence services; that these separate estimates have often been subjective and biased, that the capabilities of potential enemies have frequently been interpreted as their intentions, and that a more comprehensive collection system, better coordination and more mature and experienced evaluation are imperative.[19]

A number of recommendations were made for change, notably the suggestion that a top-level evaluation board be established to produce national estimates.

The need for such a board had become painfully evident during the period of the Berlin Blockade in 1948. It persisted throughout the earlier stages of the Korean War, and effective corrective steps were not taken until 1950 when General Walter Bedell Smith set up the formal estimating mechanism, the earlier described Board of Estimates.[20]

The survey which reported to the President in 1951 was conducted by a three-man group headed by Allen Dulles, then Deputy Director of CIA.[21] The findings of this group were never made public, but its study apparently spanned several years, "watchdogging" the intelligence community at the request of President Truman and the National Security Council. The Dulles group helped to straighten out organizational and administrative difficulties which beset the institution of a new centralized intelligence system. It also attempted to referee some of the bitter interdepartmental battles over the intelligence function in the period when jurisdictional lines were not clearly drawn.[22]

The second special survey was conducted by a four-man board headed by retired Air Force Lieutenant General James H. Doolittle.[23] This study came at a time when Senator Joseph McCarthy was threatening an investigation of CIA. It also followed closely upon the apparent defection to the Communists of Dr. Otto John, former West German security chief, who had been in a position to know of detailed operations of Western intelligence agencies. Just before disappearing into Russia in the spring of 1954, Dr. John had spent some time in the United States on a semiofficial visit, meeting with officials of the State and Defense Departments and the Federal Bureau of Investigation.[24] These and other events motivated the appointment of a special group to look into CIA operations for the President.

The Doolittle group reported to President Eisenhower in October 1954. Through the White House a brief report was issued by General Doolittle, stating that the CIA was doing a "creditable job," but that there were "important areas in which the CIA organization, administration and operations can and should be improved." Specific recommendations made by the Board to the President were not disclosed.[25] As the *New York Times* commented at the time of the Doolittle report: "For Congress, which must appropriate funds for C.I.A., and for the general public, the verdict would have to be accepted pretty much on faith."[26]

In 1955 the Hoover Commission Task Force on Intelligence Activities, headed by General Mark W. Clark (U.S.A., Ret.), conducted an extensive survey of the intelligence community and produced two reports. One, dealing with organizational aspects, was made public, and the other, dealing with operations, was stamped TOP SECRET. The published report recommended more intensive linguistic training (a long-time glaring weakness in the community); the transfer to CIA from the Department of State the responsibility for procurement of foreign publications and scientific intelligence (thus giving CIA more operational tasks); utilization of more retired military officers in CIA; salary increases and funds for new CIA headquarters. Also, the CIA director was reminded of "certain administrative flaws" which had developed in the CIA and was mildly rebuked for having "taken upon himself too many burdensome duties and responsibilities on the operational side of CIA's activities."[27]

The Clark Task Force took special note of the relative freedom from surveillance enjoyed by CIA and commented that liaison between Congress and the agency through the Armed Services committees' channel lacked the essential "wide scope of service and continuity." To fill this void the Hoover Commission recommended creation of a civilian watchdog board and a "Joint Congressional Committee on Foreign Intelligence, similar to the Joint Committee on Atomic Energy."[28]

Based on the first of these recommendations, monitoring by the executive branch was established on February 6, 1956, when President Eisenhower appointed an eight-man civilian watchdog group, the President's Board of Consultants on Foreign Intelligence Activities. This board, headed by President James R. Killian, Jr., of the Massachusetts Institute of Technology, was a part-time survey group charged with conducting periodically "an objective review of the foreign intelligence activities of the Government and of the performance of . . . the Central Intelligence Agency."[29] In February 1958, on Mr. Killian's retirement, the chairmanship was assumed by General John E. Hull, a retired army officer. When John Kennedy became President in January 1961, the board was automatically dissolved, and the new President made no move to continue or reconstitute it, presumably thinking that the CIA would be under presidential surveillance through other means. After the Bay of Pigs disaster, however, Kennedy reconstituted the board, renaming it the President's Foreign Intelligence Advisory Board. On May 2, 1961, James R. Killian was reappointed chairman. Later, under both Kennedy and Johnson, the chairmanship was taken over by Clark Clifford, an attorney and veteran adviser to Democratic presidents, who became Defense Secretary early in 1968. His successor as board chairman was General Maxwell D. Taylor.

Spurred on by the controversy surrounding the downing of a U-2 aircraft deep within the Soviet Union in May 1960, the Bureau of the Budget initiated a study of all U. S. intelligence activities.

The study was conducted by a special task force headed by the Director of Central Intelligence and comprising representatives from State, Defense, the White House, the Budget Bureau, and CIA. The CIA representative, Lyman B. Kirkpatrick, Jr., served as chairman of a study group charged with the responsibility of preparing a comprehensive report to outgoing President Eisenhower prior to the end of 1960.[30] The group toured foreign and domestic bases, concerning itself in particular with military intelligence organization and procedures. One motivating force behind the desire of the President and the Budget Bureau for such a study was the need for consolidating various Pentagon intelligence activities. According to the group's chairman, writing later, many different views on what outsiders might call vested interests were discussed. After much heated debate, conflict, and compromise, the Study Group in its report made forty-three major recommendations.[31]

The precise nature of these recommendations has never been disclosed but the Study Group's report resulted in the subsequent creation of the Defense Intelligence Agency, to eliminate the duplication of intelligence activities in the Pentagon, and a corresponding reorganization of the U. S. Intelligence Board. The separate armed services lost their individual representation on the board; the Director of the Defense Intelligence Agency came to be the sole representative of the Pentagon on the "Supreme Court" of the intelligence community—the U. S. Intelligence Board. This development was resisted by the intelligence services of the separate armed forces, particularly the Navy, which has long been a foe of greater centralization in the defense establishment. As a result, representatives of each of the armed services have continued to sit with the board, although technically no longer members. Though centralizing military representation in the highest intelligence councils, the Pentagon was nonetheless urged to develop intelligence into a more prestigious and attractive military career. The enormous growth of the intelligence system after World War II created an unprecedented number of high-ranking officer "billets." It has been a common practice from the beginning, for example, that either the Director or Deputy Director of Central Intelligence be a military officer. Similarly, the huge National Security Agency is normally headed by a high-ranking officer. And with the establishment of the Defense Intelligence Agency, six assignments carrying the rank of general were made available to ambitious officers. Efforts to create incentives making intelligence a desirable profession in the armed services have greatly increased, but many persons continue to doubt whether that profession yet recruits the talent commensurate with the importance of intelligence.

Not all of the Study Group's forty-three recommendations were put into effect. Indeed, some of them called for further study. Each of the major intelligence agencies of government, in fact, was urged to prepare a long-range plan for its future development.

Early in 1962, still another organizational study of the CIA and the intelligence community was undertaken. This study was initiated by John A. McCone shortly after his appointment as Director of Central Intelligence. Again, Lyman Kirkpatrick, Jr., was in charge of the study task force, with a mission centered more directly upon CIA, still suffering shock from the Bay of Pigs disaster in 1961. Kirkpatrick was instructed to study McCone's duties as Director of Central Intelligence, his relation to the White House and to the other government departments. He was also to study "the organization of the intelligence community and the work of the CIA and make recommendations to [McCone] on all of these subjects."[32] Apparently McCone's principal motive for commissioning such a study was to have his authority clarified by a presidential directive.

Such a clarification was made in a carefully worded letter from President Kennedy to the Director. This letter, drafted in the agency, was perhaps the principal product of the Kirkpatrick study, although there followed some significant structural changes within the CIA. The President's letter stated clearly that McCone, as Director of Central Intelligence, was the "Government's principal foreign intelligence officer," and it was his responsibility to guide and coordinate the intelligence effort of the United States.[33] The letter strengthened McCone's hand somewhat, but evidently it was not as strong as some CIA officials wanted it to be. The Director was ordered in the Presidential directive to give "effective guidance" rather than "to direct" the government's total foreign intelligence effort. The CIA would have preferred a less ambiguous assignment of authority. Such is the Washington bureaucratic jungle, where separate kingdoms remain inviolate from centralized direction. On such matters, the State, Defense, and Justice Depart-

ments—each with a slice of the intelligence pie—have to be negotiated with, and any reorganization is likely to be a compromise
that continues the confederative principle. To cite the view of a
partisan CIA veteran: "Since the creation of CIA there has been
almost constant sniping at the organization by those that wanted to
make it 'just another one of the intelligence agencies.' "[34]

Other consequences of the McCone study included strengthening
of the Agency Controller's office, ultimately to be combined, in
1963, with other duties within the newly created office of Executive
Director; the creation of a new division in CIA under a Deputy
Director for Science and Technology; and the adding of a cost-
analysis system of decision-making, adapted from the Pentagon's
new techniques under Secretary Robert McNamara, along with
other cost-conscious management methods. In 1963, when the
President began to insist on budget-cutting among agencies, the
CIA ceased to do any appreciable hiring above the junior professional trainee level.

In 1965 the CIA undertook another significant study, this time
initiation of Admiral William Raborn, who succeeded McCone as
director. Raborn undertook the formulation of a 15-year plan for
the CIA. Lyman Kirkpatrick again was CIA's director for the
study, his last action after twenty-two years of service in U. S.
intelligence work, beginning with the OSS in World War II. CIA's
long-range plan was completed in September 1965. Details of its
substance were never revealed, as has been the case in all such
studies except those by the Hoover Commissions. Undoubtedly the
plan stressed the importance of an intelligence capability to forecast scientific and technological developments and their impact
upon future intelligence collection techniques and requirements and
the political, economic, and military configurations of power in
world politics. But in the absence of hard information, one can
only speculate on the nature of the American intelligence system
foreseen for the year, say, 1984—that ominous-sounding date.

Up to the present, then, CIA surveillance has come largely from
internal self-studies and from specially appointed presidential
groups, plus the few congressmen serving on the two Hoover Commissions and the handful of members of Congress on the CIA subcommittees of the Armed Services and Appropriations committees.

Surveillance, at best, has been sporadic. During its first twenty years of existence, no one was given the full-time responsibility of intelligence surveillance for the President. He, of course, could not possibly give constant attention to the intelligence system, calling to mind Dean Acheson's foreboding in 1947 when he advised President Truman that no one would be in a position to know what CIA was doing or to control it.

Public Relations

Proposals for closer auditing of CIA and the intelligence community have not always been directed at establishing outside surveillance over intelligence activities. The 1955 Hoover Commission insisted that one of the aims of its watchdog groups was to assure the public of the "essential and trustworthy accomplishments of our Intelligence forces, and to enlist public support and participation in the Intelligence effort."[35]

The Hoover Commission was justifiably concerned about the lack of prestige the intelligence establishment held in the minds of both policy makers and public. Representative Daniel Flood also once highlighted this problem at the House hearings on Army appropriations: "The average American thinks . . . that our intelligence is a laughing stock . . . that the British are the finest intelligence people in the world, that the Germans are great, but that we do not have anybody on this intelligence business."[36] Congressman Flood, expressing his own confidence in United States intelligence, inquired about what might be done to change this attitude without compromising intelligence techniques and sources. The Army G-2 representative squirmed at this suggestion, replying that he was in no position "to start a television program or a radio program publicizing United States intelligence activities." Nor had the presidential advisory board, early or later, revealed any plans to educate the public about the intelligence establishment. No report to the President of its surveillance of foreign intelligence operations has ever been publicly disclosed; nor is it likely to be. Whether the intelligence services will ever even approach the public esteem generated by skillful public relations techniques for the FBI seems questionable. Whether this would be proper in a democratic society is even more questionable. As it stands, the intelligence function continues to provide fodder only for novels, plays, and dramatized television thrillers.

CIA's public relations problem was described by its director, Allen Dulles, in 1957:

> I am the head of the silent service and cannot advertise my wares. Sometimes, I admit, this is a bit irksome. Often we know a bit more about what is going on in the world than we are credited with, and we realize a little advertisement might improve our public relations. For major reasons of policy, however, public relations must be sacrificed to the security of our operations.[37]

Public relations aside, central intelligence inevitably must remain in essence a silent service. This is so because, in part, it is a *staff arm* of the presidency; in part, because it deals in the shadowy realm of espionage and backstage foreign political action. Yet this secrecy must somehow be made compatible with responsible democracy. An invisible branch of government possessed of superior knowledge is a source of great potential power. American political liberties are theoretically safeguarded by the checks and balances of constitutional government. The intelligence apparatus must not be allowed in the future to operate as freely as it seems to have done since 1947 beyond the careful scrutiny and control of the President, his principal deputies, and indeed from Congress.

CHAPTER X

The "CIA Problem"
Some Conclusions

Scandal is the word best characterizing the context in which most citizens have viewed, in recent times, the intelligence establishment, particularly the CIA. The problems and scandals that have beset the intelligence system are the result of entanglements of definitions, purpose, organization, and policy. An overlay of mythology further beclouds the subject. Perhaps the best way to symbolize this mythology is to cite the observation by Trevor-Roper that in the popular mind the chief of a contemporary intelligence system is seen as a "super-spy." In reality he is a bureaucrat.[1] He works within a political system, and his office is the locus of great potential influence.

The heart of the definitional problem is that "intelligence" has come to be used as a term to label two disparate activities: information gathering and secret political action. This semantic confusion is so pervasive that it extends into the highest levels of government and obfuscates conceptual—and thus organizational—clarity on the subject. A simpler way of saying this is that the government does not always know what it is doing in the "intelligence" field. If so, officials do not in reality control intelligence operations. This allows intelligence men to exert an undue, and often unseen, influence on policy.

Governmental confusion about intelligence relates and contributes to the additional problem of defining organizational purpose. Organizations and functions of government should not be justified or evaluated in their own terms; they must be related to purpose. Intelligence activities sometimes are undertaken for no other reason, it would seem, than that an intelligence apparatus stands by, awaiting an assignment. And much of the time both the "purpose" of a mission and the information on which it has been planned are secret and cannot be publicly discussed. Indeed, in some instances purpose and mission are not even discussed in high government councils because of "security."

Purpose in turn relates to organization. A principal technique of secret intelligence is the use of "cover," the pretense that something is what it is not. Possibly there is a relation between the widespread use of "cover" and the absence of conceptual and organizational clarity. For example, a commercial airline pretends to be privately operated when it is in fact a government airline, secretly sponsored. The CIA has become more than an intelligence agency because not only does it operate airlines, "free" radio stations, and phony foundations, but it is also engaged in underground political action and psychological warfare in foreign areas. It can be found directing undeclared wars in distant lands, oblivious to international law, the "rules of war," or the Geneva Conventions. Also it has penetrated deeply into American domestic institutions. This multiplicity of roles blurs conceptual thinking about the intelligence system and about relating organization to purpose.

This ambivalence, in turn, affects policy, for policy comes to be formulated in the midst of conceptual and semantic confusion. The results are likely to be inefficient, sometimes even counterproductive. But such inefficiency will be difficult to recognize because the criteria for evaluation are confused, if they exist at all. One enters, therefore, the realm of Alice in Wonderland, where confusion is compounded by definitional and conceptual caprice. Efficiency is difficult to judge for the further reason that "intelligence activities" in their countless forms are so compartmental, as illustrated in earlier sections of this book, that the total picture is never visible; measures of efficiency are difficult to devise and to apply.

One might hypothesize a symposium of two dozen of the best-informed men in the United States on the subject of intelligence activities. Their communication would be hampered to some degree by isolated compartments of knowledge, definitional confusion, and differing "images" about the nature of an intelligence system. This, in fact, has proved to be the case in the experience of this writer. Public information and understanding are even more severely obscured by these limitations. Much more than other aspects of government and politics, then, intelligence systems defy controlled observation and full understanding. Consequently, they may also defy the policy controls implicit in a democratic system.

Stereotypes of the Intelligence System

A number of competing images, or stereotypes, about intelligence activities have emerged from the mélange of fiction and half-truth and from the fact that espionage and associated activities are now a major international industry.

One among the prevalent stereotypes depicts the world's second oldest profession as resembling a vintage Marx Brothers movie. In this view intelligence activities involve a lot of adventuresome, slapstick activity, adding up to very little. There appear to be large numbers of those who believe, or pretend to believe, that intelligence activities are little more than something to be joked about; not to be taken seriously.

A more pervasive stereotype is a second one, casting the spy or secret agent in the role of the suave superman, conducting his business with British manners, a cool efficiency, and ruthless power to obtain his objective. It could be argued that these stereotypes have only broad cultural impact and do not affect the serious business of state policy or international relations. But consider the fact that Adolph Hitler and his henchman Heinrich Himmler had been readers of "novelettes" about the exploits of the British Secret Service which they apparently came to believe were instrumental in the creation of the British world empire. Misled by a set of fiction-based illusions, Hitler determined to have a secret service of the

"British kind" to help him gain his empire. His hopes of a "gigantic, ubiquitous, infallible, secret service, like the British Secret Service of his imagination," according to Hugh Trevor-Roper, were never fulfilled.[2] But the whole world was profoundly affected by these, among others, of Hitler's illusions.

Still a third view of the subject depicts the world of espionage populated by the small-minded, sadistic policeman, dealing in the back alleys of world politics with chiselers or mentally unstable ideologues. Thus the picture is that of an espionage system populated by a group of small-time international racketeers.

As in most stereotypes, there is an element of truth in each of these. Stereotypes aside, one may view secret intelligence and political action as a growing international industry, profoundly influenced by technology and organized now into high government bureaucracies capable, by their activities, of either causing or preventing trouble in a dynamic international political arena.

Terminological confusion is compounded by designating as "intelligence operations" actions that more accurately should be called secret political intervention. This confusion is institutionalized in the United States, as earlier explained, by housing two disparate functions, intelligence and secret political operations, under the same CIA roof.

Interventionism Added to Intelligence Role

In 1947 Allen Dulles wrote that "intelligence work in time of peace differs fundamentally from that in time of war" (see Appendix A). Since that time, Americans have become increasingly aware that distinctions between war and peace have become blurred. Since the Korean War a consensus has developed that national security required the indefinite maintenance of a military establishment, designed both for deterrence and "flexible response." The collapse of the World War II alliance with Russia and its dissolution into an ideological–power conflict between the United States and the Soviet Union, created the cold war. The American objective became the "containment" of Soviet power, which meant that the United States had to develop an organization within the intelligence system to counter subversion, and to wage or to counter various forms of psychological warfare. These activities would supplement the intel-

238

ligence, that is to say informational, needs generated by an upward-spiraling arms race.

To sustain a strategy of containment sometimes-by-intervention has required decision making founded on carefully developed forecasts of what is likely to happen in the future or estimates of what can be made to happen. Demands upon the central intelligence system have, consequently, continued to increase.

While playing the role of "sentinel-on-duty"—a product of the "Pearl Harbor complex"—the intelligence system has the opportunity of shaping the "pictures in the mind" of the nation's decision makers. The fact that the intelligence apparatus has been given the operational functions of underground foreign political action and psychological warfare has further compounded the "CIA problem." It has become a problem of such dimensions that one observer wrote in 1968 that, excepting Vietnam actions, "nothing the U. S. Government had done in recent years in the field of foreign policy has created so much controversy as its intelligence operations, especially the secret subsidizing of private American institutions."[3]

A Storm of Bad Publicity

In trying to meet America's global commitments, the CIA came to be assigned roles far beyond the intent of congress in 1947 when it created the CIA as part of the National Security Council. From the start, definitional confusions and organizational entanglements characterized the missions of this "most peculiar agency." Prior to 1960, however, the CIA generally received a "good press." For the most part, Americans knew little of what the agency's functions were, or what it had achieved. Its apparent failures—to anticipate, for example, the onset of the Korean War, to predict Soviet attainment of nuclear power, or in the Middle East crisis of 1956—were not highly publicized. Such "failures," moreover, could be interpreted as deficiencies in the *use* of information by policy makers as much as in the provision of accurate estimates.

The 1960s proved to be the CIA's decade of degradation. Publicized trouble began with the U-2 affair in May 1960, on the eve of a carefully planned summit meeting with the Soviet Union. While the U-2 is now generally regarded as a notable technical achievement in intelligence gathering, the government's handling of the

U-2 episode raised widespread criticism of policy, professionalism, organization, and control. Moreover, the incident dramatized the inherent incompatibility of diplomacy and espionage. This was followed, in 1961, by the Bay of Pigs invasion, which raised even more penetrating questions about the CIA—this time from some of its former supporters. The press dropped its critical restraint in writing about the agency and published all information that could be obtained. For the first time the CIA and its leadership became "cover story" material in the mass media.

The destruction of the intelligence ship *U.S.S. Liberty* in the June 1967 Arab-Israeli war, with the loss of thirty-four American lives, and the North Korean capture of a similar ship, the *U.S.S. Pueblo*, and its crew in 1968, followed later by the loss of a Navy espionage aircraft, dramatized to the public some of the costly risks intelligence agencies were taking. Perhaps most perplexing of all were the disclosures early in 1967 that the CIA had been secretly subsidizing, for more than fifteen years, several dozens of American private institutions, to support various overseas programs of those organizations.[4] Another major shock to public sensitivities came in the summer of 1969, when through a murky picture of charge and countercharge, fact and allegation, it appeared that the CIA was involved, while collaborating with Army Special Forces "Green Berets," in political assassinations in Vietnam. Disclosures such as these caused some persons to wonder where the distinctions lay between our own and totalitarian systems.

Where Did the CIA Go Wrong?

The sentiments and confusions of many Americans, even before the increasing number of disclosures, were perhaps best expressed by former President Truman: "There is something about the way the CIA has been functioning that is casting a shadow over our historic position, and I feel that we need to correct it."[5] Since Truman wrote in 1963, the CIA has remained the uncorrected problem child of American foreign policy. From Vietnam to Czechoslovakia, from the Congo to the "Green Berets" disclosures, American secret agents continue to leave the impression with many persons at home and abroad that they do more harm than good. Our adversaries laugh at CIA and claim that the letters stand for "Caught in the

Act." Our friends abroad, however, are frightened. One writer in the British publication, *The New Statesman*,[6] for example, saw America "dangerously near conducting international relations through a secret police all but completely independent of elected authority." Too many others have the same view, even if rarely based upon adequately detailed knowledge. Where did the CIA go wrong?

A few weeks before his death, President John F. Kennedy denied in a press conference that CIA was operating overseas independently. Referring to Vietnam, he stated bluntly that CIA was operating "under my instructions." Although Kennedy had voted for a joint congressional committee on intelligence in the unsuccessful Senate move in 1956, as President he no longer favored such a proposal. He was, he said, "well satisfied" with existing controls. His true concern, however, is revealed by the fact that shortly before he died he was in process of creating a task force to survey the global intelligence and other secret operational activities of the United States, to improve coordination and efficiency. Perhaps, too, he was concerned with the quality of information from Vietnam where, as we now know, the lives of so many have been sacrificed to the ignorance of so few. As in most previous studies, however, the intelligence community was investigating itself. The three-man task force initiated by President Kennedy represented only the State Department, the Pentagon, and the CIA. It remained for President Johnson to receive the report, and no publicity was given it. Doubts and misgivings have remained, not only about the coordination, but about policy control and the competence of the CIA and other intelligence agencies. No major organizational changes, however, were visible to outsiders following that study, other than semiofficial intimations that the CIA's budgets had been reduced in the years since the Bay of Pigs.

Trauma Over Secret CIA Subsidies

Perhaps the greatest dismay and trauma over the activities of CIA came with disclosures of the agency's vast program of secret subsidies. Early in 1967, the public and Congress learned something of the scope of the agency's involvement with private domestic organizations. Prior to these disclosures, a very limited amount of public knowledge existed about CIA's special links since 1952 with some private foundations, university research centers, book publishers, labor and cultural organizations. But the scope of such programs and specific details were well-kept secrets until February 1967, when *Ramparts* magazine disclosed the specifics of CIA's financing, for nearly 15 years, of the overseas programs of the National Students Association, a student-managed organization comprising more than 300 member colleges and universities in the United States. Between 1952 and 1967, it was later learned, the NSA received more than $3 millions in CIA secret funds for its international programs. In one year, more than three fourths of NSA's total budget was from the CIA, supplied through "front" and "conduit" foundations. Moreover, the NSA headquarters building in Washington, D. C., was subsidized by mortgage payments from the CIA. Funds were provided primarily so that the United States could be "properly" represented by college students at various international youth conferences abroad, in which the Communist movement was strongly represented. Such projects were organized under the CIA's division for Psychological, Political, and Paramilitary programs (PPPM). Money was provided also by PPPM to allow the initiation and promotion of non-Communist youth organizations in some of the developing nations. Similar subsidies, it became known, were supplied by CIA to dozens of other private American organizations, including academic, labor, church, legal, and literary groups, for their overseas programs.[7] Defenders of such programs argued that they were necessary expedients in the psychological warfare of cold war; that the Communists had to be fought with their own weapons.

Reactions to these revelations varied widely. There were demands for congressional investigations and for a reorganization of the CIA. Some critics proposed CIA's abolition. Many of its defenders were willing to admit that the publicity had further damaged the agency's image and had created serious complications for American students and researchers working overseas. CIA's supporters were quick to note that such programs resulted from policies made at the highest levels under every president since Truman. The CIA, it was argued, had not undertaken secret subsidization "on its own," as some seemed to believe. One of CIA's harshest critics, Walter Lippmann, acknowledged the need for a Central Intelli-

gence Agency but would sharply limit its role to foreign information gathering. Not since the crisis over the Bay of Pigs in 1961 had
the agency been involved in so much public controversy. Vice-
President Humphrey declared he was not at all happy about the
CIA. Senator Richard Russell of Georgia, Chairman of the Senate's
"watchdog" subcommittee on the CIA and long its defender from
congressional critics, urged reforms in the system.

Responding to the congressional, editorial, and public criticism,
President Johnson ordered CIA financing of the National Students
Association to be ended. On February 15, 1967, he named a three-
man committee to review the secret subsidy programs. Under-
Secretary of State Nicholas Katzenbach was appointed chairman;
others serving were John Gardner, Secretary of Health, Education
and Welfare, and Richard Helms, Director of Central Intelligence.
Perhaps to assure access to crucial facts, the CIA always is represented on bodies charged with investigating the agency—a questionable arrangement. A public version of the committee's report
was issued on March 29, 1967, accompanied by a presidential
statement accepting its findings. President Johnson promised to consider the recommendation "that the Government should promptly
develop and establish a public-private mechanism to provide public
funds openly for overseas activities." Toward this end, he appointed
Secretary of State Dean Rusk to head an 18-member committee
comprising public and private representatives, including one college student, to make more detailed recommendations for alternative means of subsidizing certain foreign operations.

The Katzenbach Committee recommended, and the President
accepted, a policy statement stipulating that "no Federal agency
shall provide any covert financial assistance or support, direct or
indirect, to any of the nation's educational or private voluntary
organizations." Any existing support was to be terminated, in
most cases by the end of 1967. Future exceptions to such a policy
might be permissible "only where overriding national security
interests so require," and on specific approval by the Secretaries
of State and Defense. But the committee's most pointed reference
to the whole scandal was, in effect, an admission of wrong-doing in
the past, to wit: "In no event should any future exception be approved which involves any educational, philanthropic, or cultural
organization." Alternatives to secret subsidies awaited the report of

the Rusk Committee, and any subsequent congressional action. The committee has rendered no public report, nor had Congress taken any action well into 1969.

The most profound political and moral problems have been raised by the secret subsidy disclosures. A university or organization which only pretends to be open, or whose true means of support is falsified, raises fundamental questions about leadership judgment. Such camouflage can poison the academic wells, just as it can spoil open access for the American professor innocently seeking data in scholarly research overseas. The Center for International Studies at MIT, for example, was at its founding financed in part by the Central Intelligence Agency. But its links to CIA were not publicly revealed in 1951-1952, when this secret support was initiated. Recall ironically, that for a number of years in which the research center at MIT received secret CIA funds, the institution's president, Dr. James Killian, served as chairman of a special presidential board designed to provide public, nongovernmental surveillance of the CIA and related agencies. It could be argued that MIT was in one sense providing "cover" for CIA. This kind of arrangement was ultimately abandoned by MIT, yet suspicions continuing into the present were generated about other academic research institutes which then or now may have provided "cover."

One of the greatest dangers of the cold war mentality is that it tends to ape the adversary. Certainly our scholars, books, foundations, universities, and others in the private sector ought to remain free of the suspicion that they are available for use as "cover" by secret agencies. The U. S. Government, at the end of 1967, announced that it had discontinued all secret subsidies to private voluntary institutions in the United States. Some alternative means of governmental support will be required for those overseas projects that serve both American ideals and the national interest. The form of subsidy used, and the CIA as the disbursing agency, are unacceptable for the future, for they represent a step toward a totalitarian society. The waters of American free institutions have already been muddied by these ill-advised experiments of 1947-1967. It would be hard to demonstrate that the national security would have been seriously endangered had such programs not been undertaken. It is somewhat easier to demonstrate that the American free society has been injured by what was done.

244

A few headlines from the *New York Times* point to one aspect of the damage done: "Asia Foundation Banned by India" (February 16, 1968); "Mexican Theories on Unrest Blame Both C.I.A. and the Reds" (October 14, 1968); "Iraqi Public Links the C.I.A. to Coup" (July 28, 1968); "Italian Premier Backed on [C.I.A.] Intelligence Scandal" (February 2, 1968); "Passer of Che's Diary, Due to Return to Bolivia, Pledges Disclosures on C.I.A." (August 17, 1968); and "Iraq Executes 4 as Spies for C.I.A." (April 14, 1969). Most significant, from the domestic point of view, is the fact that since 1966 CIA recruiters have been unable to hold scheduled interviews on the campuses of a number of American universities because of student protest and, in some cases, because of actual violence. The point is less the question of domestic protest, and more the fact that what is being protested is a supposedly secret activity of government.

Many have asked, "What is the danger; what's wrong with this?" One answer has been given by Professor Henry Steele Commager in testimony before the Senate Committee on Foreign Relations, February 20, 1967. The danger of the secret subsidy, he said,

is that it substitutes the immediate advantage for the long run disadvantage; that it uses great things like scholarship, science, the community of learning, truth, for immediate purposes, which it doubtless thinks are worthy, but which, in the long run, are not to be compared with the larger purposes of learning, scholarship, literature, art, and truth.

Put more simply, why destroy what you are trying to protect?

Problems of Policy, Organization, and Control

As of this writing, fundamental organizational changes have continued to be resisted by the leadership of the intelligence community. Clearly lacking since 1955 has been a thoroughgoing inquiry of the "Hoover Commission" type into the government's total intelligence system, including covert operations overseas. Such a nonpartisan inquiry, parts of which would necessarily proceed in secret, ought to be made at least every five years.

Focus of such an inquiry would be the major agencies, including the CIA, the Pentagon's Defense Intelligence Agency, the

National Security Agency, and the Department of State. One of its investigative tasks would be to take a close look at the sponsorship of research by these agencies and by such organizations as the Agency for International Development, the armed services, the Arms Control and Disarmament Agency, and others.

The problems which would be surveyed by such an inquiry center upon issues of organization, policy control, "cover," and secrecy.[8]

Organization. Is the intelligence establishment properly organized? There is strength in the argument that espionage, counterespionage, and clandestine political action overseas need to be under unified direction and control. But it is of questionable validity to combine these activities with the massive research and analysis performed by the CIA and continue to call the organization an intelligence agency. This combination of research and analysis intelligence work with covert political action and psychological warfare has made it patently impossible to maintain secrecy for that which ought to be secret; has made it difficult to recruit high-quality personnel for research and analysis; and has prompted serious duplication and conflict in some overseas operations. Not only has a large and possibly duplicating Defense Intelligence Agency grown up in the Pentagon, but the FBI is sometimes tempted to reassert its claim for an overseas intelligence role, at least in Latin America, where it had extensive World War II experience.

The Central Intelligence Agency ought to be divided so that the branch for covert operations is separated from that for research and analysis. The aim of such a division of functions would be (1) to disentangle the organization that produces "finished intelligence" from that which carries out operations, sometimes based crucially upon the evaluated information supplied; (2) to bring back some respectability to the CIA—a respectability that has gradually diminished with the increased public knowledge that one of its arms is essentially a "Department of Dirty Tricks," a fact that has caused much alienation between the intellectual community and the intelligence system; (3) to diminish the vulnerability of the CIA to critics at home and abroad who commonly characterize the agency as a sinister force in foreign affairs; (4)

and, finally, to enable the truly secret branch of government to preserve such secrecy more effectively.

The arguments in favor of separating the dual functions of the CIA are more persuasive than a number of counterarguments frequently put forth by defenders of the organizational status quo: (1) that secret agents and analysts can benefit from close organizational proximity; (2) that the ability of CIA to gain generous appropriations from Congress would be sharply reduced if the glamourous "action" arm were removed from its jurisdiction; (3) that serious problems would be raised about the role of the Director of Central Intelligence if the two major functions were separated; and (4) that there is no other feasible place to assign the covert operations of government which now use the CIA, in effect, for "cover."

The most generalized and persuasive argument for radical change is that the present system has not worked; it has tended to be self-defeating. The CIA has become a foreign policy liability, and its status at home remains under a serious and debilitating cloud of suspicion.

Control. Is CIA controlled adequately at the highest governmental level? As just noted, there are difficult problems about where best to place the intelligence and secret operations functions within the policy-making structure. But the most serious question involves the control by responsible political authority of espionage, counterespionage, and political warfare overseas. No foreign secret action should be undertaken until after the most careful weighing of risks against possible gains, and particularly a careful and realistic analysis of the prospects for secrecy and the consequences of public exposure. The State Department, acting for the President, or the President himself, should have a meaningful veto in this regard.

Beyond a certain point the secret agent, whether spy, secret propagandist, or guerrilla warrior cannot be controlled. To set loose expensive networks of secret agents is to open a Pandora's box of potential blunders, misfortunes, and uncontrollable events. To pack off a secret agent with a satchel of money to intervene, say, in a Brazilian election, and expect to maintain tight operational control of him is a dubious expectation. Failure to understand this may in part explain the lack of effective coordination and control that characterized some secret operations under the Eisenhower administration. Under Kennedy, there was a promise of stronger presidential coordination and leadership in foreign affairs.[9] Yet the Bay of Pigs, the greatest public disaster to befall the CIA, revealed continuing weaknesses in foreign operational concept, command, and control. The State Department remained in the shadows, failing to exercise its proper authority, while the Pentagon and CIA were in the forefront, playing an ill-defined but patently decisive role. As Theodore Sorensen recalls, Kennedy felt that State had a "built-in inertia which deadened initiative and that its tendency towards excessive delay obscured determination."[10] A question never adequately explored is the extent to which CIA activism may have been a consequence of State Department inactivity. There is little visible evidence that these problems have been of serious concern to either the Johnson or Nixon administrations.

Defenders of the secret intelligence system are quick to insist that there has always been an elaborate set of policy controls on all secret operations. Some have argued that intelligence and other secret operations are perhaps the most tightly controlled activities in all of government.

One cannot examine the evidence on this point, but experienced former officials of the intelligence system argue, sometimes persuasively, that CIA officials have always been required to seek and gain prior approval from policy makers before initiating any secret operations. In the earliest days of the system, procedures for approving secret operations were less formal than in more recent years. Even in recent times, however, it would seem that programs, once initially approved, were rarely given intensive scrutiny, particularly when the question of their continuation came up for policy review. The U-2 incident and more recently the *Pueblo* case are examples of dangerous routinization of operations.

Since the early years of the Eisenhower Administration, which established elaborate procedures for all kinds of national security decisions, covert political activities have been reviewed and approved (or rejected) by a group representing the highest levels of government: the President's Special Assistant for National

Security Affairs, the Number Two man in the Pentagon and in the State Department, and the Director of Central Intelligence. This group has been called at various times the "54-12 Group," "Special Group," and more recently the "303 Group." Other supervisory groups have existed for the review of more technical intelligence operations. Forms and procedures for policy review and control have always existed; CIA leaders have never felt that they were free to operate "on their own." Even before special projects or secret operations come to the highest level for review (if the "303 Group" so recommends, the matter can be passed directly to the President's desk), proposals have run the gamut of interdepartmental review at the lower administrative echelons, perhaps at the level of the Assistant Secretary or even of the "country desk." Ambassadors in the countries involved theoretically, as of 1969, have a veto under normal circumstances, in any proposed secret operations within their jurisdiction.

When hundreds of secret operations are projected by a nation with world-wide commitments and extensive operational forces, true control will be determined by three factors: (1) the basic assumptions or "state of mind" of those at the highest policy levels; (2) the intelligence they possess, which is mainly supplied by the same system they are supposed to be controlling; and (3) the energy and determination of top policy makers to make this control effective. One may seriously doubt whether their "span of attention"—given a vast array of other duties and of decisions they must make—can actually result in effective policy control. And, further, it should be kept in mind that operational management of a secret agent may be at once the most important and most difficult to exercise. Control, as it has existed through much of CIA's history, has perhaps been more a matter of form than actuality. At any rate, the results have been less than the nation should demand.

Cover. Secret warriors and intelligence agents depend heavily upon "the art of cover," as they term it. They must often shield their true identity, purpose, and operations. As noted earlier, World War II had produced a vast international apparatus for applying American power around the world, including an Office of Strategic Services. When the war ended, its Director, General Donovan, proposed that the secret part of this apparatus be made permanent.

According to Donovan's assistant, Robert H. Alcorn, in referring to the OSS director's postwar plan:

> We were everywhere already, he argued, and it was only wisdom and good policy to dig in, quietly and efficiently, for the long pull. Overseas branches of large corporations, the expanding business picture, the rebuilding of war areas, Government programs for economic, social and health aid to foreign lands, all these were made to order for the infiltration of espionage agents.[11]

And so the CIA took advantage of numerous opportunities for "cover" in the postwar years. And espionage, after the Truman Doctrine, was easily transferred to political action.

The CIA and the higher level "controllers" have shown themselves to be inadequately sensitive to issues raised by such activity. One example of how far CIA has gone in the infiltration of other American overseas agencies for the purpose of "cover" is to attempt to make use of the Peace Corps. In the Corps' formative days, a determined effort was required to forestall CIA infiltration attempts. With a few possible exceptions, the threat was successfully resisted, but it is astounding that the CIA threat existed at all, particularly in the face of Communist claims that the Peace Corps was no more than an espionage front.

Use of legitimate agencies for intelligence cover is a traditional gambit of almost all governments. But how far should CIA be allowed to go in using for cover the diplomatic service, foreign economic aid missions, including university-operated technical assistance missions in foreign countries, and other agencies? The answer is: not as far as they have gone. Even more serious are the questions raised by CIA's invasion of the domestic private sector, its secret use of foundations, universities, publishers, and others for the agency's purposes. Most universities undertaking government-financed defense research have done so openly, although some of the work done might remain "classified." A healthy shift of university policy away from secret research in recent years indicates that important basic values of scholarly independence are being reasserted.

Secrecy. The CIA director is responsible "for protecting intelligence sources and methods from unauthorized disclosure." Even with secrecy oaths, binding after employment with the agency, lie-detector tests as commonplace personnel routine, and "top secret" labels profusely applied, the CIA has been patently unsuccessful in keeping its proper secrets. To combine research and analysis with covert strategic services requires a blanket of secrecy over the entire agency. The blanket has proved to be riddled with holes. One important reason for this has been a lack of respect among journalists, on Capitol Hill, and in other branches of government for the agency's efficiency and the validity and propriety of some of its operations. Another reason may be Allen Dulles's lack of a passion for anonymity while CIA chief, particularly during President Eisenhower's administration. While head of CIA, Dulles made more than sixty major public addresses on a variety of foreign policy topics. More recent directors, John McCone, Admiral William F. Raborn, and Richard Helms, have, commendably, gone about their job more quietly.

The disclosure in 1965 by Prime Minister Yew of Singapore that a CIA agent had been involved in a $3 million bribe attempt to cover up an unsuccessful CIA effort to penetrate Singapore's intelligence service is a case in point. An enormous risk of disclosure was involved as compared with any possible gain. Another example of confusion in CIA, this time on the home front, was a CIA press conference in January 1964, at which CIA spokesmen gave their estimates of Soviet economic growth rates to demonstrate that Russia was falling behind her own expectations. The agency unwisely had entered the policy sphere. It was, at best, doing the job of (a) the White House, (b) the State Department, or (c) the nation's propaganda agency.

Role of the Press

No public press in recent history has been as full of details about its government's secret services as that in the United States. In Great Britain, an open society, as we have seen, the press cooperates with proper governmental requests for secrecy. In a closed society like the Soviet Union or China, disclosure of state secrets by the mass media is never a problem.

Time was when the American press exercised considerable restraint in publishing information about intelligence activities. Prior to 1960, important segments of the American press knew of U-2 aircraft overflights of the Soviet Union (as did the Soviet Government) but refrained from disclosure. And prior to the Bay of Pigs disaster in 1961, James Reston reports that newsmen knew "all about" the Kennedy Administration's plan, but some withheld the information. In retrospect, Kennedy told the then managing editor of the *New York Times* that he wished the press had disclosed much more information than it had revealed about the plan. This, he suggested, might have forced cancellation of a patently bad plan. Significantly, the President held this view only in retrospect.[12]

So it is debatable whether press disclosures about CIA activities have from the agency's point of view been a liability or an asset. On the liability side, some have argued, as has William J. Barnds, that these "disclosures have created a public awareness that the U.S. Government has, at least at times, resorted to covert operations in inappropriate situations, failed to maintain secrecy, and failed to review ongoing operations adequately. The public revelation of these weaknesses, even though they are now [1969] partially corrected, hampers CIA (and the U.S. Government) by limiting those willing to cooperate with it and increasing [the number of] those opposed to it and its activities."[13]

From the public's point of view, it can be argued that the press leadership is as competent to judge the national interest as any government group. The press can, and probably will, show restraint—even self-censorship—when this is seen to be in the national interest and if the press maintains confidence in the competence and good judgment of the government in its planning and conduct of secret operations. These are indeed big "ifs," and rarely is there unanimity on foreign policy issues. But most important of all, a secret operation, if justified, should only be planned and authorized by highest authority, and then only if chances of maintaining secrecy are strong enough to justify the risks of disclosure. If not, some other instrument of policy should be chosen, or no action taken. There are, of course, no formulas for easy decision making.

Another problem involves the posture to be taken by the government if "caught in the act" of a secret operation. In the past, U.S. officials have issued denials which on occasion have caused acute embarrassment when the charge was proved by evidence, as in the case of the U-2 aircraft downed within the Soviet Union. The policy of most governments in these situations is to refuse any comment on the matter. This would seem to be the wisest policy for the American government to follow in the future, along with a very conservative attitude toward mounting secret operations in the first place.

The foregoing pages have described in detail the American government's organizational response to the worldwide information explosion and to the shifting requirements of the nation's world power position. I have chosen to apply to the variety of intelligence organizations the descriptive term "intelligence establishment." By this I have not meant to suggest a monolithic "invisible government" but a set of agencies with common missions and great potential power in shaping the picture of the external environment in the decision maker's mind. I do not pretend to have found a way to measure this power but I see it existing and growing, often in league with a military-industrial-labor complex. And thus the problem grows of controlling these new loci of power, for uncontrolled political power is incompatible with democratic government.

Finally, to summarize my prescriptions: (a) organizational mistakes which have combined foreign information gathering and political action need to be repaired by surgery; (b) covert political operations should only be undertaken to prevent a direct threat to national security and as an alternative to overt military action; and (c) the President and State Department should exert effective policy control over secret foreign operations at all times. Put another way, the President and National Security Council must effectuate their authority to know what the intelligence establishment is doing and to control it.

Can Man Survive Technology?

Paradoxically, intelligence, in both its principal meanings, will be required if man is to survive technology. An intelligence establishment is both a threat and a possible savior to any nation's legitimate political system. It is a threat in an age of information explosion, when policy makers must depend heavily upon the system to collect, analyze and interpret, and communicate information, often at great speed. Thus the intelligence establishment possesses the power potentially to control the informational assumptions of a decision. Intelligence is a possible savior because correct decisions for the future cannot be expected, barring luck, to result from inadequate information. A decision rarely can be better than the information upon which it is based. But the required information is not likely to be forthcoming in the absence of a clearly defined purpose, supplemented by rational information policies, strategies, and organizations.

The threat of a gargantuan intelligence establishment can best be contained by an alert press, and by vigilance on the part of Congress, the public, and the scholar about what will certainly be a continuing problem. And the promise of an intelligence system is intimately related to an acknowledgment of its dangers and closer attention than previously given to its proper policy, organization, and control.

Appendices
Bibliography
Notes
Index

Appendix A. Views on Central Intelligence of Allen W. Dulles, Director 1953-1961

Note: Contemporary officials of the CIA are expectedly reticent in discussing the agency's structure and functions. The memorandum which follows is of basic historic importance because it provided the conceptual foundation for the agency when established in 1947. This statement was prepared for Congress when it was considering the National Security Act of 1947, which contains the charter of the agency. This memorandum is extracted from Hearings, "National Defense Establishment," Senate Committee on Armed Services, 80th Congress, 1st Session, on S.758, Washington, D. C., 1947, pp. 525-528.

MEMORANDUM RESPECTING SECTION 202 (CENTRAL INTELLIGENCE AGENCY) OF THE BILL TO PROVIDE FOR A NATIONAL DEFENSE ESTABLISHMENT, SUBMITTED BY ALLEN W. DULLES, APRIL 25, 1947

I

To create an effective Central Intelligence Agency we must have in the key positions men who are prepared to make this a life work, not a mere casual occupation. Service in the Agency should not be viewed merely as a stepping stone to promotion in one of the armed services or other branches of the Government. The Agency should be directed by a relatively small but elite corps of men with a passion for anonymity and a willingness to stick at that particular job. They must find their reward primarily in the work itself, and in the service they render their Government, rather than in public acclaim.

Intelligence work in time of peace differs fundamentally from that in time of war. In time of war military channels and military facilities, and consequently military personnel, can effectively be employed in far greater measure than in peacetime. In time of peace, intelligence with respect to foreign countries must come largely through civilian channels.

Because of its glamour and mystery, overemphasis is generally placed on what is called secret intelligence, namely, the intelligence that is obtained by secret means and by secret agents. During war this form of intelligence takes on added importance but in time of peace the bulk of intelligence can be obtained through overt channels, through our diplomatic and consular missions, and our military, naval, and air attachés in the normal and proper course of their work. It can also be obtained through the world press, the radio, and through the many thousands of Americans, business and professional men and American residents of foreign countries, who are naturally and normally brought in touch with what is going on in those countries. A proper analysis of the intelligence obtainable by these overt, normal, and aboveboard means would supply us with over 80 percent, I should estimate, of the information required for the guidance of our national policy. An important balance must be supplied by secret intelligence which includes what we now often refer to as "Magic."

II

I believe that the agency which is to be entrusted with assembling and analyzing intelligence should be predominantly civilian rather than military and under civilian leadership.

Whoever takes the post of Director of Central Intelligence should make that his life work. If previously a military man, he should not look forward to resuming a position in one of the armed services. The same should be true of his top staff. Whatever may have been their previous professions, whether military or civilian, once they take high position in the central intelligence organization they should, if military, divest themselves of their rank as soldiers, sailors, or airmen and, as it were, "take the cloth" of the intelligence service.

The success of the FBI has been due not only to the ability of the director and the high qualities of his chief assistants, but to the fact that that director has been on that particular job for a sufficient period of years to build up public confidence, and esprit de corps in his organization, and a high prestige. We should seek the same result for our intelligence service, which will operate in the foreign field, and on items of foreign information.

I do not suggest that the legislation should lay down a hard and fast rule that the chief of the Intelligence Agency must come from civilian life. Certainly there are many men of military training who are competent to hold that job. But if a military man takes the job, he should operate from that time on as a civilian. Further, he must be assured, subject to good performance, a specified term of duty, which should be subject to extension as long as he carried out his task efficiently. Appointment as Chief of Central Intelligence should be somewhat comparable to appointment to high judicial office, and should be equally free from interference due to political changes. In fact, the duties the Chief will have to perform will call for the judicial temperament in high degree. An appointee must gain that critical faculty which can only come of long experience and profound knowledge to enable him to separate the wheat from the chaff in the volume of information which will pass through his office.

Of course, the Central Intelligence Agency should also have attached to it a substantial number of men from the armed forces as well as from civilian life, many of whom will not make it a life career but who can perform useful functions for a term of years.

Much of our thinking relating to an intelligence agency is colored by our recent dramatic war experiences. Intelligence work in time of peace will require other techniques, other personnel, and will have rather different objectives. The prime objectives today are not solely strategic or military, important as these may be. They are scientific—in the field of atomic energy, guided missiles, supersonic aircraft, and the like. They are political and social. We must deal with the problem of conflicting ideologies as democracy faces communism, not only in the relations between Soviet Russia and the countries of the west, but in the internal political conflicts within the countries of Europe, Asia, and South America. For example, it may well be more important to know the trend of Russian communism and the views of individual members of the Polit Bureau than it would be to have information as to the locations of particular Russian divisions.

Having this conception of the task of a central intelligence agency, I am skeptical as to the wisdom or adequacy of the provisions in the bill to provide for a national defense establishment with respect to central intelligence. These provisions seem to me to set up what, in effect, is likely to become merely a coordinating agency for the military intelligence services, G-2, A-2, ONI. This is useful, and this function should be performed by the agency, but it is not enough.

The constant changes in the chiefs of the military intelligence services has crippled their efficiency and lessened their prestige. As these services are a part of a professional career, of which intelligence is only one segment (and too often it has been a stepchild), such changes are somewhat inevitable. But this precedent should not be carried over to the new Central Intelligence Agency. There, provision must be made for permanence and continuity . . .

Hence I would recommend that any legislation provide long-term tenure for the Chief of the Agency, with the establishment of a precedent that his chief subordinates should also have that degree of permanence which is necessary to insure team play between the Chief and his immediate assistants. The Chief should not have men imposed upon him for political or other like reasons. He should have the right to pass upon his assistants. The legislation should provide that the Chief and his immediate assistants, so long as they are attached to the Central Intelligence Agency, should act in a civilian and not in a military capacity.

III

Under the legislation as proposed, the Central Intelligence Agency is to operate under the National Security Council, the stated purpose of which is "to advise the President with respect to the integration of foreign and military policies, and to enable the military services and other agencies of the Government to cooperate more effectively in matters involving national security." This Council will have at least six members, and possibly more, subject to Presidential appointment. From its composition it will be largely military, although the Secretary of State will be a member. If precedent is any guide, it seems unlikely, in view of the burden of work upon all the members of this Council, that it will prove to be an effective working body which will meet frequently, or which could give much supervisory attention to a central intelligence agency. It would seem preferable that the Chief of Central Intelligence should report, as at present, to a smaller body, of which the Secretary of State would be the chairman, and which would include the Secretary of National Defense, and a representative of the President, with the right reserved to the Secretaries of State and of National Defense to be represented on this small board by deputies, who should have at least the rank of Assistant Secretary. And this board must really meet and assume the responsibility for advising and counseling the Director of Intelligence, and assure the proper liaison between the Agency and these two Departments and the Executive.

IV

In time of peace, intelligence will probably be of more importance in the day-by-day operations of the Department of State than any other agency of the Government, even the Department of National Defense. Further, in time of peace, intelligence can only be properly collected if there are the closest working arrangements with the Department of State, as the bulk of the intelligence collected abroad will come through the facilities of that Department.

The proposed intelligence set-up in the draft legislation is overweighted on the side of the military department of the Government, as contrasted with the State Department. This is natural because it appears in a bill for our National Defense Establishment. This fact, however, should not blind us to the realities of the situation.

The State Department, irrespective of the form in which the Central Intelligence Agency is cast, will collect and process its own information as a basis for the day-by-day conduct of its work. The armed services intelligence agencies will do likewise. But for the proper judging of the situation in any foreign country it is important that information should be processed by an agency whose duty it is to weigh facts, and to draw conclusions from those facts, without having either the facts or the conclusions warped by the inevitable and even proper prejudices of the men whose duty it is to determine policy and who, having once determined a policy, are too likely to be blind to any facts which might tend to prove the policy to be faulty. The Central Intelligence Agency should have nothing to do with policy. It should try to get at the hard facts on which others must determine policy. The warnings which might well have pointed to the attack on Pearl Harbor were largely discounted by those who had already concluded that the Japanese must inevitably strike elsewhere. The warnings which reportedly came to Hitler of our invasion of North Africa were laughed aside. Hitler thought he knew we didn't have the ships to do it. It is impossible to provide any system which will be proof against the human frailty of intellectual stubbornness. Every individual suffers from that. All we can do is to see that we have created the best possible mechanism to get the unvarnished facts before the policy makers, and to get [them] there in time.

V

Any Central Intelligence Agency (in addition to having access to the intelligence collected by the State Department and the armed services, to intelligence gained through intercepted messages, open and deciphered alike, and from the results of its own secret and overt intelligence operations) must have a corps of the most competent men which this country can produce to evaluate and correlate the intelligence obtained, and to present it, in proper form, to the interested Government departments, in most cases to the State Department, in many cases to the Department of National Defense, or to both.

It is important to avoid splitting up and dissipating the personnel available for this work through having over-all specialized intelligence evaluating agencies in both the State Department and the Central Intelligence Agency. If close working relations are established between the Central Intelligence Agency and the State Department—as is essential if the Agency is to function properly—it would seem desirable, for reasons of economy and efficiency, that the task of evaluation should be delegated to the Central Intelligence Agency without, of course, affecting the work in the geographical and other divisions of the State Department. This would mean that the specialized intelligence agency within the State Department should be coordinated with, or amalgamated into, the branch of the Central Intelligence Agency devoted to the analysis and evaluation of intelligence.

VI

In addition to these basic considerations, the Central Intelligence Agency should have the following powers and attributes:

1. Control its own personnel but with the right to co-opt personnel from other departments of the Government, with the consent of the head of the department in question but without affecting the rank, civil-service status, or pay of the employee assigned for temporary duty.

2. Have its own appropriations but with the possibility of supplementing these appropriations from available funds of the Department of State or the Department of National Defense under conditions to be provided by law, in order to carry on certain special operations which may, from time to time, be deemed necessary by the President, the Secretary of State, or the Secretary of National Defense.

3. Have exclusive jurisdiction to carry out secret intelligence operations.

4. Have access to all intelligence information relating to foreign countries received by all departments of the Government, including "Magic."

5. Be the recognized agency for dealing with the central intelligence agencies of other countries.

6. Have its operations and personnel protected by "official secrets" legislation which would provide adequate penalties for breach of security.

VII

It has truthfully been said that intelligence is our first line of defense. The European countries more immediately exposed to danger in the past have realized this, and have spared no pains to develop adequate intelligence services. Among them the British have had signal success, and this success, in no small part, has been responsible for pulling them through periods of the direst danger. The British system has behind it a long history of quiet, effective performance, based on a highly trained personnel with years of service and great technical ability. In this country we have the raw material for building the greatest intelligence

service in the world. But to accomplish this we must make it a respect-
able, continuing, and adequately remunerated career. The personnel
need not be very numerous. The operation of the service must be neither
flamboyant nor overshrouded with the mystery and abracadabra which
the amateur detective likes to assume.

With the proper legislative backing, a correct technical set-up, and
adequate leadership, all that is required for success is hard work, dis-
criminating judgment, and common sense. Americans can be found who
are not lacking in these qualities.

Appendix B. CIA Policy on
Public Disclosure

Note: The following regulations are self-explanatory. They are re-printed from U. S. Senate, Judiciary Subcommittee on Constitutional Rights, "Withholding of Information from the Public and the Press." Committee Print, 86th Congress, 1st Session, Washington, D. C., 1960, pp. 124-125.

July 7, 1958

Hon. Thomas C. Hennings, Jr.,
Chairman, Subcommittee on Constitutional Rights,
U. S. Senate, Washington, D. C.

Dear Mr. Chairman: I have your letter of June 26, 1958, requesting that the Agency supply answers to the following questions:

1. What types of information and records in the possession of your department or agency are not available to members of the public or press upon request?
2. On the basis of what authority do you withhold such information or limit the availability of such records?

The following types of information and records within the Agency are not available to members of the public or press: Information relating to intelligence sources and methods or that information which tends to reveal intelligence sources and methods; information officially designated as "classified" either by the Central Intelligence Agency or by other agencies of the Government pursuant to appropriate statutes and Executive orders; and information concerning the functions and organization of the Agency or the names, official titles, salaries, or numbers of personnel employed by the Agency with certain exceptions.

The statutory basis for protecting such information is as follows: Section 102(d) (3) of the National Security Act of 1947, as amended (50 U.S.C. 401), provides "That the Director of Central Intelligence shall be responsible for protecting intelligence sources and methods from unauthorized disclosure." Further statutory authority appears in section 7 of the Central Intelligence Agency Act of 1947, as amended (50 U.S.C. 403(a)), which provides:

In the interests of the security of the foreign intelligence activities of the United States and in order further to implement the proviso of section 102(d)(3) of the National Security Act of 1947 (Public Law 253, 80th Cong., 1st sess.) that the Director of Central Intelligence shall be responsible for protecting intelligence sources and methods from unauthorized disclosure, the Agency shall be exempted from the provisions of sections 1 and 2, chapter 795 of the act of August 28, 1935 (49 Stat. 956, 957; 5 U.S.C. 654), and the provisions of any other law which requires the publication or disclosure of the organization, functions, names, official titles, salaries, or numbers of personnel employed by the Agency: *Provided,* That in furtherance of this section, the Director of the Bureau of the Budget shall make no reports to the Congress in connection with the agency under section 607, title VI, chapter 212, of the act of June 30, 1945, as amended (5 U.S.C. 947(b)).

The classification of information affecting the national defense within the meaning of sections 793 and 794 of title 18 of the United States Code is in accordance with the procedures specified in Executive Order 10501 with which I am sure the subcommittee is familiar.

We are enclosing for your information a copy of the Agency Regulation 10-290 entitled "Protection and Disclosure of Information." It is hoped that the above will be helpful to your subcommittee in its current study.

Sincerely,

Allen W. Dulles, *Director*

REGULATIONS

Protection and Disclosure of Information

1. AUTHORITY

Under the National Security Act of 1947 and the Central Intelligence Agency Act of 1949, and under direction of the National Security Council, the Director of Central Intelligence is responsible for protecting intelligence sources and methods from unauthorized disclosure.

2. PROTECTED INFORMATION

The problem of determining what information relates to the protection of intelligence sources and methods is of such complexity that no final determination can be made in regard to any single piece of information within the Agency or the other intelligence components except at the Director's level. Under his responsibility for protection of such information there have been established overall policies and detailed procedures for the appropriate dissemination of information and for its protection in the executive branch of the Government. Every request for information outside of the system designed to serve the excutive branch becomes a special problem requiring specific determination by or on behalf of the Director. Therefore, all files, documents, records, and information (whether or not reduced to writing) in the offices of the Central Intelligence Agency, including the several field offices, or acquired by any person as a result of service with or on behalf of the Agency, are to be regarded in the first instance as protected information.

3. POLICY

All persons are hereby prohibited from disclosing or using protected information for any purpose other than the performance of duties for or on behalf of the Agency, unless the Director of Central Intelligence or his designee has authorized the disclosure or use as not being contrary to the public interest. When deemed advisable by the Director, requests for protected information will be referred to the National Security Council for a decision on disclosure.

4. SUBPOENA FOR PROTECTED INFORMATION

a. Any person who is served with a subpoena requiring the disclosure of protected information to a court or the Congress shall promptly inform the General Counsel of the service of the subpoena, the nature of the information sought, and any circumstances which may bear upon the desirability of making available the information, in order that the General Counsel may advise the Director. Any action in response to the subpoena shall be taken only in accordance with advice of the General Counsel. Disclosure may be authorized only by the Director or Deputy Director of Central Intelligence.

b. If circumstances make it necessary for the Director to decline in the public interest to furnish the information, the person on whom the subpoena is served (acting in accordance with advice of the General Counsel) or the General Counsel or his designee will appear in answer thereto and respectfully state that he is complying with specific instructions of the Director of Central Intelligence in refusing to furnish the information requested.

C. P. Cabell,
Lieutenant General, USAF,
Acting Director of Central Intelligence

Appendix C. Authority of Director of Central Intelligence Clarified

Note: The following letter is considered of fundamental importance because it redefines the authority of the Director of Central Intelligence. This letter was written in 1962, signed by President John F. Kennedy, and directed to John A. McCone, who had succeeded Allen W. Dulles as Director in late 1961. Prior to this letter, uncertainty had prevailed among the various units in the intelligence community as to whether the DCI was simply head of another agency or chief of the entire system. The letter reaffirms that the Director is both the President's personal representative and the government's chief intelligence officer. This letter is reprinted from Lyman B. Kirkpatrick, Jr., *The Real CIA* (Macmillan, 1968, pp. 237-239).

In carrying out your newly assigned duties as Director of Central Intelligence it is my wish that you serve as the Government's principal foreign intelligence officer, and as such that you undertake, as an integral part of your responsibility, the coordination and effective guidance of the total United States foreign intelligence effort. As the Government's principal intelligence officer, you will assure the proper coordination, correlation, and evaluation of intelligence from all sources and its prompt dissemination to me and to other recipients as appropriate. In fulfillment of these tasks I shall expect you to work closely with the heads of all departments and agencies having responsibilities in the foreign intelligence field.

In coordinating and guiding the total intelligence effort, you will serve as Chairman of the United States Intelligence Board, with a view to assuring the efficient and effective operation of the Board and its associated bodies. In this connection I note with approval that you have designated your deputy to serve as a member of the Board, thereby bringing to the Board's deliberations the relevant facts and judgments of the Central Intelligence Agency.

As directed by the President and the National Security Council, you will establish with the advice and assistance of the United States Intelligence Board the necessary policies and procedures to assure adequate coordination of foreign intelligence activities at all levels.

Appendix C

With the heads of the Departments and Agencies concerned you will maintain a continuing review of the programs and activities of all U. S. agencies engaged in foreign intelligence activities with a view to assuring efficiency and effectiveness and to avoiding undesirable duplication.

As head of the Central Intelligence Agency, while you will continue to have over-all responsibility for the Agency, I shall expect you to delegate to your principal deputy, as you may deem necessary, so much of the direction of the detailed operation of the Agency as may be required to permit you to carry out your primary task as Director of Central Intelligence.

It is my wish that you keep me advised from time to time as to your progress in the implementation of this directive and as to any recommendations you may have which would facilitate the accomplishment of these objectives.

Appendix D. Report on CIA Secret Subsidies, 1967

Note: Under the glare of publicity about CIA's secret subsidies, from the early 1950s into the 1960s, of a large number of American private organizations, President Lyndon B. Johnson appointed a committee to review such programs in 1967. The committee consisted of Undersecretary of State Nicholas Katzenbach as chairman, Secretary of Health, Education and Welfare John W. Gardner, and CIA Director Richard Helms. Their report, as published in the *Department of State Bulletin* (April 24, 1967, pp. 665-668) follows.

Text of Report

Dear Mr. President:

The committee which you appointed on February 15, 1967 has sought, pursuant to your request:

—To review relationships between government agencies, notably the Central Intelligence Agency, and educational and private voluntary organizations which operate abroad; and

—To recommend means to help assure that such organizations can play their proper and vital role abroad.

The committee has held a number of meetings, interviewed dozens of individuals in and out of government, and reviewed thousands of pages of reports. We have surveyed the relevant activities of a number of federal agencies. And we have reviewed in particular and specific detail the relationship between CIA and each relevant organization.

Our report, supplemented with supporting classified documents, follows.

In summary, the committee offers two basic recommendations:

1. It should be the policy of the United States Government that no federal agency shall provide any covert financial assistance or support, direct or indirect, to any of the nation's educational or private voluntary organizations.

2. The Government should promptly develop and establish a public-private mechanism to provide public funds openly for overseas activities of organizations which are adjudged deserving, in the national interest, of public support.

269

Appendix D

1. A New Policy

The years immediately after World War II saw a surge of communist activity in organizations throughout the world. Students, scientists, veterans, women, and professional groups were organized into international bodies which spoke in the cadences, advocated the policies, and furthered the interests of the communist bloc. Much of this activity was organized, directed, and financed covertly by communist governments.

American organizations reacted from the first. The young men and women who founded the United States National Student Association, for example, did so precisely to give American youth the capacity to hold their own in the international arena. But the importance of students as a force in international events had yet to become widely understood and NSA found it difficult to attract private support for its international activities. Accordingly, the United States Government, acting through the Central Intelligence Agency, provided support for this overseas work.

We have taken NSA as an example. While no useful purpose would be served by detailing any other CIA programs of assistance to private American voluntary organizations, one fundamental point should be clearly stated: such assistance was given pursuant to National Security Council policies beginning in October, 1951, and with the subsequent concurrence of high-level senior interdepartmental review committees in the last four Administrations. In December, 1960, in a classified report submitted after a year of study, a public-private Presidential Committee on Information Activities Abroad specifically endorsed both overt and covert programs, including those assisted by CIA.

Our study, undertaken at a later time, discloses new developments which suggest that we should now re-examine these policies. The American public, for example, has become increasingly aware of the importance of the complex forms of international competition between free societies and communist states. As this awareness has grown, so have potential sources of support for the overseas work of private organizations.

There is no precise index to these sources, but their increase is suggested by the growth in the number of private foundations from 2,220 in 1955 to 18,000 in 1967. Hence it is increasingly possible for organizations like NSA to seek support for overseas activities from open sources.

Just as sources of support have increased, so has the number of American groups engaged in overseas work. According to the Agency for International Development, there has been a *nine-fold* increase just among voluntary organizations which participate in technical assistance abroad, rising from 24 in 1951 to 220 in 1965. The total of *all* private American voluntary groups now working overseas may well exceed a thousand.

CIA Secret Subsidies

The number of such organizations which has been assisted covertly is a small fraction of the total. The vast preponderance have had no relationship with the government or have accepted only open government funds—which greatly exceed funds supplied covertly.

The work of private American organizations, in a host of fields, has been of great benefit to scores of countries. That benefit must not be impaired by foreign doubts about the independence of these organizations. *The committee believes it is essential for the United States to underscore that independence immediately and decisively.*

For these reasons, the committee recommends the following:

STATEMENT OF POLICY

No federal agency shall provide any covert financial assistance or support, direct or indirect, to any of the nation's educational or private voluntary organizations. This policy specifically applies to all foreign activities of such organizations and it reaffirms present policy with respect to their domestic activities.

Where such support has been given, it will be terminated as quickly as possible without destroying valuable private organizations before they can seek new means of support.[1]

We believe that, particularly in the light of recent publicity, establishment of a clear policy of this kind is the only way for the government to carry out two important responsibilities. One is to avoid any implication that governmental assistance, because it is given covertly, is used to affect the policies of private voluntary groups. The second responsibility is to make it plain in all foreign countries that the activities of private American groups abroad are, in fact, private.

The committee has sought carefully to assess the impact of this Statement of Policy on CIA. We have reviewed each relevant program of assistance carried out by the Agency in case-by-case detail. As a result of this scrutiny, the committee is satisfied that application of the Statement of Policy will not unduly handicap the Agency in the exercise of its national security responsibilities. Indeed, it should be noted that, starting well before the appearance of recent publicity, CIA had initiated and pursued efforts to disengage from certain of these activities.

The committee also recommends that the implementation of this policy be supervised by the senior interdepartmental review committee which already passes on proposed CIA activities and which would review and assist in the process of disengagement.[2]

[1] On the basis of our case-by-case review, we expect that the process of termination can be largely—perhaps entirely—completed by December 31, 1967.

[2] If the Statement of Policy is to be effective, it must be rigorously enforced. In the judgment of this committee, no programs currently would justify any exception to this policy. At the same time, where the security of the nation may be at stake, it is impossible for this committee to state categorically now that there will never be a contingency in which overriding national security interests may require

2. New Methods of Support

While our first recommendation seeks to insure the independence of private voluntary organizations, it does not deal with an underlying problem—how to support the national need for, and the intrinsic worth of, their efforts abroad.

Anyone who has the slightest familiarity with intellectual or youth groups abroad knows that free institutions continue to be under bitter, continuous attack, some of it carefully organized and well-financed, all of it potentially dangerous to this nation.

It is of the greatest importance to our future and to the future of free institutions everywhere that other nations, especially their young people, know and understand American viewpoints. There is no better way to meet this need than through the activity of private American organizations.

The time has surely come for the government to help support such activity in a mature, open manner.

Some progress toward that aim already has been made. In recent years, a number of federal agencies have developed contracts, grants, and other forms of open assistance to private organizations for overseas activities. This assistance, however, does not deal with a major aspect of the problem. A number of organizations cannot, without hampering their effectiveness as independent bodies, accept funds directly from government agencies.

The committee therefore recommends that the Government should promptly develop and establish a public-private mechanism to provide public funds openly for overseas activities of organizations which are adjudged deserving, in the national interest, of public support.

Such a mechanism could take various forms. One promising proposal, advanced by Mr. Eugene Black, calls for a publicly funded but privately administered body patterned on the British Council.

The British Council, established in 1934, operates in 80 countries, administering approximately $30,000,000 annually for reference libraries, exhibitions, scholarships, international conferences, and cultural exchanges. Because 21 of its 30 members are drawn from private life, the Council has maintained a reputation for independence, even though 90 percent of its funds are governmental.

According to the UNESCO Directory of Cultural Relations Services, other nations have developed somewhat similar institutions. The Indian

an exception—nor would it be credible to enunciate a policy which purported to do so.

We therefore recommend that, in the event of such unusual contingencies, the interdepartmental review committee be permitted to make exceptions to the Statement of Policy, but only where overriding national security interests so require; only on a case-by-case basis; only where open sources of support are shown to be unavailable; and only when such exceptions receive the specific approval of the Secretaries of State and Defense. In no event should any future exception be approved which involves any educational, philanthropic, or cultural organization.

Council for Cultural Relations, for example, is entirely government-financed but operates autonomously. The governing body of the Swedish Institute for Cultural Relations consists of both government and private members. This institute receives 75 percent of its funds from the government and the remainder from private contributions.

The experience of these and other countries helps to demonstrate the desirability of a similar body in the United States, wholly or largely funded by the federal government. Another approach might be the establishment of a governmental foundation, perhaps with links to the existing Federal Inter-Agency Council on International Education and Cultural Affairs.

Such a public-private body would not be new to the United States. Congress established the Smithsonian Institution, for example, more than a century ago as a private corporation, under the guardianship of Congress, but governed by a mixed public-private Board of Regents.

The committee began a preliminary study of what might be the best method of meeting the present need. It is evident, however, that, because of the great range both of existing government and private philanthropic programs, the refinement of alternatives and selection among them is a task of considerable complexity. Accordingly, we do not believe that this exclusively governmental committee is an appropriate forum for the task and we recommend, instead, the appointment of a larger group, including individuals in private life with extensive experience in this field.

The basic principle, in any event, is clear. Such a new institution would involve government funds. It might well involve government officials. But a premium must be placed on the involvement of private citizens and the exercise of private judgments, for to be effective, it would have to have—and be recognized to have—a high degree of independence.

The prompt creation of such an institution, based on this principle, would fill an important—and never more apparent—national need.

Respectfully,

John W. Gardner
Secretary of Health, Education and Welfare

Richard Helms
Director of Central Intelligence

Nicholas deB. Katzenbach
Undersecretary of State, Chairman

A Selected Bibliography

As a bibliographical subject, foreign intelligence activities lead off into endless directions. The bibliography that follows is highly select, limited primarily to United States problems of policy, organization and control of the intelligence establishment. Some attention is paid to the British experience and to generalized studies. But no attempt has been made to cover the literature dealing primarily with military intelligence, or with other highly technical subjects. Nor is there detailed coverage of the voluminous and highly uneven work on espionage and counterespionage, psychological warfare, propaganda, counterrevolutionary warfare and related topics. To pursue these subjects, a forthcoming publication, *A Bibliography of Intelligence Activities,* by William R. Harris, will be essential. On a number of specific topics, items cited in the notes are not included in my bibliography. The notes should be considered an essential part of the source material for my book.

1. UNITED STATES

A. BOOKS

Ford, Corey, and Alastair MacBain. *Cloak and Dagger: The Secret Story of the OSS.* New York: Random House, 1946.
  A melodramatic account of the activities during World War II of the Office of Strategic Services. A later book by Ford, *Donovan of OSS* (Boston: Little, Brown) is a biography of the chief of the OSS.
Goulden, Joseph C. *Truth is the First Casualty.* Chicago: Rand McNally, 1969.
  An excellent journalistic account of the Gulf of Tonkin affair. Part II is of special interest, dealing with "the dangerous business of electronic espionage."
Hilsman, Roger. *To Move a Nation.* New York: Doubleday, 1967.
  Part II, Chapters 6, 7 and 8 deal with President Kennedy and the CIA. As a high-ranking State Department official during the Kennedy Administration and as a student of intelligence doctrine, Hilsman offers here an incomplete memoir of how President Kennedy tried to deal with the CIA during 1961-63.
————. *Strategic Intelligence and National Decisions.* Glencoe, Ill.: The Free Press, 1956.
  Hilsman served with OSS and CIA. His book is based in part on interviews with State Department, CIA, and other officials. A valuable

treatise on the relationship between intelligence and the decisional process.

Ind, Colonel Allison. *Allied Intelligence Bureau: Our Secret Weapon in the War against Japan.* New York: McKay, 1958.

Johnson, Haynes. *The Bay of Pigs.* New York: W. W. Norton, 1964.
One of several accounts of the Bay of Pigs operation in April 1961. Leans heavily upon interviews with Cuban exiles involved in the CIA-planned misadventure.

Kent, Sherman. *Strategic Intelligence for American World Policy.* Princeton, N. J.: Princeton University Press, 1949, 1951.
The classic primer on strategic intelligence written by a former professor of history at Yale, one-time OSS and State Department intelligence official, and later a high official of CIA. Somewhat outdated, but it remains a practical professional analysis of intelligence problems and techniques on the national strategic level and a good appraisal of what can and should be expected of the intelligence community.

Kim, Young Hum, ed. *The Central Intelligence Agency: Problems of Secrecy in a Democracy.* Lexington, Mass.: D. C. Heath, 1968.
A collection of twelve articles dealing with the problem of controlling a secret agency within a democratic society. Designed for teaching in political science courses, this is a useful collection of essays, *pro* and *con.*

Kirkpatrick, Lyman B., Jr. *The Real CIA.* New York: Macmillan, 1968.
Provides valuable insight into the organizational history and internal administrative struggles of the CIA. The author was employed by the CIA for more than twenty years, serving as its Inspector General and Executive Director before his retirement.

Meyer, Karl E., and Tad Szulc. *The Cuban Invasion.* New York: Praeger, 1962.
A competent journalistic account of the Bay of Pigs fiasco in April 1961.

Office of Strategic Services assessment staff (Henry A. Murray and others). *Assessment of Men.* New York: Rinehart, 1947, 1950.
A detailed report by psychologists and psychiatrists who worked at the various stations established during World War II for testing and assessing the qualifications of men and women recruited for a variety of tasks performed by OSS during the war. Offers valuable insight into OSS and various concepts of the tasks of secret intelligence and special operations and the personal qualities required for such assignments.

Pettee, George S. *The Future of American Secret Intelligence.* Washington, D. C.: Infantry Journal Press, 1946.
Written by a World War II intelligence specialist, this book contains more critical opinions on specific intelligence substantive and organizational problems than either Kent's or Hilsman's. Outdated somewhat, this book nevertheless remains of value.

Pinkerton, Allan. *The Spy of the Rebellion.* New York: G. W. Carleton, 1886.
An autobiographical account by the famous detective who was, for a time and under the *nom-de-guerre* of Maj. E. J. Allen, Chief of General

McClellan's Union Army intelligence service. This book reveals some of the ineptness with which this job was handled by Pinkerton, who had no experience qualifying him to lead a military intelligence service. See especially pp. 151ff.

Platt, Washington. *Strategic Intelligence Production: Basic Principles.* New York: Frederick A. Praeger, 1957.

An attempt to establish basic principles of strategic intelligence production, written by an Army reserve officer experienced in military intelligence. The specific structure and role of the contemporary intelligence community are not discussed.

Ransom, Harry Howe. *Can American Democracy Survive Cold War?* Garden City, N. Y.: Doubleday, 1963. Doubleday, Anchor, 1964.

Chapters VI and VII deal with some basic problems of an intelligence system in a democratic society and with the nature of strategic intelligence. Contains a case history of intelligence in the Korean War.

Wise, David and Thomas B. Ross. *The Invisible Government.* New York: Random House, 1964.

A very revealing book based upon a highly simplistic theme, which overstates the influence of the CIA and contains errors in fact and interpretation. The book has been widely used by unfriendly foreign powers as anti-American propaganda. In the muck-raking tradition, by two resourceful journalists.

Wohlstetter, Roberta. *Pearl Harbor, Warning and Decision.* Stanford: Stanford University Press, 1962.

The most detailed case study available of a major intelligence failure. A major work, developing the useful concept of information "noise" which drowns out the essential facts.

Yardley, Herbert O. *The American Black Chamber.* Indianapolis: Bobbs-Merrill, 1931.

The "Black Chamber" was the American Cryptographic Bureau, which operated out of the Department of State in the decade after the First World War. It monitored the secret correspondence of foreign nations and was abolished as a "dirty business" early in 1929 by a new Secretary of State, Henry L. Stimson. Mr. Yardley was its director.

Zacharias, Ellis M. *Behind Closed Doors, The Secret History of the Cold War.* New York: G. P. Putnam's Sons, 1950.

An account of intelligence activities from 1945 to 1950 coupled with a foray into American foreign policy problems.

————. *Secret Missions.* New York: G. P. Putnam's Sons, 1946.

Personalized account by a senior naval intelligence officer of ONI operations before and during World War II, with considerable background on Navy's psychological warfare campaign waged against Japan.

Zlotnick, Jack. *National Intelligence.* Washington, D. C.: Industrial College of the Armed Forces, 1964.

A CIA staff member gives a detailed, if discreet, description of the organization of the national intelligence community and some of its operating principles.

B. PERIODICALS

Baldwin, Hanson W. Series of five articles in *The New York Times* on intelligence:

A Selected Bibliography

July 20, 1948: "Intelligence—One of the Weakest Links in our Security
Survey Shows—Omissions, Duplications."

July 22, 1948: "Older Agencies Resent a Successor and Try to Restrict
Scope of Action."

July 23, 1948: "Intelligence III: Errors in Collecting Data Held Exceeded by Evaluation Weakness."

July 24, 1948: "Competent Personnel Held Key to Success—Reforms
Suggested."

July 25, 1948: "Broader Control Set-Up is Held Need With a 'Watch-
Dog' Committee for Congress."

Barnds, William J. "Intelligence and Foreign Policy: Dilemmas of a Democracy." *Foreign Affairs,* 47 (January 1969), 281-295.
A general discussion of the "CIA problem" by a sophisticated analyst.

Chamberlain, John. "OSS." *Life,* November 19, 1945, pp. 119-130.
Capsule history of OSS and General William J. Donovan's role in its
wartime activities.

Donovan, William J. "Intelligence: Key to Defense." *Life,* September 30,
1946, pp. 108-120.
Critique of pre-war intelligence and of wartime OSS by its founder and
director together with suggestions for post-war organization.

Evans, Allan. "Intelligence and Policy Formation." *World Politics,* October
1959, 84-91.
A long-time State Department intelligence official discusses the intelligence problem in the context of several books dealing with the subject.

Fischel, Edwin C. "The Mythology of Civil War Intelligence," in *Civil War
History,* vol. 10, no. 4. University of Iowa at Ames, December 1964.
There are many legends about espionage on both sides in the American
Civil War. Careful research has indicated that most of the popular
tales cannot be verified. This essay analyzes the problem.

Harkness, Richard and Gladys. "The Mysterious Doings of CIA." *Saturday
Evening Post,* October 30, November 6 and 13, 1954.
A journalistic but impressively detailed three-part account of CIA activities and organization. Security regulations prevent confirmation or
denial of article, but tone indicates CIA may have "assisted" in this
publicity *tour de force.*

Hilsman, Roger. "Intelligence and Policy Making in Foreign Affairs." *World
Politics,* October 1952, pp. 1-45.
A detailed argument about the role of intelligence in policy making. A
forerunner of Hilsman's book, *Strategic Intelligence and National Decisions.*

Hobbing, Enno. "CIA: Hottest Role in the Cold War." *Esquire,* September
1957, pp. 31-34.
A journalistic account of CIA organization and activities, with some
interesting detail on how CIA recruits and uses defectors from behind
the Iron Curtain.

Kendall, Willmoore. "The Function of Intelligence." *World Politics,* July
1949, pp. 542-552.
A critical analysis of Sherman Kent's book, *Strategic Intelligence.*
Professor Kendall challenged the prevalent view of the function, organization, and role of intelligence.

A Selected Bibliography

Knorr, Klaus. *Foreign Intelligence and the Social Sciences.* Center of International Studies, Princeton, N. J. Research Monograph No. 17, Princeton University Press, 1964.

―――. "Failure in National Estimates: The Case of the Cuban Missiles." *World Politics,* April 1964, pp. 455-467.
Analyzes and defends the intelligence system's "failure" to give earlier warning of the Soviet emplacement of nuclear missiles in Cuba in 1962.

Ransom, Harry Howe. "How Effective Is Central Intelligence?" *Christian Science Monitor,* December 1, 1958, p. 13.
A general discussion of the intelligence function and description of its evolution in the United States after World War II.

―――. "How Intelligent is Intelligence?" *The New York Times Magazine,* May 22, 1960, pp. 26, 80-83.
A discussion of the problem of managing espionage activities in a democratic society, written shortly after the downing of an American U-2 reconnaissance plane over the Soviet Union in early May 1960.

―――. "Secret Mission in an Open Society," *The New York Times Magazine,* May 21, 1961, pp. 20, 77-79.
An analysis of the problem of responsible political control of secret operations, written in the wake of the Bay of Pigs fiasco.

Robinson, Donald. "They Fight the Cold War Under Cover." *Saturday Evening Post,* November 20, 1948, pp. 30ff.
Written within the first year of CIA's existence and apparently with help from inside government sources, this article reveals the extensive overseas political operations of CIA agents as early as 1948.

Unna, Warren. "CIA: Who Watches the Watchman?" *Harper's,* April 1958, pp. 46-53.
A well-informed journalistic account of CIA's role in the Washington decision-making process in the 1950s. Emphasis is placed upon the question of Congressional surveillance.

Wicker, Tom, and other members of the Washington, D. C., staff of the *New York Times.* "CIA: Maker of Policy or Tool?"
Five-part series running on consecutive days, April 25 through April 29, 1966. A very revealing series contributed to by the world-wide staff of the *New York Times.* Discusses specific operations as well as policy, organization, and controls.

Wohlstetter, Roberta. "Cuba and Pearl Harbor." *Foreign Affairs,* vol. 43, no. 4 (July 1965), pp. 691-707.
A comparison of the strategic surprises at Pearl Harbor, and two decades later, the Soviet emplacement of missiles in Cuba in 1962.

C. GOVERNMENT DOCUMENTS

(a) *U. S. Congress*

House Committee on Armed Services. "Amending the Central Intelligence Act of 1949," *Report,* August 11, 1966, to accompany H. R. 16306, 89th Cong., 2nd sess. Washington, D. C.: G.P.O., 1966.

House Committee on Armed Services. "Inquiry Into the U.S.S. Pueblo and EC-121 Plane Incidents," *Report,* July 28, 1969, No. 91-12. 91st Cong., 1st sess. Washington, D. C.: G.P.O., 1969.

A Selected Bibliography

Senate Committee on Armed Services, *Hearings,* "National Defense Establishment," 80th Cong., 1st sess., on S.758, 3 parts. Washington, D. C., 1947.
Part 3 contains testimony on central intelligence.
Senate Committee on Government Operations, Subcommittee on National Policy Machinery, *Intelligence and National Security,* Report, 86th Cong., 2nd sess. Washington, D. C.: G.P.O., 1960.
Senate Committee on the Judiciary, Subcommittee to Investigate the Administration of the Internal Security Act, *Hearings, Communist Forgeries.* Washington, D. C.: G.P.O., 1961.
Senate Committee on the Judiciary, Subcommittee to Investigate the Internal Security Act of 1950, *The Wennerstroem Spy Case, How It Touched the U. S. and NATO,* 88th Cong., 2nd sess. Washington, D. C.: G.P.O., 1964.
Senate Committee on Naval Affairs, *Report* to the Secretary of the Navy, "Unification of the War and Navy Departments and Postwar Organization for National Security" (Eberstadt Report), 79th Cong., 1st sess., 1945, pp. 12-13, 159-163.
Brief account of World War II intelligence organization and Navy proposals for postwar reorganization.
Senate Committee on Rules and Administration, *Report,* "Joint Committee on Central Intelligence Agency," Senate Report No. 1570, 84th Cong., 2nd sess. Washington, D. C., February 23, 1956.
The Committee supports, by an eight-to-one vote, the proposal to establish a Joint Congressional Committee on CIA. Contains the outlines of the argument in favor of such a move as well as the dissenting argument.
Senate Judiciary Internal Security Subcommittee, *Hearing,* "Interlocking Subversion in Government Departments," 83rd Cong., 1st sess. Washington, D. C., June 25, 1953, Part 13.
Contains testimony and important documents and memoranda relating to intelligence organization within the Department of State, 1945-1947. See especially pages 854-882.
Dulles, Allen W. "Memorandum Respecting . . . Central Intelligence Agency . . . ," submitted to Senate Committee on Armed Services, April 25, 1947. Printed in *Hearings,* "National Defense Establishment," 80th Cong., 1st sess., on S.758, Washington, D. C., 1947, pp. 525-528.
A concise statement of Mr. Dulles' views on a central intelligence organization as of 1947, reprinted in Appendix A of this book.
Act to Provide for the Administration of the CIA . . . And for Other Purposes (Public Law 110, 81st Cong., 1st sess., June 20, 1949, 63 Stat. 208).
This act was designed to strengthen the administration of CIA. It gave additional powers to the Director, both in protecting the secrecy of CIA operations and in the unvouchered expenditure of money.

(b) *Other Documents*

Commission on Organization of the Executive Branch of the Government (Hoover Commission), 1949: *Task Force Report on Foreign Affairs* (Appendix H), January 1949, p. 95; *Foreign Affairs, A Report to*

279

Congress, February 1949, pp. 15, 16, 56, 57; *Task Force Report, National Security Organization,* Appendix G, January 1949, pp. 4, 32, 76-78.

Commission on Organization of the Executive Branch of the Government (Hoover Commission), "Intelligence Activities," *A Report to the Congress* (containing the Commission and Clark Task Force Reports), June 1955.

Department of State: "Coordination of Foreign Intelligence Activities," *Department of State Bulletin,* February 3, 1946, pp. 174-175; "Intelligence Objectives," *Bulletin,* May 12, 1946; *Intelligence, A Bibliography of Its Functions, Methods and Techniques,* Part I. *Bibliography No. 33,* December 20, 1948 (mimeographed). Part II (Periodical and Newspaper Articles), *Bibliography No. 33.1,* April 11, 1949 (mimeographed), Office of Intelligence Research.

National Security Act of 1947 (Public Law 253, July 26, 1947, 80th Congress, 1947, 61 Stat. 495, 50 U.S.C. Supp. 403).
Section 102 contains provisions establishing CIA. This is CIA's basic charter.

U. S. Bureau of the Budget, "Intelligence and Security Activities of the Government," A Report to the President. Washington, D. C., September 20, 1945 (mimeographed).

2. GREAT BRITAIN

Babington-Smith, Constance. *Air Spy: The Story of Photo Intelligence in World War II.* New York: Harper and Bros., 1957.
A detailed personal narrative of British photo reconnaissance and interpretation, so vital to the intelligence on which Allied bombing operations were planned in World War II.

Cookridge, E. H. *Set Europe Ablaze.* New York: Crowell, 1967.
This is a popular account of the work of the British Special Operations Executive, the secret agency in World War II for sabotage, espionage, and subversion in Nazi-occupied territory.

Foot, M. R. D. *SOE in France, An Account of the Work of the British Special Operations Executive in France, 1940-1944.* London: H.M.S.O., 1966.
A volume in the official British "History of the Second World War" series. Although officially sanctioned, this outstanding work has no peer on the American OSS side. A very valuable history of the British wartime experience in secret operation in France in World War II.

Jones, R. V., "Scientific Intelligence," *Journal of the Royal United Service Institution,* August 1947, pp. 352-369.
A brilliant and revealing account of a scientist's experience with British intelligence in World War II. The author was particularly concerned with air and scientific intelligence.

McLachlan, Donald. *Room 39, A Study in Naval Intelligence.* New York: Atheneum, 1968.
The story of British Naval Intelligence in World War II, emphasizing the central direction of the "hard" intelligence effort directed, on the Navy's side, from Room 39 in the Admiralty. An authoritative, al-

A Selected Bibliography

though not a definitive, account. The author was a member of the British Naval Intelligence Staff in Room 39.

Montagu, Ewen. *The Man Who Never Was.* Philadelphia and New York: J. B. Lippincott Co., 1954.
Brief story of the famed British deception operation for Sicilian invasion involving faked body and papers of an English officer.

Page, Bruce, David Leitch, and Phillip Knightley. *The Philby Conspiracy.* Garden City, N. Y.: Doubleday, 1968.
A remarkable account of the case of H. A. R. Philby, British intelligence official who was recruited early in his career by the Soviet intelligence system. This book is not only the most detailed account of the bizarre Philby episode but contains more information than ever previously published about the British intelligence system; thus an important publishing landmark.

Philby, Kim (H. A. R.). *My Silent War.* London: MacGibbon and Kee, 1968.
Philby surely ranks as one of the most notorious "double-agents" of the twentieth century. He was a member of the British Secret Intelligence Service (MI-6) for two decades, holding high rank and important assignments while in the pay also of the Soviet intelligence service. Before being apprehended he escaped to Moscow, where this book was written. It must be assumed that this account was motivated by a desire to further the Soviet cause.

Ransom, Harry Howe. "Great Britain's Secret, Secret Service." *Midway,* vol. 8, no. 1 (June 1967), pp. 19-35.
A general survey of the British system and how secrecy has been maintained.

Read, Conyers. *Mr. Secretary Walsingham and the Policy of Queen Elizabeth.* 3 vols. Cambridge, Mass.: Harvard University Press, 1925.
A detailed three-volume biography of Sir Francis Walsingham, Queen Bess's principal State Secretary who operated an extensive intelligence network.

Richings, M. G. *Espionage: The Story of the Secret Service of the English Crown.* London: Hutchinson and Co., 1934.
An historical account of government secret service operations in England from the fourteenth to the twentieth century, from the Plantagenet kings to the period of the First World War.

Strong, Sir Kenneth. *Intelligence at the Top, The Recollections of an Intelligence Officer.* London: Cassell, 1968.
After forty years in British military intelligence work, Sir Kenneth offers a personal memoir giving a considerable amount of detail about the British system. Stresses military intelligence and the period through World War II.

Sweet-Escott, Bickham. *Baker Street Irregulars.* London: Methuen, 1965.
An apparently authentic account of many of the episodes and organizational and policy details of the British Special Operations Executive, a secret strategic service in World War II.

Trevor-Roper, Hugh. *The Philby Affair.* London: Kimber, 1968.
The noted British historian has had substantial experience in and maintains apparently close contacts with the British intelligence system.

A Selected Bibliography

In addition to a most perceptive commentary not only on the Philby affair but on the nature of the intelligence system, he reprints a valuable essay on Admiral Canaris, for nine years head of the German Secret Service, or *Abwehr*, under Hitler.

Williams, David. *Not in the Public Interest*. London: Hutchinson, 1965.
British scholars have paid scant attention to the history and operation of official secrets policy in Great Britain. This book is an exception, written by a law don now at Cambridge University.

3. GENERAL WORKS

Australia. *Report of Royal Commission on Espionage*. Sydney: Commonwealth of Australia, A. H. Pettifier, 1955.
A devastatingly documented account of Soviet espionage operations conducted in Australia. Based on testimony from former MVD agent Vladimir Petrov. An excellent sequel to the Canadian report (see below), indicating types of Soviet intelligence targets and the elaborate collection system employed by the Russians.

Blackstock, Paul W. *The Strategy of Subversion*. Chicago: Quadrangle, 1964.
A largely historical survey of covert political operations abroad, stressing the role of the CIA in such operations and questioning the utility of this instrument and concern about its proper control. The author is one of the few scholars who have written in this difficult field.

Carroll, John M. *Secrets of Electronic Espionage*. New York: Dutton, 1966.
A description, for the non-expert reader, of various electronic developments that have affected the gathering of information of all kinds.

Cottam, Richard. *Competitive Interference and Twentieth-Century Diplomacy*. Pittsburgh, Penn.: University of Pittsburgh Press, 1967.
An attempt to provide a theoretical base for analyzing foreign intervention short of war, particularly after 1947.

Dallin, David J. *Soviet Espionage*. New Haven, Conn.: Yale University Press, 1955.
A leading authority on Soviet Russia discusses in detail the Soviet espionage system, its evolution, its theory, and its operational code. The book contains certain "area studies" of Soviet espionage, particularly Europe and North America. This is one of the most comprehensive and authoritative studies of the subject.

Canada. *Report of Royal Commission to Investigate Disclosures of Secret and Confidential Information to Unauthorized Persons*. Ottawa: Clouthier, 1946.
A well-documented case study of Soviet methods, individual agents, and organization emerges in this Royal Commission probe of atomic-espionage operations conducted through the USSR Embassy in Ottawa.

Daugherty, William E., with Morris Janowitz. *A Psychological Warfare Casebook*. Baltimore, Md.: The Johns Hopkins Press, 1958.
Chapter 7 deals with the "Role of Intelligence, Research, and Analysis in Psychological Warfare" (pp. 425-549). This section contains selected writings by scholars on the subject. The premise is that "psychological warfare depends on intelligence for all aspects of its operation."

282

A Selected Bibliography

Deriabin, Peter, and Frank Gibney. *The Secret World*. Garden City, N. Y.: Doubleday, 1959.

A personal memoir of a former staff officer of the Russian KGB, revealing many details of the Soviet security and intelligence services. While it is not possible to judge the authenticity of books such as this, it has a realistic ring and gives many organizational details.

Dulles, Allen W. *The Craft of Intelligence*. New York: Harper & Row, 1963.

By the man most influential in determining the doctrine, organization, and style of the CIA as its Director, 1953-1961. Not a systematic book, but the author's experience and access to the facts requires that it be placed among the basic literature. Tendency toward a CIA recruiter's handbook.

————, editor. *Great True Spy Stories*. New York: Harper & Row, 1968.

Thirty-nine selections dealing with the principal espionage and counter-intelligence cases from all periods, with emphasis on the years since the beginning of World War II. A "bedside reader" which tends to stress the most dramatic episodes and thus to romanticize the grim and ruthless business of secret operations.

————. *The Secret Surrender*. New York: Harper & Row, 1966.

An account of the OSS role in bringing about the surrender of German armed forces in Italy in World War II. Dulles was the OSS chief in Switzerland during that period. The author expands upon his 1947 book, *Germany's Underground*.

Farago, Ladislas. *War of Wits, The Anatomy of Espionage and Intelligence*. New York: Funk and Wagnalls, 1954.

Journalistic opus on intelligence doctrines and operations written by a newspaperman and wartime reserve officer in the Office of Naval Intelligence.

Felix, Christopher (pseud.). *A Short Course in the Secret War*. New York: Dutton, 1963.

An anonymous but ostensibly experienced writer delves into the various forms of covert foreign intervention, with apparent authenticity and concrete examples. A very revealing book. See also this author's "The Unknowable CIA," *The Reporter*, April 6, 1967, pp. 20-24, defending the CIA against its many critics.

Goudsmit, Samuel A. *Alsos*. New York: Henry Schuman, 1947.

The *Alsos* mission, of which the author of this book was the scientific head, was to follow Allied armies in the invasion of Europe to determine precisely how much the Germans knew about the atomic bomb and how much progress the Germans had made. This is the story of one important aspect of scientific intelligence by American forces in World War II.

Gramont, Sanche de. *The Secret War*. New York: Putnam, 1962.

A popularized exposé of many of the supposedly secret espionage activities of the CIA and foreign secret agencies, emphasizing the tense cold war years of the 1950s. Deals with a number of specific espionage and internal security cases as well as with Soviet secret operations.

Kahn, David. *The Code Breakers, History of Secret Communication*. New York: Macmillan, 1967.

A Selected Bibliography

The only comprehensive history of code making and code breaking. A journalistic but very thorough effort, containing more details on the National Security Agency (Chapter 19) than any other publication.

McGovern, James. *Crossbow and Overcast.* London: Hutchinson, 1965.
A revealing account, with concrete detail, of the Allied experience in gathering intelligence on German "V-weapons" (pilotless bombs) during World War II.

Moyzisch, L. S. *Operation "Cicero."* London: Wingate Press, 1950.
German version of the story of the valet to the British Ambassador to Turkey. Known as "Cicero," this valet worked for German intelligence to steal important documents.

Penkovskiy, Oleg. *The Penkovskiy Papers.* Garden City, N. Y.: Doubleday, 1965.
With an introduction and commentary by Frank Gibney, this volume gives intimate details from inside the Soviet intelligence and security system. This controversial memoir has provoked some skepticism about its authenticity or at least some doubt as to what degree it has been edited to serve the purposes of intelligence services in the West. Nonetheless, an interesting document.

Ransom, Harry Howe. "Intelligence, Political and Military," *International Encyclopedia of the Social Sciences,* vol. 7. New York: Macmillan and Free Press, 1968, pp. 415-421.
A general survey, stressing definitions, basic literature and suggestions for further social science research.

de Rivera, Joseph H. *The Psychological Dimension of Foreign Policy.* Columbus, Ohio: Merrill, 1968.
A psychologist applies concepts from his field to the decision-making processes, demonstrating how perceptions, personality, and interpersonal relations affect the use of information. Useful in understanding intelligence failures.

Rowan, Richard W. *The Story of Secret Service.* Garden City, N. Y.: Doubleday, Doran, 1937.
An eighty-eight chapter survey of espionage covering "thirty-three centuries." This is a popular survey of the activities of spies and counterspies in all major periods of world history. A useful general survey prior to the beginning of World War II.

Ruggles, Richard, and Henry Brodie. "An Empirical Approach to Economic Intelligence in World War II," *Journal of the American Statistical Association,* March 1947, pp. 72-91.
An account of the technique developed by the Economic Warfare Division of the American Embassy in London to analyze markings and serial numbers from captured German equipment in order to obtain estimates of German war production and strength. This was used in the selection of air targets in World War II; at other times it gave indication of German tank and rocket strength.

Schellenberg, Walter. *The Labyrinth.* New York: Harper and Bros., 1956.
Memoirs of an important Nazi intelligence official. One of the most revealing accounts of the Nazi espionage system and the complex of Nazi internecine intrigue.

A Selected Bibliography

Scott, Andrew M. *The Revolution in Statecraft: Informed Penetration.* New York: Random House, 1965.
An attempt to provide a theoretical base for analysis of foreign intervention in the modern world.

Scott, John. *Political Warfare, A Guide to Competitive Co-Existence.* New York: John Day, 1955.
Part 5, "Intelligence" (pp. 139-157), presents a concise general survey of techniques and problems.

Vagts, Alfred. *Defense and Diplomacy.* New York: King's Crown Press, 1956, chap. 3, "Diplomacy, Military Intelligence, and Espionage," pp. 61-77.
Traces the historical experience of intelligence concluding with a section on "American Intelligence in the 'Cold War.'"

Wilensky, Harold L. *Organizational Intelligence.* New York: Basic Books, 1967.
A sociologist examines perceptively the use and misuse of intelligence in governmental and business organizations. Provides valuable insight into the intelligence function in complex organizations.

Wise, David, and Thomas B. Ross. *The Espionage Establishment.* New York: Random House, 1967.
Sketches of the espionage systems of the United States, Great Britain, Russia and China, by the authors of *The Invisible Government* and, in the same vein, sensationalized yet informative journalism.

Notes

CHAPTER I: INTELLIGENCE IN THE SPACE AGE

1. As recounted in James M. Burns, *Roosevelt: the Lion and the Fox,* (New York: Harcourt, Brace, 1956), p. 392.
2. James Forrestal, *Forrestal Diaries,* ed. Walter Millis (New York: Viking, 1951), p. 320.
3. *New York Times,* April 25, 1966, p. 20.
4. *Ibid.*
5. Commission on Organization of the Executive Branch of the Government, Hon. Herbert Hoover, chairman, *Intelligence Activities,* Report to Congress, June 1955, p. 26.
6. "What's 'CIA'?" *U. S. News and World Report,* July 18, 1966, p. 74.
7. Remark attributed to Admiral Arthur Radford, in *Time,* February 25, 1957, p. 27.
8. *Dictionary of United States Military Terms for Joint Usage,* Washington, D. C., Departments of the Army, Navy, and Air Force, May 1955, p. 53.
9. Hoover Commission, *Intelligence Activities,* p. 25.

CHAPTER II: THE NATURE OF INTELLIGENCE

1. *U. S. News and World Report.* Copyright Interview, March 19, 1954, p. 65.
2. Sherman Kent, *Strategic Intelligence* (Princeton, N. J.: Princeton University Press, 1951), p. viii.
3. George S. Pettee, *The Future of American Secret Intelligence* (Washington, D. C.: Infantry Journal Press, 1946). See also Mark S. Watson, *The War Department: Chief of Staff, Prewar Plans and Preparations,* Department of the Army, Office of the Chief of Military History (Washington, D. C.: Government Printing Office, 1950), pp. 505-519.
4. *U. S. News and World Report,* March 19, 1954, p. 65.
5. William J. Donovan, "Intelligence: Key to Defense," *Life,* September 30, 1946, p. 114.
6. Harold Nicholson, "Intelligence Services: Their Use and Misuse," *Harper's,* November 1957, pp. 18-19.
7. Captain Ellis M. Zacharias, USN, *Secret Missions, the Story of an Intelligence Officer* (New York: G. P. Putnam's Sons, 1946), pp. 117-118.
8. Senator Richard B. Russell, *Congressional Record* (daily edition), April 11, 1956, p. 5413.

9. Quoted in *U. S. News and World Report,* May 25, 1956, p. 52.

10. Quoted in David Wise and Thomas B. Ross, *The Invisible Government* (New York: Random House, 1964), p. 208.

11. Details of this affair are given dramatically but with apparent authenticity in L. G. Moyzisch, *Operation Cicero* (London: Wingate Press, 1950). When this book was published, British Foreign Secretary Ernest Bevin admitted that these events had occurred in Ankara during the war. See *The Times* (London), October 19, 1950; also *New York Times* of same date.

12. Alexander McKee, *Black Saturday* (New York: Holt, Rinehart & Winston, 1960).

13. *U. S. News and World Report,* March 19, 1954, p. 62.

14. See the *Report* of the Canadian Royal Commission to Investigate Disclosures of Secret and Confidential Information, Ottawa, 1946; also *Report* of the Australian Royal Commission on Espionage, Sydney, 1955; also for details on United States, *Subversive and Illegal Aliens in the U. S.,* Progress Report of Senate Internal Security Subcommittee, 82nd Cong., 1st sess. Washington, D. C., 1951.

15. *New York Times,* August 8, 1957.

16. *Ibid.,* August 10, 1957. For a detailed description of Abel and his activities, see Frank Gibney, "Intimate Portrait of a Russian Master Spy," *Life,* November 11, 1957, pp. 123-130.

17. See Robert Eunson, "How We Nabbed Russia's No. 1 Spy," *Saturday Evening Post,* September 25, 1954, pp. 27ff. See also "How Red Titans Fought for Supreme Power," *Life,* November 29 and December 6, 1954, pp. 18-21 and 174-176.

18. Quoted in *Subversive and Illegal Aliens in the United States, p.* 1.

19. *Congressional Record* (daily edition), May 6, 1953, pp. 6547-6548.

20. Department of State Press Release, No. 411, July 22, 1960.

21. Details emanating from the trial of the Oxford students are found in *The Times* (London) for May 22, 1958.

22. Department of State Press Release, No. 246, May 19, 1964.

23. "The CIA—Maker of Policy, or Tool?" April 25, 1966, p. 20.

24. Senator Leverett Saltonstall, *Congressional Record* (daily edition), April 9, 1956, p. 5291.

25. Harry S Truman, *Memoirs,* vol. I, *Year of Decisions* (Garden City, N. Y.: Doubleday, 1955), p. 226.

26. Hanson W. Baldwin, *The Price of Power,* Council on Foreign Relations (New York: Harper, 1947), p. 205.

27. See, for example, Hanson Baldwin's article "Myopia on Intelligence," *New York Times,* June 3, 1954. Over the years the *Times* has been sharply critical of the intelligence system.

28. Harry S Truman, *Memoirs,* vol. II: *Years of Trial and Hope* (Garden City, N. Y.: Doubleday, 1956), p. 452.

29. "Exposé of Soviet Espionage," prepared by the Federal Bureau of Investigation, 86th Cong., 2nd sess., Senate Document no. 114, July 2, 1960, p. 7.

30. Interview with Allen W. Dulles, "We Tell Russia Too Much," *U. S. News and World Report,* March 19, 1954, p. 62; see also Murray Green, "Intelligence for Sale at the Corner Newstand," *Air Force,* November 1955, pp. 82-86.

31. Dulles, *The Craft of Intelligence,* p. 240.

32. Quoted in Arthur M. MacMahon, *Administration in Foreign Affairs* (University, Ala.: University of Alabama Press, 1953), p. 86.

33. For a detailed discussion of these categories see Kent, *Strategic Intelligence,* pp. 11-68.

34. *Ibid.,* p. 11.

35. Admiral William F. Raborn, *U. S. News and World Report,* July 18, 1966, p. 76.

36. Kent, *Strategic Intelligence,* p. 38.

37. For a discussion of this problem between members of Congress and Air Force officials in 1957, see *Hearings,* "Department of Defense Appropriations for 1958," House Subcommittee on Appropriations, 85th Cong., 1st sess., pt. I, Washington, D. C., 1957, pp. 1062-1064, 1121.

38. "Documentation, Indexing and Retrieval of Scientific Information," *Report,* Senate Committee on Government Operations, 86th Cong., 2d sess., May 24, 1960, p. 16.

39. *Ibid.,* pp. 63-65.

40. Hoover Commission, *Intelligence Activities,* p. 66.

41. For a full discussion of this system and the problems of evaluation see Kent, *Strategic Intelligence,* pp. 168-174. The system more recently in use by CIA is very likely more elaborate than the one here described.

42. Theodore Sorensen, *Kennedy* (New York: Harper & Row, 1965), p. 673.

43. Truman, *Memoirs,* II, 306.

44. Pettee, *American Secret Intelligence,* p. 78.

45. Admiral Arthur Radford, in *Hearings,* "Study of Airpower," Senate Armed Forces Subcommittee on the Air Force, 84th Cong., 2nd sess., pt. XIX, Washington, D. C., June 21, 1956, p. 1460.

46. In *Time,* August 28, 1950; quoted in Alfred Vagts, *Defense and Diplomacy* (New York: King's Crown Press, 1956), p. 77, n.92.

47. *Report,* Joint Committee on the Investigation of the Pearl Harbor Attack, 79th Cong., 2nd sess., 1946, pp. 179-181.

48. *Report,* Pearl Harbor Attack, p. 225.

49. Walter Lord, *Day of Infamy* (New York: Henry Holt, 1957), pp. 174-175.

50. Truman, *Memoirs,* II, 58.

51. *Hearings,* "Department of Defense Appropriations for 1958," House Subcommittee on Appropriations, 85th Cong., 1st sess., pt. I, Washington, D. C., 1957, pp. 962-963.

CHAPTER III: UNITED STATES INTELLIGENCE: HISTORICAL BACKGROUND

1. *Hearings.* "Department of Armed Forces," 79th Cong., 1st sess., Senate Committee on Military Affairs, October 18, 1945, Washington, D. C., 1945, p. 61.

2. Numbers 13:20.

3. Allen W. Dulles, *The Craft of Intelligence,* p. 13.

4. Michael Prawdin, *The Mongol Empire* (London: G. Allen, 1940), p. 254, quoted in R. Ernest Dupuy and Trevor N. Dupuy, *Military Heritage of America* (New York: McGraw-Hill, 1956), p. 56.

5. R. V. Jones, "Scientific Intelligence," *Journal of Royal United Service Institution,* August 1947, p. 352.

6. Quoted in Alfred Vagts, *Defense and Diplomacy* (New York: Columbia University Press, 1956), p. 62.

7. For a general survey of diplomacy, military intelligence, and espionage over the past several centuries, see Vagts, *Defense and Diplomacy,* pp. 61-71.

8. Roger Hilsman, Jr., *Strategic Intelligence and National Decisions* (Glencoe, Ill.: Free Press, 1956), p. 19.

9. Vagts, *Defense and Diplomacy,* p. 65.

10. Department of the Army, *American Military History, 1607-1953,* ROTC Manual 145-20, Washington, D. C., 1956, p. 491.

11. *The Craft of Intelligence,* p. 37.

12. See Jacob D. Cox, *Military Reminiscences of the Civil War* (New York: Scribner's, 1900), I, 250ff.; also Bruce Catton, *This Hollowed Ground* (Garden City, N. Y.: Doubleday, 1956), pp. 87, 138; James D. Horan and Howard Swiggett, *The Pinkerton Story* (New York: Putnam, 1951), esp. chap. 4. For a colorful account of intelligence activities within the Confederacy, see Harnett T. Kane, *Spies for the Blue and Gray* (Garden City, N. Y.: Hanover House, 1954).

13. Quoted in Richard Fenno, *The President's Cabinet* (Cambridge, Mass.: Harvard University Press, 1958), p. 101. See also Josephus Daniels, *The Wilson Era* (Chapel Hill: University of North Carolina Press, 1946), II, 628-629, 615-632.

14. Peyton C. March, *The Nation at War* (Garden City, N. Y.: Doubleday, Doran, 1932), p. 226.

15. March, *The Nation at War,* p. 229.

16. General Orders No. 80, War Department, August 26, 1918, quoted in Otto L. Nelson, *National Security and the General Staff* (Washington, D. C.: Infantry Journal Press, 1946), p. 264.

17. General Orders No. 80, quoted in Nelson, *National Security and the General Staff,* p. 265.

18. "The Military Intelligence Division," *Journal of the United States Artillery,* April 1920, p. 296, quoted in Nelson, *National Security and the General Staff,* p. 265. For a fuller discussion of military intelligence, but one which did not appreciate the need for coordinated, national intelligence, see, Lt. Col. Walter C. Sweeney, *Military Intelligence* (New York: Stokes, 1924).

19. Dwight D. Eisenhower, *Crusade in Europe* (Garden City, N. Y.: Doubleday, 1948), p. 32.

20. Eisenhower, *Crusade in Europe,* p. 32.

21. Sir John Slessor, *The Central Blue* (London: Cassell, 1956), p. 402.

22. Quoted in Pettee, *American Secret Intelligence,* pp. 36-37.

23. Elias Huzar, *The Purse and the Sword* (Ithaca, N. Y.: Cornell University Press, 1950), p. 211.

24. Industrial College of the Armed Forces, *Emergency Management of the National Economy,* vol. XV: *Economic Intelligence and Economic Warfare* (Washington, D. C., 1954), p. 37.

25. General Omar N. Bradley, *A Soldier's Story* (New York: Henry Holt, 1951), p. 33.

26. John P. Marquand, *Melville Goodwin, U. S. A.* (Boston: Little, Brown, 1951), p. 346.

27. See Report, Joint Committee on the Investigation of the Pearl Harbor Attack, 79th Cong., 2nd sess., Senate Document No. 244, July 20, 1946. See also Samuel Eliot Morison's account in his *History of United States Naval Operations in World War II,* vol. III: *The Rising Sun in the Pacific* (Boston: Little, Brown, 1941), chap. 5. A large number of other books deal with this episode.

28. The degree of surprise is clearly seen in Walter Lord, *Day of Infamy.*

29. For a detailed account of naval intelligence available prior to the attack, see Walter Millis, *This is Pearl!* (New York: Morrow, 1947); also, Ellis M. Zacharias, *Secret Missions,* pp. 253ff.

30. Roberta Wohlstetter, *Pearl Harbor: Warning and Decision* (Stanford, Calif.: Stanford University Press, 1962), p. 387.

31. *Ibid.,* p. 389.

32. "Cuba and Pearl Harbor: Hindsight and Foresight," RAND Memorandum RM-4328-ISA, April 1965, p. vi.

33. Quoted in Arthur M. Schlesinger, Jr., *A Thousand Days* (Boston: Houghton Mifflin, 1965), p. 800.

34. *Intelligence Activities,* pp. 29-30.

35. For an account of the intelligence failure at Pearl Harbor, see Rear Adm. Robert A. Theobald, *The Final Secret of Pearl Harbor* (New York: Devin-Adair, 1954), esp. pp. 32-125. One need not accept his implausible thesis regarding President Roosevelt's motives in this episode to appreciate his detailed account of events.

36. Donovan, "Intelligence: Key to Defense," *Life,* September 30, 1946, p. 110. Other than popularized accounts there are few authentic sources depicting the history of the OSS. One useful but uncritical study, based upon some of the private "Donovan Papers" is an unpublished doctoral dissertation by James G. Kellis, "The Development of U. S. Intelligence, 1941-1961," Georgetown University, Washington, D. C., October 26, 1962.

37. See "Unification of the War and Navy Departments and Postwar Organization for National Security," Report to Secretary of the Navy [Eberstadt to Forrestal], Committee Print of the Senate Committee on Naval Affairs, 79th Cong., 1st sess., Washington, D. C., 1945 (hereafter cited as Eberstadt Report). See esp. pp. 159-163.

38. For a brief review of these arrangements, see Eberstadt Report, pp. 159-163.

39. See Allen W. Dulles, *Germany's Underground* (New York: Macmillan, 1947).

40. Allen W. Dulles, *Secret Surrender* (New York: Harper & Row, 1966). Chapter 1 gives a brief sketch of the origins of OSS.

41. An interesting post-factum intelligence operation was the United States Strategic Bombing Survey, which surveyed Allied bombing in Europe, following closely behind advancing Allied armies. The aim was to produce intelligence useful in the strategic bombing of Japan. But victory in the Pacific soon followed, and a comparable USSBS study was made in Japan. The resulting analyses comprise 208 separate published items for the European Theater and 108 for the war in the Pacific. For a concise analysis

of these surveys, see Bernard Brodie, *Strategic Air Power in World War II*, Research Memorandum 1866, RAND Corporation, Santa Monica, California, February 4, 1957.

42. For an argument, bitterly stated, that adequate intelligence was available prior to the Battle of the Bulge but that commanders ignored it, see Robert S. Allen, *Lucky Forward* (New York: Vanguard, 1947), pp. 206-217.

43. See Louis Morton, "The Decision to Use the Atomic Bomb," *Foreign Affairs*, January 1957, pp. 342-344.

44. See James G. Kellis, "The Development of U. S. National Intelligence, 1941-1961," 1963, p. 48ff.

45. The Donovan Papers, as cited in Kellis (see n. 44).

46. The Donovan Papers, January 3, 1943, OSS Reorganization Order, as quoted in Kellis (see n. 44), p. 60.

47. These are the words of Stewart Alsop and Thomas Braden in their *Sub Rosa* (New York: Reynal and Hitchcock, 1946), p. 23.

48. Henry A. Murray and others of the assessment staff, Office of Strategic Services, *Assessment of Men* (New York: Rinehart, 1947, 1950), p. 10.

49. For personal and somewhat melodramatic accounts, in addition to the valuable Kellis dissertation cited above, see: Stewart Alsop and Thomas Braden, *Sub Rosa;* Corey Ford and Alastair MacBain, *Cloak and Dagger* (New York: Random House, 1946); and William J. Morgan, *The OSS and I* (New York: Norton, 1957).

50. For details, see Alsop and Braden, *Sub Rosa*, pp. 228 and 230.

51. *Ibid.*, p. 15. Later, in 1951, MacArthur reportedly took a dim view of CIA agents operating within his Far Eastern Command. For an explanation of MacArthur's attitude, see Maj. Gen. Charles A. Willoughby and John Chamberlain, *MacArthur 1941-1951* (New York: McGraw-Hill, 1954), pp. 144ff. Willoughby was MacArthur's intelligence chief. The book also contains a detailed account of the so-called Allied Intelligence Bureau (AIB) which operated in the Southwest Pacific during the war.

52. Baldwin, *The Price of Power*, p. 205. Baldwin's reference to Switzerland is an implicit tribute to Allen W. Dulles.

53. See M. R. D. Foot, *SOE in France* (London: Her Majesty's Stationery Office, 1966). This is the Government Series *History of the Second World War*.

54. "The Battlefields of Power and the Searchlights of the Academy," in *The Dimensions of Diplomacy*, ed. E. A. J. Johnson (Baltimore, Md.: Johns Hopkins Press, 1964), pp. 2-3.

55. Murray et al., *Assessment of Men* (New York: Rinehart, 1947, 1950).

56. Truman, *Memoirs*, II, 56.

57. *Ibid.*

58. Eberstadt Report, p. 163.

59. *Ibid.*

60. See Truman, *Memoirs*, II, 57.

61. Walter Millis, ed., *The Forrestal Diaries* (New York: Viking, 1951), p. 37.

62. A document which figured importantly in these events was "Intelligence and Security Activities of the Government," Report to the President by the Bureau of the Budget, Washington, September 20, 1945.

63. Truman, *Memoirs*, II, 58.

64. *Hearings*, "National Security Act of 1947," House Committee on Expenditures in the Executive Departments, 80th Cong., 1st sess., 1947, p. 121.

CHAPTER IV: THE CENTRAL INTELLIGENCE AGENCY: BASIC FUNCTIONS

1. See Allen W. Dulles, *The Craft of Intelligence,* chap. 15, "The Role of Intelligence in the Cold War," esp. pp. 220-225.

2. For Congressman Fred Busbey's questioning of Secretary Forrestal, see *Hearings*, "National Security Act of 1947," House Committee on Expenditures in the Executive Departments, 80th Cong., 1st sess., Washington, D. C., 1947, p. 120.

3. "The Central Intelligence Agency," brochure published by the agency, 1965 ed., p. 5.

4. Northcote Parkinson, *Parkinson's Law* (Boston: Hougton Mifflin, 1957).

5. Title I, Section 102, 61 *Stat.* 495.

6. 63 *Stat.* 308, approved by the Congress June 20, 1949.

7. The CIA is said, however, to have taken administrative measures to control strictly its expenditures, and to require a complete accounting for the use of all its funds, vouchered or unvouchered. Information about this system and details on use of funds are supplied each year to appropriations subcommittees of the House and Senate. See Senate Report No. 1570, 84th Cong., 2nd sess., "Individual Views of Mr. Hayden," February 23, 1956, p. 26.

8. For an example of such speculation see articles by Hanson W. Baldwin, *New York Times,* June 3 and August 3, 1954.

9. Quoted in Schlesinger, *A Thousand Days,* p. 276.

10. See Kent, *Strategic Intelligence,* pp. 91-94, a part of his brilliant and provocative chapter "Intelligence is Organization."

11. *A Thousand Days,* p. 428.

12. General MacArthur described such allegations as "pure bunkum," but they have persisted and seem to be verified by other accounts. See *Hearings,* "Military Situation in the Far East," Senate Armed Services and Foreign Relations Committees, pt. I, Washington, D. C., 1951, p. 241.

13. Donald Robinson, "They Fight the Cold War under Cover," *Saturday Evening Post,* November 20, 1948, p. 191. For a later account, along similar lines, see Richard and Gladys Harkness, "The Mysterious Doings of CIA," a three-part series in *Saturday Evening Post,* October 30, November 6 and 13, 1954.

14. Enno Hobbing, "CIA: Hottest Role in the Cold War," *Esquire,* September 1957, p. 31.

15. "How the CIA Put an 'Instant Air Force' Into Congo," *New York Times,* April 26, 1966, p. 1.

16. See "CIA Operations: A Plot Scuttled," *New York Times,* April 28, 1966, p. 1.

17. Truman, *Memoirs,* II, 372.

18. For a more detailed discussion see Harry Howe Ransom, *Can American Democracy Survive Cold War?* (New York: Doubleday, 1963), pp. 145-167.

19. "Interim Report on the Cuban Missile Buildup," U. S. Senate, Preparedness Investigating Subcommittee, 88th Cong., 1st sess., Washington, D. C., 1963, p. 2.

20. Kent, *Strategic Intelligence,* pp. 90-95.

21. *Ibid.,* pp. 95-96.

22. Hilsman, *Strategic Intelligence and National Decisions,* p. 33.

23. The CIA does not officially admit engagement in espionage or overseas political action, yet these clearly are functions of the agency, performed under explicit or tacit National Security Council directive.

24. Russell Baker, "The Other Mr. Dulles—of the C.I.A." *New York Times Magazine,* March 16, 1958, p. 17.

25. Quoted by Warren Unna, in "CIA: Who Watches the Watchman?" *Harper's,* April 1958, p. 46. For a detailed statement of Mr. Dulles' views on CIA, as of 1947, see Appendix A.

CHAPTER V: THE INTELLIGENCE COMMUNITY: OTHER PRINCIPAL MEMBERS

1. *Intelligence Activities,* p. 13.

2. Quoted in *Hearings,* Senate Defense Appropriations Subcommittee, 87th Cong., 2nd sess., "Department of Defense Appropriations for 1963," Washington, D. C., 1962, p. 682.

3. From Department of Defense Directive No. 5105.21, August 1, 1961.

4. This program was outlined in *Hearings,* "Department of Defense Appropriations for 1965," Senate Appropriations Subcommittee, 88th Cong., 2nd sess., pt. 2, Washington, D. C., 1964, pp. 727-730.

5. *Hearings,* "Department of Defense Appropriations for Fiscal Year 1967," Senate Appropriations Subcommittee, 89th Cong., 2nd sess., pt. 2, Washington, D. C., 1966, p. 432.

6. *Hearings,* "Department of Defense Appropriations for 1958," Senate Appropriations Subcommittee, 85th Cong., 1st sess., Washington, D. C., 1957, p. 796.

7. For a detailed account of G-2 structure and function during World War II, see Otto L. Nelson, *National Security and the General Staff,* pp. 521-535.

8. For a detailed account of the concepts underlying the 1944 reorganization, see *ibid.,* pp. 527-531.

9. For a chart of this organization, see *ibid.,* p. 333.

10. Hoover Commission, *National Security Organization,* Appendix G, Washington, D. C., January 1949, p. 77.

11. *Hearings,* "Department of Army Appropriations for 1956," House Appropriations Subcommittee, 84th Cong., 1st sess., Washington, D. C., 1955, p. 518.

12. These data are based on information given in *Hearings,* "Department of Defense Appropriations for 1958," Senate Appropriations Subcommittee, 85th Cong., 1st sess., Washington, D. C., 1957, pp. 795-796.

13. Army Regulation 10-5, Paragraph 38(a), May 1965.

14. "The Army's Newest Branch," *Army Information Digest,* August 1962, pp. 2-8.

15. This information is based upon details given in *Hearings,* "Department of the Army Appropriations for 1957," House Appropriations Subcommittee, 84th Cong., 2nd sess., Washington, D. C., 1956, pp. 409ff.

16. See *Hearings,* "Department of the Army Appropriations for 1957," *ibid.,* p. 396.

17. *Hearings,* "Department of Defense Appropriations for 1958," (n. 12 above), p. 796.

18. General Order 292, 23 March 1882 as quoted in Captain W. H. Packard, "A Briefing on Naval Intelligence," *All Hands,* April 1966, p. 15.

19. Samuel Eliot Morison, *History of United States Naval Operations in World War II,* vol. II: *Operations in North African Waters* (1947), p. 26.

20. Zacharias, *Secret Missions.*

21. *Ibid.,* p. 82.

22. *Ibid.,* p. 83.

23. Morison, *History of United States Naval Operations,* vol. III: *The Rising Sun in the Pacific,* p. 134.

24. Hoover Commission, *Intelligence Activities,* pp. 37-38.

25. Wesley F. Craven and James L. Cate, eds., *The Army Air Forces in World War II,* vol. I: *Plans and Early Operations* (Chicago, Ill.: University of Chicago Press, 1948), p. 625.

26. General Henry H. Arnold, *Global Mission* (New York: Harper, 1949), p. 169.

27. Craven and Cate, *The Army Air Forces,* vol. VI: *Men and Planes,* pp. 480-481.

28. Air University, Research Studies Institute, "Development of Intelligence Function in U.S.A.F., 1917-1950," by Victor H. Cohen, Special Studies Report, January 1, 1957. The study itself is classified SECRET.

29. These quotations are from *Third Report of the Commanding General of the Army Air Forces,* to the Secretary of War, Washington, D. C., November 12, 1945.

30. For a review of World War II problems in processing intelligence data see Maj. Charles H. Barber, "Some Problems of Air Intelligence," *Military Review,* August 1946, pp. 76-78; see also Constance Babington-Smith, *Air Spy* (New York: Harper, 1957). For an analysis of factors influencing the selection of targets see Col. John H. DeRussy "Selecting Target Systems and Targets," *Air University Quarterly Review,* Spring 1947, pp. 69-78.

31. For details of cryptography in the Renaissance see Garrett Mattingly, *Renaissance Diplomacy,* pp. 247-250; also J. W. Thompson and S. K. Padover, *Secret Diplomacy, A Record of Espionage and Double-dealing: 1500-1815* (London, Jarrolds, 1937), esp. pp. 253-263.

32. *Congressional Record,* daily ed., July 28, 1966, p. 16679.

33. Timothy W. Stanley, *American Defense and National Security* (Washington, D. C.: Public Affairs Press, 1956), p. 27, n. 24, and p. 35.

34. See *New York Times,* November 10, 1954.

35. "Security Practices in the National Security Agency," *Report,* House Committee on Un-American Activities, 87th Cong., 2nd sess., August 13, 1962, pp. 2-3.

36. David Kahn, *The Code Breakers* (New York: Macmillan, 1967), p. 694.

37. "Security Practices in the NSA" (n. 35 above), p. 4. Some additional details are disclosed in David Kahn's monumental and unique history of secret communications, *The Code Breakers*. See especially chap. 19. A more recent and superficial treatment is Andrew Tully, *The Super Spies* (New York: Morrow, 1969).

38. *New York Times,* March 22, 1966.

39. Kahn, *Code Breakers,* p. 718.

40. For speculative details, see *ibid.,* chap. 19.

41. The most detailed description and breakdown of NSA organizational structure is to be found in Kahn, *Code Breakers,* pp. 702-733.

42. *Code Breakers,* p. 677.

43. See Herbert O. Yardley, *The American Black Chamber* (Indianapolis, Ind.: Bobbs-Merrill, 1931).

44. Kahn, *Code Breakers,* p. 688.

45. James L. McCamy, *The Administration of American Foreign Affairs* (New York: Knopf, 1952), p. 282.

46. Quoted in John Osborne, "Is the State Department Manageable?" *Fortune,* March 1957, p. 112.

47. Letter reprinted in *Hearing,* "Interlocking Subversion in Government Departments," Senate Judiciary Internal Security Subcommittee, 83rd Cong., 1st sess., pt. 13, Washington, D.C., June 25, 1953, p. 870.

48. Hoover Commission, *Foreign Affairs,* Task Force Report, Appendix H, January 1949, p. 91.

49. *Foreign Affairs,* Task Force Report, pp. 92-93.

50. *Ibid.,* p. 93.

51. For a detailed argument on this and related points, see McCormack's State Department Memorandum of February 12, 1946. This is reproduced as Exhibit No. 263, *Hearing,* "Interlocking Subversion in Government Departments," pt. 13 (n. 47 above), pp. 856-860. See also counterarguments of Donald Russell and others, pp. 865-869 and passim.

52. Hilsman, *Strategic Intelligence and National Decisions,* pp. 51-55.

53. As quoted in *Look,* September 6, 1966, p. 16.

54. *Congressional Record,* daily ed., May 13, 1963, p. 7790.

55. Allan Evans, "Research in Action, The Department of State's Bureau of Intelligence and Research," Department of State Publication 7964, September 1965, p. 6.

56. *Ibid.,* pp. 10-11.

57. See Don Whitehead, *The FBI Story* (New York: Random House, 1956), pp. 166-167.

58. For details, see *ibid.,* pp. 210-220.

59. *Ibid.,* esp. p. 347, n. 3.

60. Other agencies playing an important, if lesser, role in intelligence include the Treasury Department, with its numerous subagencies; the Department of Justice; Post Office Department; Interior, Agriculture, and Commerce departments; the Agency for International Development; the Federal Communications Commission; and, not least in importance, the United States Information Agency.

CHAPTER VI: INTELLIGENCE END PRODUCT: THE NATIONAL ESTIMATE

1. *Military Review,* May 1961, p. 20. See also Lyman Kirkpatrick, *The Real CIA* (New York: Macmillan, 1968), pp. 104-106.

2. *New York Times,* August 28, 1957.

3. For details on powerful long-range radar units based in Turkey and tracking Russian missile launchings, see "How U. S. Taps Soviet Missile Secrets," *Aviation Week,* October 21, 1957, pp. 26-27.

4. See Vagts, *Defense and Diplomacy,* p. 72.

5. News conference, October 30, 1957, transcribed in *New York Times,* October 31, 1957.

6. Admiral William F. Raborn, interview, *U. S. News and World Report,* July 19, 1966, "What's CIA?" p. 77.

7. See Winston S. Churchill, *The Grand Alliance* (Boston: Houghton Mifflin, 1950), pp. 356-358.

8. This issue was touched on at the 1956 Symington Hearings when General Twining was testifying on Soviet air capabilities. Remarked Senator Symington: "We want no intelligence that is not national intelligence." See *Hearings,* "Study of Airpower," Senate Armed Services Subcommittee on the Air Force, 84th Cong., 2nd sess., p. 1814.

9. In *U. S. News and World Report,* March 19, 1954, p. 66.

10. For details, see Robert J. Donovan, *The Inside Story* (New York: Harper, 1956), pp. 40-41.

CHAPTER VII: SURVEILLANCE BY CONGRESS

1. In *U. S. News and World Report,* March 19, 1954, p. 67.

2. Interview, *U. S. News and World Report,* July 18, 1966, p. 79.

3. *Congressional Record* (daily edition), April 11, 1956, p. 5424. All *Congressional Record* references in this chapter are to the daily edition.

4. S. Con. Res. 2, 84th Cong., 1st sess., January 14, 1955.

5. For a more recent bill see, among fifteen others, H.R. 211, 85th Cong., 1st sess., January 3, 1957, by Representative Marguerite Stitt Church, "To Establish a Joint Committee on Foreign Intelligence." Senator Mansfield, with 20 co-sponsors, had introduced a similar resolution in the 83rd Congress.

6. *Senate Report No. 1570,* "Joint Committee on Central Intelligence Agency," Committee on Rules and Administration, 84th Cong., 2nd sess., February 23, 1956, p. 2.

7. *Senate Report No. 1570.*

8. *Ibid.,* pp. 17-18.

9. *Ibid.,* pp. 19-20.

10. Quotation from a letter of Senator Richard B. Russell to the Chairman of the Senate Committee on Rules and Administration.

11. *Senate Report No. 1570,* p. 24.

12. *Ibid.*

13. *Ibid.,* p. 28.

14. *Ibid.,* p. 24.

15. *Ibid.,* p. 28.

16. *Congressional Record,* April 9, 1956, p. 5298.

17. *Ibid.,* p. 5297.
18. *Ibid.,* p. 5290.
19. *Ibid.,* p. 5294.
20. *Ibid.,* pp. 5305-5306.
21. *Ibid.,* p. 5305.
22. *Ibid.,* p. 5419.
23. *Ibid.,* p. 5413.
24. *Ibid.,* p. 5292.
25. *Ibid.,* p. 5291.
26. The Armed Services Subcommittee was composed in 1956, of Senators Russell, Byrd, Bridges, Saltonstall, and Lyndon Johnson. The Appropriations Subcommittee included Senators Saltonstall, Hayden, Chavez, Russell, and Bridges.
27. *Congressional Record,* April 9, 1956, p. 5416.
28. *Ibid.,* p. 5415.
29. *Ibid.*
30. *Ibid.,* p. 5431.
31. William S. White, *The Citadel: The Story of the U. S. Senate* (New York: Harper, 1956), p. 87. As Senator Mansfield later explained his measure's defeat: "What you had was a brash freshman going up against the high brass." Quoted in Warren Unna, "CIA: Who Watches the Watchman?", p. 46.
32. *Congressional Record,* August 15, 1963, pp. 14268-14270.
33. *Ibid.,* January 29, 1962, pp. 933-935.
34. See Roger Hilsman, *To Move a Nation* (Garden City, N. Y.: Doubleday, 1967), p. 81.
35. *Congressional Record,* 89th Cong., 2nd sess., July 27, 1966, p. 14930. For a detailed account of the issue of congressional surveillance, see Gary Sperling, "Central Intelligence and Its Control: Curbing Secret Power in a Democratic Society," in 89th Cong., 2nd sess., *Congressional Record,* vol. 112, part 12, July 14, 1966, pp. 15758-15766.
36. Quoted in *New York Times,* June 12, 1966.
37. *U. S. News and World Report,* July 18, 1966, p. 79.
38. *Congressional Record,* 89th Cong., 2nd sess., July 14, 1966, p. 14930.
39. *Ibid.,* p. 14931.
40. *Ibid.,* p. 10128.
41. *Ibid.,* p. 10132.
42. *Ibid.,* p. 10123.
43. *Ibid.,* July 14, 1967, p. 14936.
44. *Time,* July 22, 1966, p. 21.
45. *New York Times,* January 8, 1967.
46. J. W. Fulbright, "We Must Not Fight Fire with Fire," *The New York Times Magazine,* April 23, 1967, p. 129.
47. See *New York Times,* February 25, 1967.

CHAPTER VIII: THE BRITISH INTELLIGENCE SYSTEM

1. This chapter is a considerably revised version of an essay published as "Great Britain's Secret, Secret Service," in *Midway,* 8:19-35 (1967), © 1967 by the University of Chicago. Published with permission.

2. "Behind the Bureaucratic Curtain," *New York Times Magazine,* October 23, 1966, pp. 74, 76.

3. *Renaissance Diplomacy* (Boston: Houghton Mifflin), 1955, p. 260.

4. *Observer* (London), May 30, 1965, p. 21.

5. *Sunday Times* (London), October 8, 1967, p. 23.

6. For details see: M. R. D. Foot, *SOE in France* (London: H.M.S.O., 1966); and E. H. Cookridge, *Set Europe Ablaze* (New York: Thomas Y. Crowell, 1967).

7. "The Philby Conspiracy," *Sunday Times* (London), October 8, 1967, p. 23.

8. New York, Atheneum, 1968.

9. The most detailed information to be found on the British intelligence system is in Bruce Page, David Leitch, and Phillip Knightley, *The Philby Conspiracy* (New York: Doubleday, 1968). See also Hugh Trevor-Roper, *The Philby Affair* (London: Kimber, 1968). Of great interest also is Kim Philby, *My Silent War* (London: MacGibbon and Kee, 1968) esp. chap. III.

10. *House of Common Debates,* May 14, 1956, 552, 5th series, column 1751.

11. *Ibid.,* column 1751.

12. *Sunday Times* (London), October 22, p. 47.

13. *British Government Observed* (London: Allen & Unwin, 1963), p. 29.

14. Dulles, *The Craft of Intelligence* (Harper & Row, 1963), p. 245.

15. London: Hutchinson, 1965, p. 208. See also Williams' "Official Secrecy in England," *The Federal Law Review,* vol. 3, no. 1, June 1968, pp. 20-50.

16. As published in Alan Watkins, "Mr. Wilson and the Press," *Spectator,* No. 7236 (March 3, 1967), p. 239.

17. For a discussion of this episode, see *Report,* Committee of Privy Counsellors appointed to inquire into "D" Notice matters, Command 3309 (London: H.M.S.O., June 1967), pp. 24-26.

18. *Daily Express* (London), February 21, 1967, p. 1.

19. See *Report,* Committee of Privy Counsellors appointed to inquire into "D" Notice matters (London: H.M.S.O., June 1967), Command 3309.

20. "The 'D' Notice System" (London: H.M.S.O., June 1967), Command 3312, p. 3. For a journalistic account of the 1967 "D-Notice" controversy, written from an antigovernment and pro-*Daily Express* viewpoint, see Peter Hedley and Cyril Aynsley, *The D-Notice Affair* (London: Michael Joseph, 1967).

21. *Ibid.*

22. Command 3312, June 1967, p. 13.

23. *Ibid.*

24. Pierre Salinger, *With Kennedy* (New York: Doubleday, 1966), p. 158

25. As quoted in Salinger, *With Kennedy,* p. 155.

CHAPTER IX: PROBLEMS OF THE INTELLIGENCE BUREAUCRACY

1. The 1955 Hoover Commission made 62 recommendations for changes in the intelligence structure and procedure within the Department of Defense

alone. A majority of these changes, most of which are classified information, had been made by early 1957. See *Hearings,* "Department of Defense Appropriations for 1958," House Subcommittee on Appropriations, Washington, 1957, pt. I, p. 166.

2. A director of the Department of State's policy planning staff from 1953-1957 has disclosed that the policy-making process starts with an "appraisal of the external situation. This is known as intelligence." For development of this point see Robert R. Bowie, "Analysis of Our Policy Machine," *New York Times Magazine,* March 9, 1958, p. 16. For more theoretical discussions of decision making, see, among others, R. C. Snyder, H. W. Bruck, and Burton Sapin, *Decision-Making as an Approach to the Study of International Policies,* Foreign Policy Analysis Project, No. 3, Princeton University, 1954.

3. Statement to United States Senate, Committee on Armed Services, February 1, 1968.

4. As an example, from a period when such figures were available, the Army's intelligence budget request was 92 million dollars in 1956; 100 million dollars in 1957; and 125 million dollars in 1958.

5. See Tom Wicker, *JFK and LBJ* (Baltimore, Md.: Penguin Books, 1968), p. 229.

6. For an authentic account of this cleverly devised and executed operation, see Ewen Montague, *The Man Who Never Was* (Philadelphia: Lippincott, 1954).

7. "U. S. Army Credits Soviet With Lead," by Jack Raymond, *New York Times,* July 7, 1957.

8. *New York Times,* March 24, 1969, p. 30.

9. Address before the Los Angeles World Affairs Council, April 13, 1956; reprinted in *Department of State Bulletin,* May 7, 1956, p. 758.

10. For an incisive account of intelligence use and abuse in this period of the Korean War, see S. L. A. Marshall, *The River and the Gauntlet* (New York: Morrow, 1953), esp. pages 1-17.

11. Robert E. Merriam, *Dark December* (Chicago and New York: Ziff-Davis, 1947), p. 99. A more recent and detailed analysis, including a defense of the intelligence performance in December 1944, is found in Sir Kenneth Strong, *Intelligence at the Top* (London: Cassell, 1968), pp. 154-180.

12. Lyman B. Kirkpatrick, Jr., *The Real CIA* (New York: Macmillan, 1968), p. 55.

13. Truman, *Memoirs,* II, 331. For another side of this story, see Willoughby and Chamberlain, *MacArthur, 1941-1951,* pp. 354ff. For a discussion of the Korean War intelligence performance, see Harry Howe Ransom, *Can American Democracy Survive Cold War?* (New York: Doubleday, 1963), chap. VI.

14. "Intelligence," first of a series of five articles, *New York Times,* July 20-25, 1948.

15. *Intelligence Activities,* Report of the Hoover Commission, p. 70.

16. For a detailed account of the selection and training of OSS agents in an earlier decade, see "A Good Man Is Hard to Find," *Fortune,* March 1946, pp. 92-95ff.; also Murray et al., *Assessment of Men.*

17. *Intelligence Activities,* p. 70. For a detailed and revealing discussion

of personnel "fringe benefits" in CIA, see *Hearings* "Consideration of H.R. 7216, to Amend the CIA Act of 1949," House Committee on Armed Services, Subcommittee No. 1, Document No. 26, Washington, D. C., July 23, 1963.

18. *Intelligence Activities,* p. 59.

19. Task Force Report, *National Security Organization,* Appendix G, January 1949, p. 76.

20. Kirkpatrick, *The Real CIA,* p. 224.

21. Others were William H. Jackson, New York lawyer and wartime intelligence officer, and Mathias F. Correa, a former OSS official.

22. For background information on these disputes see Hanson W. Baldwin, series of five articles on "Intelligence," *New York Times,* July 20-July 25, 1948.

23. Other members were William B. Franke, former Assistant Secretary of the Navy; Morris Hadley, New York lawyer; and William D. Pawley, former Ambassador to Brazil.

24. *New York Times,* October 17, 1954.

25. *Ibid.,* October 20, 1954.

26. *Ibid.,* October 24, 1954.

27. *Intelligence Activities,* p. 14.

28. *Ibid.*

29. *Senate Report No. 1570,* p. 14. In addition to Mr. Killian, who in 1957 became the President's Special Assistant for Science and Technology, the Board originally was composed of Admiral Richard L. Conolly, Lieutenant General James H. Doolittle, Benjamin F. Fairless, General John E. Hull (chairman after February 1958), Joseph P. Kennedy, Robert A. Lovett, and Edward L. Ryerson. The Board is assisted by a three-man staff, and its reports to the President are never publicized.

30. Kirkpatrick tells of the formation of this group in his memoir, *The Real CIA,* pp. 216ff. Members included Marine Lieutenant General Graves Erskine, Allan Evans, of State; James Lay, NSC; Robert Macy, Budget; and James P. Coyne and Jesmond Balmer as observers.

31. Kirkpatrick, *The Real CIA,* p. 224.

32. *Ibid.,* p. 236.

33. The text of the letter is printed below as Appendix C.

34. Kirkpatrick, *The Real CIA,* p. 240.

35. *Intelligence Activities,* p. 15.

36. *Hearings,* "Department of the Army Appropriations for 1957," House Appropriations Subcommittee, 84th Cong., 2nd sess., p. 413.

37. Allen W. Dulles, "The Communists Also Have Their Problems," address to the Advertising Council of San Francisco, September 19, 1957; reprinted in *Department of State Bulletin,* October 21, 1957, p. 639.

CHAPTER X: CONCLUSIONS

1. See Hugh Trevor-Roper, *The Philby Affair* (London: William Kimber, 1968), p. 118.

2. *Ibid.,* pp. 109ff.

3. William J. Barnds, "Intelligence and Foreign Policy: Dilemmas of a Democracy," *Foreign Affairs,* January 1969, p. 281.

4. See, for example, *New York Times,* February-March 1967 passim.

5. Syndicated article, North American Newspaper Alliance, as published in the *Washington Post,* December 22, 1963.

6. September 3, 1965.

7. Secret subsidies were given wide press coverage after the publication of the March 1967 issue of *Ramparts,* a magazine of the "new left." See also the *New York Times,* February-March 1967; and *Time* cover story "The CIA and the Students," February 24, 1969, pp. 13-17.

8. These topics were discussed, in a different context, in my essay "Containing Central Intelligence," *The New Republic,* December 11, 1965, pp. 12-15.

9. For attempts within the State Department to bring the CIA under stricter policy controls, see Roger Hilsman, *To Move a Nation* (New York: Doubleday, 1967), pp. 78-82.

10. Theodore C. Sorensen, *Kennedy* (New York: Harper & Row, 1965), p. 287.

11. As quoted in *No More Vietnams?,* ed. Richard M. Pfeffer (New York: Harper & Row, 1968), p. 66.

12. See James Reston, *The Artillery of the Press* (New York: Harper & Row, 1967), pp. 21, 30-31.

13. William J. Barnds, "Intelligence and Foreign Policy: Dilemmas of a Democracy," *Foreign Affairs,* January 1969, p. 292.

Index

Index

Index

Defense, Department of: intelligence organizations, 102-133
Defense Intelligence Agency (DIA), 103-108; responsibilities, 104-105; functions, 105-107; 230
Defense Intelligence Staff, Great Britain, 191-192
Defense Notice, Great Britain, 197-203
Defense, Secretary of, Assistant for Special Operations, 102, 103
Defoe, Daniel, 183
Denning, Vice-Admiral Norman G., 202
DIA, see Defense Intelligence Agency
Dictionary of United States Military Terms for Joint Usage: quoted, 7-8
Director of Central Intelligence: authority clarified, 267-268; *see also* Allen W. Dulles
Directorship, CIA, 99, 267-268
Disclosure, CIA policy on public, 264-266
District Intelligence Office (DIO), U. S. Navy, 119
Donovan, William J.: on intelligence work, 33; appointed to intelligence position, 61-62; and OSS organization, 66-67; personality of, 70; postwar plan, 77; and secret operations, 249-250
Doolittle, General James H., 228
Dreyfus, Captain, 51
Dulles, Allen W.: on nature of intelligence, 17; on special research, 20; on information from Soviet Union, 26; on U. S. controls of information, 32; on intelligence in American Civil War, 52; Truman Doctrine, 82; as CIA Director, 99-100; on Watch Committee, 156; on the British system, 184; on making estimates, 218; on CIA public relations, 234; on peacetime intelligence, 238; 1947 views on central intelligence, 257-263
Dulles, John Foster: quoted, 148
Dworshak, Senator Henry: quoted, 168

Eberstadt (Ferdinand) report: quoted, 77
EC-121, Navy aircraft, 214
Eden, Anthony, 194-195
Edinburgh Journal, University of, 192
Eisenhower, Dwight D.: quoted, 54, 151
Electronic intelligence, 20-23
ELINT, 21
Elizabeth I, Queen (Great Britain), 50, 183

Espionage, 17-18, 20-29
Espionage, Soviet Russian, 27
Espionage Establishment, The, by David Wise and Thomas B. Ross, 182
Establishment, national intelligence, chart, 154
Estimate, National, Chapter VI, 147-158; production of, 149-151; types of, 150
Estimate, net, 151
Estimates, Board of National (CIA), 98
Evaluation, 40-44
Evans, Allan: quoted, 142-143
Ewing, Sir Alfred, 192-193
Ezhov, Petr Y., 28

Federal Bureau of Investigation, 143-145; relations with OSS, 72; overseas liaison role, 145; report quoted, 32; Special Intelligence Service, 143-144; World War II role, 143-144
Fleming, Ian, 181; quoted, 184
Flood, Representative Daniel, 116; quoted, 233
Foreign Office, Great Britain, 206
Foreign Relations, U. S. Senate Committee on, 174-176
Forrestal, James V., 79; quoted, 80; 205-206
Fort Meade, Maryland, 127
Franklin, Benjamin, 24
Frederick the Great, 51
Fulbright, Senator J. William, 173-179, 218
Furnival-Jones, Sir Edward M., 190

Great Britain: intelligence system, Chapter VIII, 180-207; secret intelligence, 50
Green Berets, U. S. Army, 240
Greene, Graham, 184
"303 Group," 89, 249
Group, Joint Intelligence, 102
Gruening, Senator Ernest: quoted, 176
G-2 (Army intelligence), 53, 108-111, 112-116
Gaither, H. Rowan, committee, 151 (footnote)
Gaitskell, Hugh, 194-195
Gardner, John W., 243, 269
GCHQ, Great Britain, 192
General Accounting Office, 87

Harris, William R., *A Bibliography of Intelligence Activities*: cited, 274

305

Index

Hayden, Senator Carl, 163: quoted, 166-167
Helms, Richard M., 100, 243, 251, 269
Helsby, Sir Laurence, 191
Henderson, Loy: quoted, 134
Hennings, Senator Thomas C., Jr., 264
Hillenkoetter, Admiral Roscoe H., 2, 100
Hilsman, Roger: quoted, on 19th-century espionage, 51; on CIA functions, 98; on State Department intelligence, 137; on McCone's role, 173
Himmler, Heinrich, 237
Historical background of intelligence, Chapter III, 48-81
Hitler, Adolph, 237
Hoover Commission (1949): on intelligence community relationships, 227; (1955): on single index, 39; on Pearl Harbor, 60; on collection of scientific data, 93; on size of agencies, 102; on Air Force intelligence, 122; on Congressional surveillance, 164; on reorganization, 209; on personnel, 222; on need for surveillance, 226; survey of intelligence activities, 228-229
Howard, Anthony: quoted, 182
Hughes, Thomas L., 140
Hull, Secretary of State Cordell, 1
Hull, General John E., 229
Humphrey, Hubert H., 29, 243
Hollis, Sir Henry, 190
Hoover, J. Edgar: quoted, 27

India, Council for Cultural Relations, 272-273
Indications Center, 42, 155-157
Indicators, intelligence, 36
Information, storage and retrieval, 38
Information Activities Abroad, Presidential Committee on, 270
INR (Department of State), 134
Institute for Cultural Relations, Sweden, 273
Intelligence, in decision making, 3-5; definitions, 7-8, 12-13; nature of, 12-47; strategic, 13; tactical, 14; process, 15-16; sources, 17-30; collection techniques, 19-30; categories of, 33-36; processing, 37-40; evaluation, 40-44; dissemination, 44-47; historical background, 48-81; community members, 101-146; British system, 180-207; problems of policy, organization and control of, 208-254; select bibliography of, 274-285
Intelligence Advisory Committee, 89

Intelligence bureaucracy: problems of, Chapter IX, 208-234
Intelligence community: principal members of, Chapter V, 101-158
Intelligence credibility, 215-218
Intelligence Establishment, national: chart, 154; surveillance of, 226-233
Intelligence Research and Analysis, Office of, Department of State (IN-R), 134-143
Intelligence Review, U. S. Army, 115
Intelligence system, stereotypes of the, 237
Inter-Agency Council on International Education and Cultural Affairs, U. S., 273
Interdepartmental Intelligence Conference, 145

JANIS, 34
James, Sir William, 192
Joint Chiefs of Staff, 62, 66-67, 103-104, 152
Joint Congressional Committee on Atomic Energy, 164, 166-167
Joint congressional committee on intelligence activities, proposed and debated, 161-172
Japan, Pearl Harbor attack, 57-61
John, Otto, 228
Johnson, Lyndon B.: on Mansfield resolution, 168; 216; 243; 269
Joint Intelligence Agency Reception Center, 63
Joint Intelligence Committee (Great Britain), 193
Joint Intelligence Committee (U. S.), 62-63
Joint Intelligence Group (U. S.), 102

Kahn, David, 129; quoted, 132
Karamanlis, Prime Minister, 188
Katzenbach, Nicholas, 243, 269
Keeler, Christine, 190
Kell, Sir Vernon, 189
Kennedy, John F.: on controlling CIA, 89; on Mansfield Resolution, 168; on press role, 206; on CIA Directorship, 231, on Vietnam, 241; on Bay of Pigs, 252
Kennedy, Robert F.: quoted, 91
Kent, Sherman: on descriptive function, 34; on coordination, 90; on CIA role, 98
KGB (Soviet Union), 27
Khan, Genghis, 49
Khrushchev, Nikita, 23

Index

Index

Index

Sharpe, George H., 52
Sinclair, Sir John Alexander, 189
SIS (Federal Bureau of Investigation), 144
SIS (Secret Intelligence Service), Great Britain, 180-189, 203-205
Slessor, Sir John: quoted, 55
Smith, General Walter Bedell, 32, 44, 100, 149, 225, 227
Smithsonian Institution, 273
SOE. *See* Special Operations Executive, Great Britain
Sorensen, Theodore: quoted, 248
Souers, Rear Admiral Sidney W., 77, 80
Soviet Union, army of, 217
"Special Branch," Scotland Yard, 190
Special Forces, U. S. Army, 240
Special Group, U. S., 89, 249
Special Intelligence Service (FBI), 144
Special Operations Executive (SOE), Great Britain, 187-188
Speculative-evaluative intelligence, 35-36
State, U. S. Department of, 29; intelligence organization, 134-143; chart, 139; Special Studies Group, 140; Executive Staff, 141; Coordination Staff, 141; Operations Staff, 141; Research Staff, 142; Office of Current Indications, 143; Operations Center, 143
Stieber, Wilhelm, 51
Stimson, Henry L., 133
Strategic intelligence, 13-14
Strategic Intelligence for American World Policy, by Sherman Kent, 34, 90
Subsidies, Secret (1967) by CIA, 241-245; Katzenbach Committee report on, 269-273
Sunday Times (London): quoted, 185, 189, 195
Surveillance of intelligence establishment: by Congress, Chapter VII, 159-179; by the executive, 226-233, 247-251
Surveys, National Intelligence (NIS), 114-115
Sweden, Institute for Cultural Relations, 273

Tactical intelligence, 14
Taylor, General Maxwell D., 229
Technology, 253-254
Treasury, Great Britain, 182
Trend, Sir Burke, 191

Trevor-Roper, Hugh: cited, 235; quoted, 238
Truman, Harry S: misgivings about secret services, 30; on atomic intelligence, 42; creates a coordinated system, 76-80; "Doctrine," 82-83; abolishes OSS, 136; expresses surprise at CIA role, 159; Korean War surprises, 219-220; advice from Dean Acheson, 233; worries about CIA, 240
Tzu, Sun, 49

U-2 affair, 239-240
U-2 aircraft, 22
UNESCO, Cultural Relations Services, 272
USIB. *See* United States Intelligence Board
United States Air Force. *See* Air Force, U. S.
United States Army. *See* Army, U. S.
United States Intelligence Board (USIB), 3, 6, 89, 91-92, 151-157, 215, 230
United States intelligence: historical background, Chapter III, 48-81
United States Navy. *See* Navy, U. S.

Vandenberg, General Hoyt S., 80

Walsingham, Sir Francis, 183
Watch Committee, 155-157
White, Sir Dick Goldsmith, 189
Whitten, Representative Jamie: quoted, 46, 108
Wienecke, Major General Robert H.: quoted, 108
Wigg, Colonel George, 191
Williams, David: quoted, 196
Wilson, Harold, 191, 200, 201
Wilson, President Woodrow, 53
Wohlstetter, Roberta: work cited, 57, 59-60
World War I, 53
World War II, 54-76

X-2 Division (OSS), 68

Yardley, Herbert O., 133
Yew, Prime Minister, 251
Young, Senator Milton: quoted, 127

Zacharias, Ellis M., 19: quoted, 117-118